Alfred Holbrook

A new English grammar conformed to present usage

Alfred Holbrook

A new English grammar conformed to present usage

ISBN/EAN: 9783337810900

Printed in Europe, USA, Canada, Australia, Japan

Cover: Foto ©ninafisch / pixelio.de

More available books at **www.hansebooks.com**

ECLECTIC EDUCATIONAL SERIES

A

NEW ENGLISH GRAMMAR

CONFORMED TO PRESENT USAGE

WITH THE

Objective Method of Teaching the Elements of the English Language

BY

ALFRED HOLBROOK

President National Normal University

The Eclectic Press

VAN ANTWERP, BRAGG, AND COMPANY

CINCINNATI AND NEW YORK

PREFACE

I GLADLY avail myself of the opportunity presented by my publishers to make this revision of my grammars. For economy to the purchaser, I have combined two books in one, thus placing the Training Lessons for PRELIMINARY DRILL in advance of the several parts of speech to which these "Lessons" are designed to introduce the beginner. Thousands of teachers, by this "objective method" thus revealed, have converted the study of Grammar from a burdensome, hateful, useless process of memorizing definitions and rules, into an exciting and enthusiastic work of comprehending and applying principles in the correct use of the varying forms and arrangements of the English language. The study of Grammar has ceased to be a nuisance; it has become the most effective discipline for arousing the observation; for chaining attention; for sharpening discrimination; for establishing the habits of independent thought: of rapid yet cautious generalization; of acute and thorough analysis; of consecutive and earnest application; of a love for reading the best authors: in fact, the discipline thus secured by the competent and faithful teacher can not fail to introduce the pupil to the broadest field of intellectual and esthetic culture. All this has been accomplished by thousands, who have used these books in the Normal method here set forth, and can and will be by the thousands of teachers who are introducing these methods over the entire nation.

But Grammar is not the only study; other branches have undergone a similar revolution by the Normal methods, both in their processes and results.

A few additions have been made to the constructions of various parts of speech, which will be found in their appropriate places. Fuller exemplifications have also been made of the more subtle constructions in nouns, pronouns, and infinite verbs.

An enumeration of all the possible constructions of nouns and pronouns is furnished for review study; also of finite and infinite verbs.

Teachers will use the PRELIMINARY DRILLS given for introducing each part of speech and each modification, either as suggestive of oral instruction from themselves, or they will read them responsively with their pupils in preparing them to write out each successive lesson in analytic parsing at their desks.

These written parsing exercises are found to be the most infallible means of exciting a controlling interest in principles and forms of our language. They are immeasurably more effective than any of the long, tedious, almost senseless processes dubbed language lessons. But language lessons must have their day, with "object lessons," with "free-hand drawing," with "natural order" and with various other waves of spasmodic efforts accepted by "leading educators," all of which have been or will be consigned to oblivion, with the scholastics of the Dark Ages.

The index is much improved in its accuracy and fullness.

NATIONAL NORMAL UNIVERSITY,
    Lebanon, Ohio,
August 15, 1889.

LANGUAGE.

HISTORY.

	PAGE
Origin of Spoken Language	9
Origin of Written Language	9
Diversity of Languages	10
Time of Highest Development	11
Chief Difference between Ancient and Modern Languages	11
Definitions, Explanations, and Remarks	12, 13, 14

PART I.

ORTHOEPY.

Conspectus	15
Definitions, Explanations, and Remarks	15–19
Methods of Teaching Pronunciation	19–21
Physiological Chart of Articulate Sounds	20

ORTHOGRAPHY.

Definitions, Explanations, and Remarks	21–25
Advanced Methods of Teaching	26–29

PARTS OF SPEECH.—INTRODUCTORY LESSONS.—NOUNS.

	PAGE
Number	31
Gender	32
Person	33
Parsing Lesson	34
Pronouns	35–37

VERB.

Case	37
Subject and Object	38, 39
Possessive Case	40, 41
Declension of Personal Pronouns and Nouns	42
Classes of Nouns	43
Classes of Pronouns	44–46
Declension of Relative Pronoun	47

PART II.

ETYMOLOGY.—THE NOUN.

Definition	48
Classes	48
Person	49
Number	50, 51
Gender	51, 52
Case	52–56
Declension	57

(v)

CONTENTS.

THE PRONOUN.

	PAGE
Definition	57
Classes	58–61
Modifications, Person, Number, Gender, Case	62–66

CONSTRUCTIONS OF NOUNS AND PRONOUNS.

Nominative Constructions	67
Possessive Constructions	67, 68
Objective Constructions	68–70
Examples for Drill in Parsing Nouns and Pronouns	71–80

THE ADJECTIVE.—INTRODUCTORY LESSONS.

Preliminary Drill	80–82

CLASSES OF ADJECTIVES.

Pronominal	83, 84
Interrogative Pronominals	85

THE ADJECTIVE.

Definition	86
Classes	87, 88
Number	88, 89
Comparison	89–91

THE ARTICLE.

Definition	92
Classes	92, 93
Constructions	93
Recitation of Written Parsing	93–95
Tense	95–98
Perfect Tenses	98–100

MODE.

Potential	100–102
Imperative	102
Subjunctive	102

	PAGE
Transivity	103, 104
Voice	104–106
Infinitive Mode	106
Participial Mode	107
Recitation	108, 109
Classes of Verbs	110, 111, 112

THE VERB.

Definition	113
Classes	113–115
Style	115, 116
Voice	116, 117
Mode	117–119
Indicative Mode	119
Potential Mode	120
Subjunctive Mode	121
Imperative Mode	122
Infinitive Modes	123–129
Principal Parts	130
Conjugation	131
Inflection	131
Synopsis	131
Conjugation of the Verb "Be"	132–134
Conjugation of "Love"	135–145
List of Irregular Verbs	145–148

THE ADVERB.

Definition	148
Classes	149, 150
Modifications, Comparison	151

THE PREPOSITION.

Definition	152
Classes	152
List of Prepositions	153
Peculiarities	153

THE CONJUNCTION.

Definition	154
Classes	154, 155
List of Conjunctions	155

THE INTERJECTION.

	PAGE
Definition	156
List of Interjections	156

DRILL IN VARIOUS CONSTRUCTIONS.

Apposition	157, 158
Predicate Nominative	156–160
Subject of Infinitive	160–162
Predicate Objective	162, 163
Double Relative	163–165
Nominative Absolute,	165, 166

PART III.

SYNTAX.—RULES OF SYNTAX.

Rule I	167–172
Rule II	173–175
Rule III	175–177
Rule IV	177, 178
Rule V	178–180
Rule VI	181
Rule VII	181
Rule VIII	182
Rule IX	182–184
Rule X	184
Rule XI	184, 185
Rule XII	185
Rule XIII	186, 187
Rule XIV	187, 188
Rule XV	188, 189
Rule XVI	189, 190
Rule XVII	190–192
Rule XVIII	192, 193
Rule XIX	193, 194
Rule XX	195–198
Rule XXI	198
Rule XXII	198, 199
Rule XXIII	199, 200
Rule XXIV	200
Rules of Limitation	201
Rules of Connection	201
Rules of Agreement	201, 202
Rules of Government	202, 203
Rules of Independent Construction	203

PART IV.

PROSODY.

Definition	204
Figures	204
Figures of Orthography	204
Figures of Etymology	205
Figures of Syntax	205–207
Figures of Rhetoric	207–211
Punctuation	211
Rhetorical Punctuation	211–213
Etymological "	213, 214
Punctuation for Reference	214
Punctuation for Printer	214, 215

PART FIVE.

ANALYSIS.

As to Structure	216, 217
As to the Nature of the Proposition	217–219
As to Structure	219
As to Relation	220
As to the Base	220, 221
Diagrammed Analysis	221–227
Programme for Verbal Analysis	227
Verbal Analysis Exemplified	228–236
Abridgment	237–239
Examples for Parsing and Analysis	240–247
Programmes and Models for Parsing	248–266

ENGLISH GRAMMAR.

LANGUAGE—HISTORY.

ORIGIN OF SPOKEN LANGUAGE.

1. LANGUAGE is a divine gift. Spoken Language was used undoubtedly by our first parents. Adam gave names to all cattle, and to fowls of the air, and to every beast of the field, before there was a helpmeet for him; so says the Bible. He is also represented as talking directly with that Being from whom he derived the faculty of speech, and who trained him in its use.

Let teachers remember who was the first of their profession; and not only so, but that no profession has been more highly honored.

ORIGIN OF WRITTEN LANGUAGE.

2. The first account we have of Written Language, is the writing of the decalogue on the tablets of stone. It is remarked that all the Hebrew characters, except one or two unimportant points, which have since been added to the language, are found in the Ten Commandments.

Before Written Language, pictures, monuments, and medals were used to communicate events, and to some slight extent to communicate ideas between those of the same age. These forms, however, represented *things*, and not *sounds* used in words. The Romanic letters, which we use, are evidently derived from the Greek letters; while the Greek letters, according to their historians, were brought by Cadmus from Phenicia, B. C. 1493. The Phenician alphabet is similar, in some respects, to the Hebrew, as is also the Greek.

Mr. Pitman, in forming his Phonographic Alphabet, seems to have imitated the Hebrew more nearly than any other, especially in his vowel system. Thus we have in the latest and most improved form of Written Language, a restoration of the original characters to some extent, as taught to Moses on Mount Sinai.

DIVERSITY OF LANGUAGES.

3. Profane History assigns no reason for the multiplicity of languages. Sacred History gives us an account of the "confusion of tongues," at the Tower of Babel, and the consequent dispersion of mankind. This may account for the existing number and variety of languages; or, if, as many commentators suppose, the "confusion of tongues" refers to a disagreement of the builders in their plans, and the consequent irreconcilable quarrels which drove these early inhabitants into diverse parts of the earth, then the changes which take place in the pronunciation and signification of many words in a few years in modern society, even though language is fixed by written characters, and by the diversity of pronunciation in different localities in the same country, where there is much and frequent intercourse, will show that, when tribes have wandered far from each other, with no written language, with no intercourse, their language, though originally the same, will, in a few generations become so changed as to become entirely unintelligible to others than the tribe or tribes in more imme-

diate proximity. The great diversity of languages ceases to be a wonder, then, even though men were originally of one blood, used one language, and no miracle interposed to confound their language.

TIME OF HIGHEST DEVELOPMENT.

4. Both Greece and Rome, at the time of their highest political power, enjoyed the greatest refinement in the arts and sciences. Language is no exception to the rule. Gradual improvement may be traced in the style of their authors from the earliest historical dawn of those nations to the period of their highest glory, respectively. This improvement may be noticed in all the qualities which constitute excellence of language; some of which are precision, euphony, flexibility, and susceptibility of nice shades of difference in expressing thought or feeling.

At the present time, the several spoken languages have attained a higher degree of polish and power than at any previous period. Among these modern languages, the German is highly cultivated for the expression of thought, and the Italian for the exhibition of the emotions; while the English yields to no other in its strength, flexibility, and delicacy of expression for both thought and feeling.

CHIEF DIFFERENCE BETWEEN ANCIENT AND MODERN LANGUAGES.

5. This lies mainly in the mechanical structure of their verbs and nouns, the nouns of the ancient languages having more methods of declension, and each declension more terminations than any of the modern nouns. This variety of termination gives equal precision, with much greater latitude of arrangement. The cases of modern nouns are determined to some extent by their position with relation

to the verb. The cases of ancient nouns depend entirely on their termination, and not in the least on their position in the sentence. Hence the ancient languages give a better opportunity for securing harmony in the arrangement than the modern.

The verbs of the ancient languages are much more complete in their terminations, and, of course, make use of fewer auxiliary verbs. None are necessary save that denoting *being*, which is used only in the passive voice.

DEFINITIONS, EXPLANATIONS, AND REMARKS.

6. Language.—Any method of communicating thought or feeling.

7. *Natural Language.*—Instinctive methods of communicating thought or feeling.

REMARK.—Brute animals possess their own instinctive forms of language, many of which forms are understood by other species than those which use them.

8. *Artificial Language.*—That which must be learned before it can be used.

9. *Vocal Language.*—That produced by the organs of speech.

10. *Written Language.*—Any method of communicating thought by visible characters depicted on a surface.

11. *Symbolic Language.*—That form of written language in which the characters are designed to represent ideas and not sounds.

12. *Phonic Language.*—That form of written language in which the characters are designed to represent sounds.

13. *Pictorial Language.*—That form of symbolic language in which the ideas are plainly represented.

14. *Hieroglyphic Language.*—That form of symbolic language in which the ideas are so obscurely represented as to need an interpreter.

15. *Syllabic Language.*—That form of phonic language in which the characters represent syllables.

16. *Alphabetic Language.*—That form of phonic language in which the characters represent separate articulate sounds.

17. *Equivocal Alphabetical Language.*—Those in which a letter represents more than any one sound, and in which a sound is represented by more than one letter.

18. *Unequivocal Alphabetical Languages.*—Those in which the number of letters equals the number of separate articulate sounds—giving but one sound to each letter, and but one letter for each sound.

19. *Gesticulate Language.*—Any method of communicating or impressing thought or feeling, by motions, postures, or appearances of the animal form, not producing or representing articulated sounds or written characters.

GRAMMAR.

20. *General, or Universal, Grammar.*—That form of grammar which treats of all those principles and usages which are common to all languages.

21. *Particular Grammar.*—That form of grammar which treats of all those principles, usages, characters, and sounds, comprised in any particular language.

22. *English Grammar.*—That branch which treats of the English language.

23. *Orthoepy.*—That division of grammar which treats of articulate sounds, and of their correct use in pronunciation.

24. *Orthography.*—That division of grammar which treats of letters, words, and spelling.

25. *Etymology.*—That division of grammar which treats of the derivation and formation of words, and the classification of words according to their uses.

26. *Lexicography.*—That division of grammar which treats of the signification of words.

27. *Syntax.*—That division of grammar which treats of the arrangement of words in sentences.

28. *Analysis.*—That division of grammar which treats of the separation of sentences into their elements.

29. *Prosody.*—That division of grammar which treats of versification and punctuation.

PART ONE.

ORTHOEPY AND ORTHOGRAPHY.

ORTHOEPY.

CONSPECTUS.

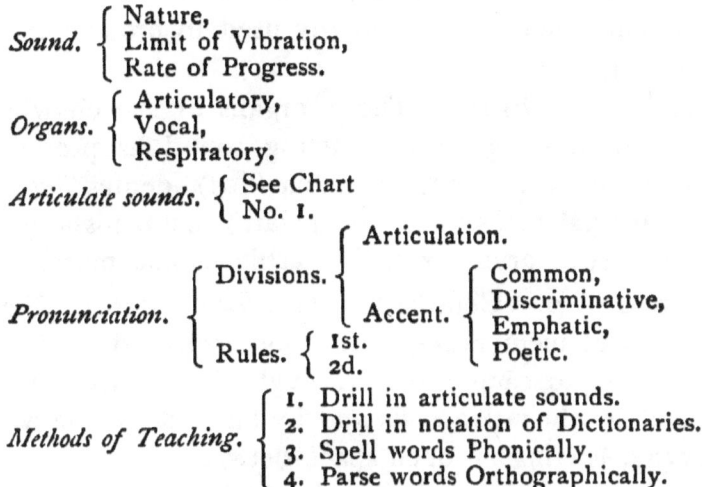

DEFINITIONS, EXPLANATIONS, AND REMARKS.

30. Orthoepy.—That division of grammar which treats of articulate sounds, and their correct use in pronunciation.

31. Sound.—A sensation produced on the auditory nerve by the rapid vibratory motion of air or other elastic substance.

REMARK 1.—The vibration that produces the sound is often called sound; as, we say "sound travels," etc.

REMARK 2.—*Limit of Vibrations.*—The fewest number of vibrations in a second that can yield a sound to the human ear, is 32. The highest number is 30,000, though other animals may perceive vibrations more or less rapid than these limits.

REMARK 3.—*Rate of Progress.*—Sound travels through air at the rate of seven hundred and sixty-three miles per hour, or eleven hundred and twenty feet per second; through liquids and solids at a rate many times greater.

32. Organs of Speech.—All those distinct parts of the human system which are necessarily used in producing the sounds of language.

33. *Articulatory Organs.*—Those organs of speech which are used in modifying or obstructing sound as produced by the other organs. They are labia (lips), dentes (teeth), palatum (hard palate), uvula (soft palate), nasal fossæ (cavities of the nose), larynx, with its cartilages and muscles.

34. *Vocal Organs.*—Chordæ Vocales (vocal chords). These are two pairs of membranes, extending backwards and forwards, opposite to each other, through the larynx. They are attached by their two ends and by one side to the walls of the larynx, leaving an open space between them, through which air is drawn in and forced out by the respiratory organs.

35. *Respiratory Organs.*—Those organs of speech used in forcing air through the other organs. They are trachea (windpipe), bronchi (bronchial tubes), pulmo (lungs), diaphragm, and the intercostal, dorsal, and abdominal muscles.

36. Voice, or Vocal Sound.—That sound produced by the vibration of the vocal chords.

REMARK.—The vibration of these chords during the emission of vocal sound, may be perceived by placing the fingers on the larynx, externally, at the projection of "Adam's apple." The vibration can be detected at no other time.

37. *Articulate Sound.*—That made by the organs of speech, and used in language.

38. *Voiced Sound, or Voice.*—A sound made by the vibration of the vocal chords.

39. *Vocal Sound, or Vocal.*—A voiced sound, modified but not obstructed by the articulatory organs.

40. *Simple Vocal.*—A vocal, made without a change in the position of the articulatory organs during its emission.

41. *Compound Vocal.*—A vocal made by a change in the position of the articulatory organs, from that required by one simple vocal to that required by another during its emission.

REMARK.—This change commences with the emission of the sound, and continues until the close; hence the elements of the compounds are not heard in their purity.

42. *Coalescent.*—An articulate sound that always precedes, and unites with, a vocal.

43. *Subvocal Sound, or Subvocal.*—A voiced sound modified and obstructed by the articulatory organs.

44. *Aspirated Sound, or Aspirate.*—An articulate sound made without the vibration of the vocal chords.

45. *Pure Aspirate.*—An aspirate modified but not obstructed by the articulatory organs.

46. *Obstructed Aspirate.*—An aspirate modified and obstructed by the articulatory organs.

47. *Labial.*—An articulate sound modified or obstructed at the lips.

REMARK.—The vocals and pure aspirates are *modified* only, while the subvocals and the other aspirates are obstructed also.

48. *Dental.*—An articulate sound modified or obstructed at the teeth or gums.

49. *Palatal.*—An articulate sound modified or obstructed at the hard palate.

50. *Guttural.*—An articulate sound modified or obstructed at the soft palate.

REMARK 1.—Sounds are obstructed at the lips by the lips only, or by the teeth and lips.

REMARK 2.—Sounds are obstructed at the teeth, gums, or hard palate, by the tip of the tongue; and at the soft palate by the root of the tongue.

51. *Abrupt (also called Explodent and Mute).* — An articulate sound made by such a *perfect contact* of the organs as entirely prevents the escape of air externally.

52. *Continuant.* — An articulate sound, made by such *partial contact* of the organs as to admit of escape of air externally.

53. *Liquid.* — A continuant susceptible of simultaneous combination with other obstructed sounds. The liquids are *l* and *r*.

54. *Nasal.* — A continuant made by the escape of air through the cavities of the nose only.

55. *Cognate Sounds.* — Those sounds made by the articulatory organs in the same positions, and differing only in the vibrations of the vocal chords.

56. Pronunciation. — The enunciation of the sounds of a word with correct articulation and accent.

57. *Articulation (joining).* — The distinct enunciation of the sounds in words.

58. *Accent.* — The greater stress given to one syllable of a word than to others; also, the greater force given to long syllables in poetry.

59. *Common Accent.* — That given in the ordinary pronunciation of a word without reference to any other word.

60. *Discriminative Accent.* — That given to words of the same articulation to distinguish different parts of speech.

   Examples. — 1. *Nouns from Verbs.* — Ac′cent, accent′; con′cert, concert′; in′sult, insult′, etc.
   2. *Adjectives from Verbs.* — Ab′sent, absent′; com′pound, compound′; fre′quent, frequent′, etc.

61. *Emphatic Accent.* — That in which the stress is transferred from the ordinary syllable to another, for the purpose of giving antithetic emphasis more distinctly.

62. *Poetic Accent.*—That which is placed on long syllables of a poetic foot, even though those syllables should be monosyllabic words.

METHODS OF TEACHING PRONUNCIATION.

63. Drill in Articulate Sound.—Commence with vocals as given in Chart, page 20.

1. Repeat each long sound twice in order.
2. Direct the class to do the same in concert with yourself.
3. Direct the class to do the same without your aid. Continue this process until the large majority make the sounds correctly, and in the order of the chart.
4. Drill individuals failing, before the class, in groups or singly, till each pupil masters all the difficulties.
5. Pursue the same course with the short vocals.
6. Repeat and vary these drills until every pupil can *go through* the vocals, long and short, and name the organ at which the sound is modified.
7. Pursue a similar course with the obstructed sounds, beginning with the aspirates, and following with the sub-vocals on Chart, page 20.

64. Spelling words Phonically.—1. This should be practiced more or less in connection with every exercise in concert, the teacher accompanying; next, the class in concert without his aid; lastly, individual pupils, always giving opportunity for the members of the class to criticise the spelling of the individuals, they first raising their hands for permission to do so.

2. Let the teacher select such phonic characters in order from the chart on page 20 as shall form words. The class will pronounce each sound as its representative is touched with the pointer, until the elements of a word are thus separately pronounced; then, a signal given, they are expected to pronounce the word together. This exercise

PHYSIOLOGICAL CHART OF ARTICULATE SOUNDS.

A Physiological Classification of the Articulate Sounds of the English Language, with the Websterian and Worcesterian Notation.

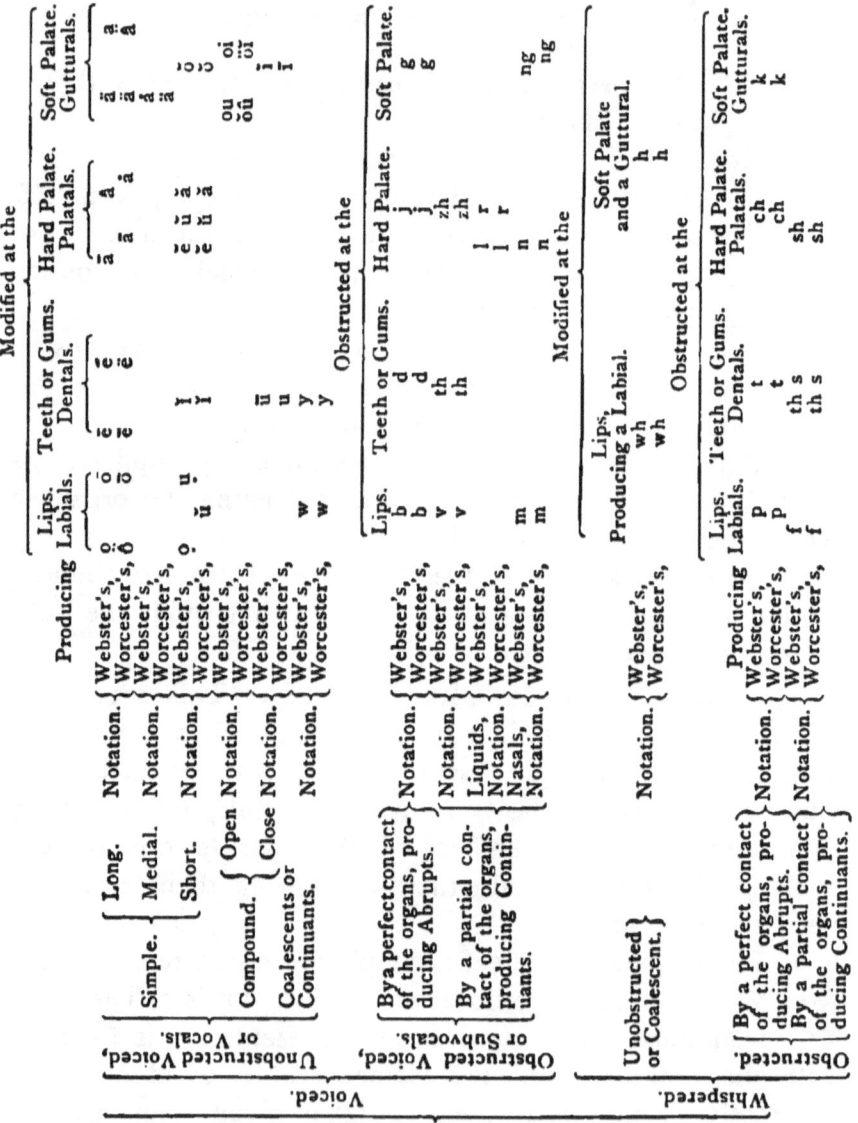

should begin with monosyllables, and from these proceed to the most complicated and difficult words.

65. Criticism on Pronunciation.—In recitation of all studies, opportunity should be given the classes for mutual criticism on pronunciation, as well as in other particulars.

This matter of criticism is managed thus:

The teacher asks, "Are there any errors in pronunciation?"

Pupils who have noticed errors, raise their hands.

The teacher calls upon such a pupil as is least in the habit of criticism, to mention the error.

The pupil does it in this form: "Mr. A. B. pronounced 'heard' 'heerd.' He should have given the close sound of *e* rather than the long." The pupil continues: "He pronounced 're*mon*'strate' '*rem*'onstrate,' accenting the first syllable instead of the second."

In case of doubt in the mind of any one, either pupil or teacher, a pupil is requested to examine the authorities, Webster's or Worcester's dictionary, which should always be on the teacher's table and in the pupil's desk.

ORTHOGRAPHY.

66. Orthography.—That division of grammar which treats of letters, syllables, words, and spelling.

67. Letter.—A visible character representing by itself, or with one or more besides, an articulate sound; also used to determine signification.

68. *Typical Forms.*—These are given in the names that distinguish them in the classification. There are many ornamental forms in use not given.

69. *Rhetorical Forms.*—These are used for emphasis or other rhetorical distinction.

70. *Power of a Letter.*—The sound which a letter represents in a word; also the influence which one letter exerts upon the representative character of another.

71. *Vowel.*—A letter used to represent a vocal sound; the basis of a syllable.

72. *Consonant.*—A letter used to represent a subvocal or aspirate sound, modifying the basis of a syllable.

73. *Aphthong, or Silent Letter.*—A letter which represents no sound, but is used either to modify the representative character of another, or merely to determine signification.

REMARK.—An aphthong may be a vowel or a consonant aphthong, according to the more common use of the letter.

EXPLANATION.—*E*, in the word *lade*, changes the sound of *a* from short to long; also *g*, in *sign*, changes the sound of *i* short to long; also *w*, in *write*, determines the signification of the word, and distinguishes it from that of *rite;* also *b*, in *dumb*, determines signification, since *dum* has no signification.

74. Diphthongs.—One or two vowels, representing a combination of two vocal sounds.

EXPLANATION.—The diphthong *i* represents a combination of Italian *a* and long *e*.
The diphthong long *u* represents a combination of long *e* and close *o*.
The diphthong *oi* represents a combination of broad *a* and short *i*.
The diphthong *ou* represents a combination of Italian *a* and close *o*.
These are all the proper diphthongs in the English language.

75. Digraphs.— *A Vowel Digraph*, or improper diphthong, is a combination of two vowels, in which only one receives a sound, the other being a modifier.

76. *A Conjoined Vowel Digraph* is one in which the two vowels are not separated by a consonant.

77. *A Disjoined Vowel Digraph* is one in which the two vowels are separated by one or more consonants.

78. *A Consonant Digraph* is a combination of two consonants, one or both of which are required to represent a sound.

REMARK.—A consonant not required to represent a sound of the word is an aphthong, whether modifying the representative character of a letter or not. Thus, in the consonant digraph *gn*, in the word *condign*, the *g* modifies the sound of *i*, but it is not necessary for the representation of the final sound, and hence is an aphthong.

79. *A Combined Digraph* is a combination of a consonant and a vowel to represent a subvocal or an aspirate sound.

EXPLANATION.—The consonant *t* and the vowel *i* are used in the terminal syllable *tion*, to represent the aspirate sound of *sh* or *ch*. *Ci*, *ce*, and *si*, are used in a similar manner.

80. Trigraphs.—*Vowel Trigraph.*—A combination of three vowels representing one or two sounds.

REMARK.—*Eau* in *beau* represents one sound; in *beauty*, it represents two combined.

81. *Disjoined Trigraph.*—One in which a consonant occurs between two of the vowels.

82. Syllables.—One or more sounds uttered at one impulse of the breath; also the letters representing any sound or sounds so uttered.

83. *Ultimate Syllable.*—The last syllable in a word.

84. *Penultimate Syllable, or Penult.*—The last syllable but one in a word.

85. *Antepenultimate Syllable.*—The last syllable but two in a word.

86. *Preantepenultimate Syllable.*—The last syllable but three in a word.

REMARK.—The syllables of a word are also described in their numerical order, commencing at the left; as, first, second, third, etc.

87. *Base of a Syllable.*—The vocal or vowel used in its formation.

88. *Modifier.*—Any sound preceding or succeeding the base of a syllable, or letter or digraph representing such sound.

89. *Antecedent.*—Any sound preceding the base of a syllable or letter or digraph representing such sound.

90. *Consequent.*—Any sound succeeding the base of a syllable, or letter or digraph representing such sound.

REMARK.—A letter representing a sound, preceding another, is parsed as an antecedent, though the order of the letter should differ from that of the sounds represented by them.

91. Word.—The received sign of an idea, expressed in one or more articulate sounds, or in visible characters representing such sounds.

92. *Simple Word.*—One which can not be divided into separate words without radically altering the signification.

93. *Compound Word.*—One which can be divided into separate words without radically altering their signification.

94. *Primitive Word.*—One which can not be reduced to simpler form without radically altering its signification.

95. *Derivative Word.*—One which can be reduced to a simpler form without radically altering its signification.

REMARK.—A compound word is considered primitive if all its parts are primitive, otherwise a derivative. A derivative is considered simple unless it plainly comes under the definition of a compound.

96. *The Base of a Compound Word* is that word representing the fundamental idea.

97. *The Modifier in a Compound Word* is that word which describes the other.

98. *The Base of a Derivative Word* is the primitive word from which it is derived.

99. *The Modifiers in a Derivative Word* are the prefixes or suffixes, or both. Both are called affixes.

100. *Prefix.*—One or more syllables not used as a word of similar meaning in the English language, but placed before words to modify their signification.

101. *Suffix.*—One or more syllables, not used as a word of similar meaning in the English language, but placed after words to modify their signification.

102. *Monosyllable.*—A word of one syllable.

103. *Dissyllable.*—A word of two syllables.

104. *Trisyllable.*—A word of three syllables.

105. *Polysyllable.*—A word of more than three syllables.

106. *Accented Syllable.*—One that is pronounced with more force than others in the same word.

REMARK 1.—Accent may be primary when it is greater than that received by any other syllable in the same word; or secondary when it is less than that received by some other syllable in the same word.

REMARK 2.—In Prosody, an accented syllable is long in quantity, an unaccented syllable short in quantity, *i. e.*, of time taken to pronounce it.

107. Spelling.—A distinct expression of the letters or sounds of a word in their proper order.

108. *Orthographic Spelling.*—The expression of the letters of which a written word is composed, and in their proper order, according to the received authority.

109. *Phonic Spelling.*—The separate expression of the elementary sounds of which a word is composed, and in their proper order, according to established usage.

110. General Rules for Spelling.—*Rule* 1. Write no word unless sure of its orthography and signification.

Rule 2. Consult the dictionary in case of doubt.

Rule 3. Apply the rules for derivatives.

REMARK.—The *special rules* for spelling are to be found on page 28, and need *special attention*. All grades, except primary, should be thoroughly *drilled* in their use. It is not enough *to memorize* them. More than one half the bad spelling found in school exercises, as well as in business operations, may be justly charged to ignorance of these special rules.

H. Gram.—3.

ADVANCED METHODS OF TEACHING.

111. Teaching Orthography by the Chart.—The methods of using the chart are explained in sections 63 to 65.

This chart can be copied in an enlarged form by the teacher or by pupils, on one or more large sheets of printing-paper, with a crayon. Charts of orthography are sold frequently for two dollars. Such a chart would cost the teacher not over a half-dime, including paper and crayon, and will serve as good a purpose as the most expensive. If pupils are permitted to make such a chart, they have the advantage of learning by the process, and of cultivating their taste in drawing and writing.

112. Teaching Orthography by Derivatives.—It is an excellent practice to give spelling lessons in the derivatives. Let the teacher propose two or three roots for a lesson; as, *press*, *act*, etc. The pupils, at the recitation, are required to write as many derivatives as they have been able to obtain, either on their slates or on the blackboard. They should, of course, be provided with dictionaries in the preparation of such a lesson. They can also make use of tables of prefixes and suffixes. They will also bring into use the *special rules* for spelling derivatives.

The definitions of the derivatives should be required as a part of the exercise. The exercise can be made very profitable with the use of the dictionary, prefixes and suffixes being defined.

113. Examples in formation of derivatives, with the special rules for spelling, are given on page 28.

WITH SUFFIXES.

Act.—A primitive word, signifying to do or to make.
Actor.—The person who acts.
Actress.—The female who acts.
Action.—The result or process of acting.
Acts.—Does act.
Actest.—Dost act.
Acteth.—Does act.
Acted.—Did act.
Acting.—Continuing to act.
Actionable.—Admitting of an action.

Actionably.—By admitting an action.
Actionary. } —A person who has a share in an action.
Actionist. }
Active.—Inclined to act.
Activity. } Rule 4. } —The state or quality of being active.
Activeness. } Rule 3. }
Actively.—Rule 3.—In an active manner.
Actual.—Real in acting or being.
Actuality. } —The state of being actual.
Actualness. }
Actually.—In an actual manner.
Actuate.—To cause to act.

WITH PREFIXES AND SUFFIXES.

Coact.—To act together with force.
Coaction.—The process of coacting.
Coactive.—Inclining to coact.
Counteract.—To act against.
Counteraction.—The process of acting against.
Enact.—To act in making a law.
Enactment.—The process or result of enacting.
Inactive.—Without action.
Inaction.—An inactive state.
Inactively.—Rule 3.—In an inactive manner.
Inactivity.—Rule 4.—An inactive state.
Exact.—Verb.—To act in forcing out of.
Exacting.—Continuing to exact.
Exaction.—The process or result of exacting.
Exactor.—The person who exacts.
Exact.—Adjective.—Acting from rule; accurate.
Exactly.—In an exact manner.
Exactness. } —The state of being exact.
Exactitude. }
React.—To act again; to act back.
Reacting.—Continuing to react.
Reaction.—The process of reacting.
Reactive.—Inclining to react.
Reactively.—Rule 4.—In a reactive manner.
Sub-action.—The process of acting to place under.

114. *Pel.*—An inseparable radical word, signifying *to drive* or *force.* From *Pello, Pulsus.*

Pulsion.—The act of driving.

With prefixes and suffixes—

Compel, Compelled—Rule 1; *Compelling*—Rule 1; *Compulsion, Compulsive, Compulsively*—Rule 4; *Compulsiveness*—Rule 4; *Compulsory.*

115. From the root *Press* nearly two hundred derivatives can be obtained. From the inseparable root *Gress* a long list can be formed.

These two examples, *Act* and *Pel*, will be sufficient to illustrate the method of spelling by the use of prefixes and suffixes in forming derivatives from separable and inseparable primitives.

116. Rules for Spelling.—1. Words which *end* with a single consonant, preceded by a single vowel, and which are accented on the last syllable, double the final letter on taking an additional syllable beginning with a vowel.

REMARK.—*X* and *h* are never doubled.

2. Words which end with a consonant, preceded by a diphthong, or a digraph representing a vowel sound, and words which are *not* accented on the last syllable, do not double the final letter on taking an additional syllable.

3. Words which end with *e*, generally retain it on taking an additional syllable beginning with a consonant.

EXCEPTIONS.—*Judgment, lodgment, abridgment, acknowledgment.*

REMARK.—When the *e* is preceded by a vowel, it is sometimes retained and sometimes dropped; as, *true, truly; rue, rueful; shoe, shoeless,* etc.

4. Words which end with *e* generally omit it on taking an additional syllable beginning with a vowel.

EXCEPTIONS.—Words ending with *ce* or *ge* retain *e* before the terminations *able* and *ous*, to preserve the soft sound of *c* and *g*; as, *peace, peaceable, courage, courageous,* etc. *Dyeing* retains the *e* to distinguish it from *dying.*

5. Words which end with *ie* drop the *e* and change *i* into *y* on taking the syllable *ing.*

6. Words which end with *y*, preceded by a consonant, change *y* into *i* on taking an additional syllable.

EXCEPTIONS.—Before *ing*, *y* is retained; as, *pity, pitying.*

7. The digraph *ei* follows *c* soft; *ie* is found after the other consonants. *Ei* begins words; *ie* is found at the end of words.

117. Drilling on the Special Rules for Spelling.—1. The class should be required to memorize these as they are given on page 28, with the exceptions and remarks. They should so memorize them that they can give them as they are called for by the teacher promiscuously. They should then be required to write, or to spell orally, words as they are dictated, or pronounced, from examples selected by the teacher, under each rule in order, until every pupil shows that he is able to apply the rules correctly.

2. Sentences may then be dictated for writing, containing derivative words coming under the rules promiscuously.

3. Sentences may be written on the board by the teacher in which these rules are violated. The pupils are expected to rewrite the sentences on slates or paper, with reference, by number, to the rules which were violated.

4. This course should be pursued day after day for weeks, until the pupils have formed the habit of noticing the application of these rules in spelling.

5. We find that the larger part of misspelling in the compositions of advanced pupils is in violation of these rules, until they have been thoroughly drilled in them.

118. Use of Capital Letters.—Capital letters are used:
1. To begin the first word of a sentence.
2. To begin all proper names.
3. To begin all titles of honor.
4. To begin the first word of every line of poetry.
5. To begin the names of objects personified.
6. In writing the pronoun I and interjection O.
7. To begin appellations of the Deity.
8. To begin the names of the days of the week, and of the months.
9. To begin direct quotations.
10. To begin words derived from proper names.
11. To begin the chief words in the titles of books, headings of divisions of books, chapters, discourses, etc.
12. To begin words of special importance.

PARTS OF SPEECH.

INTRODUCTORY LESSONS—NOUNS.

119. Names of Material Objects.—1. The boys study grammar.

2. The ship sails on the ocean.
3. The birds sit on the tree.

Teacher. "Pupils, we have here three sentences. As many as can give me the names in the first sentence, 'The boys study grammar,' may raise their hands."

All hands are up.

Teacher. "James, you may give them."

James. "Boys and grammar."

Teacher. "Right. These names are nouns. All names are nouns. What nouns in the next sentence, 'The ship sails on the ocean'?"

Some hands come up.

Teacher. "Mary, you may give them."

Mary. "Ship and ocean."

Teacher. "Class, you may think of other nouns or names, and give them as I call on you. Susan."

Susan. "Horse, dog, cat."

Teacher. "These words are nouns, but the things they are the names of, are not nouns: they are animals. James, why is the word *dog* a noun?"

James. "Because it is a name."

Teacher. "Hattie, what is the dog itself?"

Hattie. "An animal or a thing."

120. Names of Immaterial Objects.—*Teacher.* "Thus far, Class, we have had the names of only those things we can see. In the following sentences we have names of things we can not see."

1. Our life is very uncertain.
2. Your minds are improving.
3. Health is a great blessing.

Teacher. "In the first sentence, 'Our life is very uncertain,' what is the noun? Henry."

Henry. "Life."

Teacher. "But you never saw nor heard a life."

Henry. "No; but I have life; I am not dead."

Teacher. "Very good. In the second sentence, 'Your minds are improving,' Samuel, what is *minds?*"

Samuel. "I don't know, sir."

Teacher. "Well, Samuel, you believe you have a mind as well as body and clothes? Since you have a mind, we must have a name for it, and all names are what, Samuel?"

Samuel. "Nouns."

Teacher. "And now, Class, all together, what is *minds?*"

Class. "A noun."

Teacher. "You may think of some other such nouns, and give them as I call on you. Charles."

Charles. "Truth and good."

Teacher. "Charles, why is *truth* a noun?"

Charles. "Because it is the name of something."

Teacher. "Very well. But did you ever have a *good?*"

Charles. "We had a good teacher last winter."

Teacher. "True; but what sort of thing is the *good* without the teacher? Your last teacher had a quality of heart which made her good. Can you tell me the name of that quality?"

Hands are up.

Teacher. "Jane."

Jane. "Goodness."

Teacher. "Right. Goodness is, then, a noun, because it is the name of the quality which your teacher had."

121. Distinction of Number.—*Teacher.* "Now, Class, when I say, 'Boys run,' do I mean one or more than one boy? All together."

Class. "More than one."

Teacher. "Right. What would I say, if I meant but one?"

Class. "Boy."

Teacher. "When we have a noun which means but one, the grammarians say it is in the singular number; but if it means more than one, they say the noun is in the plural number. In the sentences which follow, you may point out all the nouns and give their number."

1. The girls in the house.
2. My book is torn.
3. We play croquet with mallets and balls.

Teacher. "You may give, in concert, the plural of *house.*"
Class. "Houses."
Teacher. "Plural of *book.*"
Class. "Books."
Teacher. "The singular of *mallets.*"
Class. "Mallet."
Teacher. "The plural of *fan.*"
Class. "Fans."
Teacher. "*Pan.*"
Class. "Pans."
Teacher. "*Man.*"
Class. "Mans——Oh, men."
Teacher. "Try again. Give the plural of *youth.*"
Class. "Youths."
Teacher. "*Truth.*"
Class. "Truths."
Teacher. "*Tooth.*"
Class. "Tooths——no, no, teeth; ha, ha!"

122. Distinction of Gender.—"Pupils, I wish you now to learn something about that property of nouns, called gender. John is a noun of the masculine gender or kind, because it is the name of a male. All names of males are masculine nouns. Susan is in the feminine gender, because the name of a female. Names of females are feminine."

1. Charles is an intelligent boy.
2. Sarah is a good girl.
3. My slate is broken and my pencil lost.

Teacher. "As many as can tell me the gender of the noun 'Charles,' may raise their hands."
All hands are up.
Teacher. "Mary."
Mary. "Masculine."
Teacher. "Gender of 'Sarah' in the sentence, 'Sarah is a good girl.' All together."
Class. "Feminine."

Teacher. "In same sentence, what is the gender of the noun 'girl'? Samuel."

Samuel. "Feminine."

Teacher. "Why?"

Samuel. "Because it is the name of a female."

Teacher. "Class, all together, in what gender is the noun 'boy' in the sentence, 'Charles is an intelligent boy'?"

Class. "Masculine."

Teacher. "Why, James?"

James. "Because the name of a male."

Teacher. "Pupils, can you give me the gender of the nouns 'slate' and 'pencil,' in the sentence, 'My slate is broken and my pencil lost'?"

Class. "No, sir."

Teacher. "Because these nouns have no sex, the grammarians say they are of the neuter gender or kind. John, in what gender, then, is 'stone'?"

John. "Neuter."

Teacher. "Gender of stove? William."

William. "Neuter."

Teacher. "All nouns, then, which are names of neither males nor females are in what gender? Class, all together."

Class. "Neuter."

Teacher. "Nouns which are both masculine and feminine are in the common gender; as, parent, child, etc."

123. Distinction of Person.—*Teacher.* "Pupils, you seem so eager to learn, I will give you one more distinction of nouns, and then give you a parsing lesson. Nouns which denote the speaker or writer, are in the first person. Those which represent the person spoken to are in the second person. The person or thing spoken of is in the third person. For example: 'I, John, saw the balloon.' Here 'John' is in the first person, because it is the name of the speaker. 'O Mary! what have you done?' 'Mary' is in the second person, because it is the name of the person spoken to. In the sentence, 'The horse is a useful animal,' 'horse' and 'animal' are both in the third person, because names of things spoken of."

1. I, William, am sovereign of United Germany.
2. James, hand me that book.

Teacher. "Class, all together, in what person is 'William'?"

Class. "First person."

Teacher. "Why, Charles?"

Charles. "Because it is the name of the person speaking."

Teacher. "In the sentence, 'James, hand me that book,' in what person is 'James'? All together."

Class. "Second person."

Teacher. "Why?"

Class. "James is spoken to."

Teacher. "In what person is 'book'?"

Class. "Third."

Teacher. "Why, Henry?"

Henry. "Book is spoken of."

124. First Parsing Lesson.—1. John loves study.

2. Mary has beautiful flowers.

3. We love the songs of birds.

4. I, the king, command it done.

5. O Mary! come and see my new book.

6. O Lord, we will serve thee.

Teacher. "Pupils, I will give you a programme for parsing nouns in writing.[1] In this way I will parse 'John' in the sentence, 'John loves study':

"*John,* (Species?) noun, (Person?) third, (Number?) singular, (Gender?) masculine. The words in parenthesis ask the questions, 'what species?', 'what person?', etc. Since these are in the programme before you, you may omit them in your own parsing. We will then give it thus: *John* is a noun, third, singular, masculine. Now, I would like to have you take your slates, and parse 'flowers' in the sentence, 'Mary has beautiful flowers.' Sarah, you may go to the board and parse 'flowers' while the rest use their slates.[2]

---

[1] The teacher will place on the board and explain this programme:

Species? Person? Number? Gender?

[2] The teacher will examine slates and give all commendation possible, as far as consistent with honesty.

NOTE.—Reasons for writing parsing lessons:

(1.) It improves penmanship.

(2.) A means of teaching spelling.

(3.) Prepares the way for composition.

(4.) It secures faithful study from *every* member of the class, and thus provides against laziness, mischief, and deception.

"Now, how many think they can parse the other nouns in these sentences? As many as can, may raise their hands."

All hands up.

Teacher. "Very well. I am pleased with your attention this morning, and for your next recitation you may parse, in writing, the nouns given in the sentences above. You will use the last page of your writing-book, making it the first page of your Grammar Exercise-book. These nouns you will parse according to the programme I have given you, and at the next recitation bring in your books, when I shall be glad to see how correctly and neatly your work is done."

PRONOUNS.

125. Recitation.

126. Preliminary Drill.—*Teacher.* "When Mary came from Mary's seat, Mary forgot Mary's grammar. How many can improve this sentence?"

All hands are up.

Teacher. "Charles, I would like to have you give this sentence as you would speak it."

Charles. "When Mary came from her seat, she forgot her grammar."

Teacher. "Very good. James, what words are used instead of Mary?"

Some means of supplying paper:

(1.) Some will prefer to buy a blank-book especially for this exercise.

(2.) The teacher may be able to induce the parents of every pupil to furnish a suitable book.

(3.) Use copy-book as explained above, since the pupil will make vastly more improvement in penmanship this way than by only writing after copies.

(4.) The above failing, the true teacher will provide paper at his or her own expense.

With a class of ordinary ability, the live teacher can accomplish the work of this lesson in a class drill of thirty minutes. If the teacher lack ingenuity or enthusiasm, or if the class be somewhat backward or irregular, or if the time for the grammar exercise be too limited, the teacher may find it necessary to divide this lesson, and make two or more of it.

James. "Her, she, and her, again."

Teacher. "Right. The grammarians call these words pronouns because they are used for nouns. In the sentence, 'When the sun rose it went into a cloud,' what word is used for the noun 'sun'? Mary."

Mary. "It."

Teacher. "Right. 'It' is also a pronoun because it stands for the noun 'sun.' In the sentence, 'When James came to school, his sister came with him,' what words are used for 'James'? Sarah."

Sarah. "'His' and 'him.'"

Teacher. "Mary, see if you can give that sentence, and use 'James' for 'his' and 'him.'"

Mary. "When James came to school, James's sister came with James."

Teacher. "Very good. 'His' and 'him,' then, are used instead of what, Henry?"

Henry. "Instead of 'James.'"

Teacher. "Words used for nouns are called what? Class, all together."

Class. "Pronouns."

Teacher. "In the sentence, 'When James came to school, his sister came with him,' 'his' and 'him' are what?"

Class. "Pronouns."

Teacher. "Very good. Now, I will give you a programme for parsing pronouns in writing.

(Teacher will place on the board, *Species? Antecedent? Agreement in what Person? Gender? Number? Rule?*)

In the sentence, 'When the sun rose, it went into a cloud,' I will parse 'it' according to this programme, thus: *It* is a pronoun, agrees with its antecedent, 'sun,' in third, singular, neuter, Rule 5, page 201, 'A pronoun must agree with its antecedent in person, number, and gender.' You may now parse the same, in concert, as I point to the steps in the programme."

Class. "*It* is a pronoun, agrees with its antecedent, 'sun,' in third, singular, neuter, Rule 5."

Teacher. "Very good. I would like to have one of you parse, in the same way, 'his,' in the sentence, 'When James came to school, his sister came with him.' Who would like to try it?"

Several hands up.

Teacher. "Well, Mary, you may parse 'his,' and the class will watch closely that Mary makes no mistake."

Mary. "*His* is a pronoun, agrees with its antecedent, 'James,' in the third, singular, masculine, Rule 5."

Teacher. "Very well. You may all memorize this rule as a part of the next lesson. How many think they can now parse pronouns?"

All hands up.

Teacher. "Now, I will ask you to parse, in writing, for your next recitation, the words in italics in the sentences below. Some are nouns: some are pronouns. Try to parse them according to the programmes which I shall leave on the blackboard, as they now stand."

1. Mary, *you* have been a good *girl.*
2. John bought a new book, but *he* gave *it* to *his* sister.
3. *She* can now parse a great many *words.*
4. Susan and *her* sister have come; *we* are so glad to see *them.*

127. Recitation.

Examination of papers with necessary corrections and full measure of approbation, especially of the slower pupils, grading each pupil's work in the teacher's class-book, according to merit.

THE VERB.

128. Preliminary Drill: Case.—*Teacher.* "Pupils, you have seen that nouns and pronouns have three different modifications—person, number, and gender. I will now give you another, more difficult to understand; but before I do so, it will be necessary to show you something about the verb. When I say, 'The boy studies,' what word tells what the boy does? All together."

Class. "Studies."

Teacher. "The word 'studies' is called the verb, or principal word, because it tells what the boy does. What, then, is the verb in this sentence, 'The girls read'? All together."

Class. "Read."

Teacher. "Why?"

Class. "Because it tells what the girls do."

Teacher. "In the sentence, 'James plowed the garden,' which is the verb? As many as can tell, may raise the hand."

Hands up.

Teacher. "John."
John. "Plowed."
Teacher. "Right. A verb is a word which denotes action, also being, or state of being. I will now give you some short sentences, and you may find the verbs."

1. The birds sing in the trees.
2. The rain falls in large drops.
3. The stars appear at night.
4. The dog runs after the rabbit.
5. John remains, but his sister has gone.

Teacher. "In the sentence, 'The birds sing in the trees,' James, what is the verb, and why?"
James. "Sing, because it tells what the birds do."
Teacher. "Yes; and now you may use the definition I just gave you. In this sentence, 'sing' denotes action. If I should say 'The birds rest on the ground,' the verb 'rest' does not denote an action, but simply a state of being. In the sentence, 'The rain falls in large drops,' what is the verb, and why? Mary."
Mary. "Falls, because it denotes action."
Teacher. "Very good. You will notice that 'appear,' in the third sentence, and 'remains,' in the fourth, are verbs, because they denote being or state of being; and all these words are verbs, because they assert something."

129. Subject and Object.—*Teacher.* "Pupils, if I should say 'The horse ran away,' what is the subject of my remark—what is the principal thing talked about? As many as can tell, may raise their hands."
Hands up.
Teacher. "Samuel."
Samuel. "Horse."
Teacher. "Right. The subject of a sentence is that about which the verb asserts something. In this sentence, what is it that ran? Why, the horse ran. So 'horse' is the subject of the verb 'ran.' Grammarians say this is in the nominative case. I would call it the subjective case, but it is better for you to follow the grammars in this instance. In the sentence, 'The boys gather apples,' what is the subject, and why? All together."
Class. "Boys, because it is that about which the verb asserts something."

Teacher. "Very good. What is the verb, and why? Henry."

Henry. "Gather, because it denotes action."

Teacher. "Yes. In the expression, 'The boy strikes the table,' what object does the boy strike? All together."

Class. "Table."

Teacher. "Right. In this, 'I see the blackboard,' what object do I see?"

Class. "Blackboard."

Teacher. "Now, I wish you to notice that those things which *receive* actions are objects, and, in grammar, those nouns and pronouns which denote things that receive action, are said to be objects; and they take different forms or are put in different positions from those words which are used as subjects, that we may be able to distinguish subjects from objects. For example, 'I saw him.' Here you easily recognize 'I' as the subject and 'him' as the object, both by the position and the form. If I should say 'Me addressed he,' you readily see both words are wrong. How should it be? All together."

Class. "I addressed him."

Teacher. "In this expression, 'I followed she,' what is wrong? How should it be?"

Class. "I followed her."

Teacher. "Yes. 'I' is in the subjective or nominative case, or form, and 'her' is in the objective case or objective form. Now, since pronouns simply stand in place of nouns, you see nouns must also have these cases; though they are distinguished only by position, and not by their form. We are now ready to enlarge our programmes for parsing nouns and pronouns so as to include case. I will put the enlarged programme on the board."

(Teacher will place on the board the following forms:)

1. For the noun—*Species? Person? Number? Gender? Case? Construction? Rule?*

2. For the pronoun—*Species? Antecedent? Agreement?* { *Person? Number? Gender?* } *Rule? Case? Construction? Rule?*

Teacher. "I will now parse, by the improved programme, 'she' in the sentence, 'She saw me.' *She* is a pronoun agreeing with its antecedent, the person spoken of, in third, singular, feminine, Rule 5, and is in the nominative case, subject of the verb 'saw,' Rule 15, 'The subject of a finite verb must be in the nominative case.' I will also parse 'me' in a similar manner. *Me* is a pronoun, agreeing with its antecedent, the person speaking, in the first, singular, common, Rule 5, and is in the objective case, the object of the verb 'saw,' according to Rule 17, 'The object of a transitive verb in the active voice must be in the objective case.'

"Pupils, I wish you to memorize, for the next recitation, these two rules just as I have given them to you. You will find them on pages 201, 202. The words 'transitive' and 'finite,' which occur in these rules, you do not now understand, perhaps, but I will explain them in a few days. I will now give some sentences, the italicized words of which you may parse in your exercise-book for the next recitation."

1. *You* borrowed a *book*, and *I* laid *it* on the desk.
2. Can *you* hear *me* as *I* study my grammar?
3. That hat is mine, but *you* may wear it.
4. Cheerful sunlight, *you* impart color to *our* cheeks.
5. They shine like diamonds.
6. What a beautiful world is *ours!* God made *it*.
7. I can paint the landscape which *you* admire.
8. *Flowers* are beautiful, but they soon fade.
9. *We* wish to live in the home of the angels.
10. Green tree and shrub and flower, *you* tell a wondrous story.

It may be well to ask for the oral parsing of one or two nouns and pronouns by the enlarged programme before the class is excused.

The teacher will be careful to use none but finite verbs in the active voice until these words are explained in due course.

POSSESSIVE CASE: DECLENSION OF PERSONAL PRONOUNS, AND OF NOUNS.

130. Criticism of Written Parsing.—Grading of each pupil on his book, and on the class register.

131. Preliminary Drill.—*Teacher.* "Pupils, you have had two cases of nouns and pronouns; I will give you one more. When I say 'This is my book,' I mean the book belongs to me, I possess it; 'my' is, then, a pronoun denoting possession. In the sentence, 'The sun's rays warm the earth,' I do not mean that the rays *belong* to the sun, but they come *from* the sun; 'sun's' is a noun in the possessive case denoting source or origin. 'This is my slate'; 'That is John's book.' Can you tell me what case the pronoun 'my' is in? Mary."

Mary. "Possessive."

Teacher. "Why, James?"

James. "Because it denotes ownership."

Teacher. "Very good. Susan, in what case is the noun 'John's,' and why?"

Susan. "Possessive, because it denotes ownership."

Teacher. "The possessive case is used to denote ownership, authorship, etc. You notice, pupils, that these possessives have a different form, to distinguish them from the nominative and objective cases. You would not say 'This is *I* slate,' or 'This is *me* slate,' but 'This is *my* slate.' Would you say 'That is *John* book,' or 'That is *John's* book?' In the sentence, 'John is a good boy,' in what case is the noun 'John'? All together."

Class. "Nominative."

Teacher. "But if I say 'This is John's ball,' what case is the noun 'John's' in?"

Class. "Possessive."

Teacher. "Right. Now, then, James, will you tell me the difference between the two forms of writing 'John'?"

James. "One has a *comma* and the letter *s* added to 'John.'"

Teacher. "Very good. The comma in that position is called an *apostrophe*. In nouns of the singular number, then, the possessive case is formed by adding an *apostrophe* and the letter *s* to the nominative form, but the possessive of plurals is formed by adding the apostrophe only; as, The horse's head, The horses' heads, etc. Pronouns do not take '*s*, but change their form to indicate the different cases. I will parse a pronoun in the possessive case. Take 'my' in the sentence 'This is my slate.' *My* is a pronoun, personal, agreeing with its antecedent, the person speaking, in first, singular, common, Rule 5, and is in the possessive case, limiting the noun 'slate,' Rule 19: 'A noun or pronoun, limiting another noun or pronoun signifying a different person or thing, is in the possessive case.' I will now give you the declensions of personal pronouns and of nouns."

Also, 'his' in the sentence, 'This is *his* hat.' *His* is a pronoun, personal, agreeing with its antecedent, the person spoken of in third, singular, common, Rule 5, and is in the possessive case, limiting 'hat,' Rule 19.

H. Gram.—4.

132. Declensions of Personal Pronouns and Nouns.—

		Singular.	Plural.
1st person.	Nom.	I,	We,
	Poss.	My or mine,	Our or ours,
	Obj.	Me.	Us.

		Singular.		Plural.
		Ordinary style.	Solemn style.	
2d person.	Nom.	You,	Thou,	You or ye,
	Poss.	Your or yours,	Thy or thine,	Your or yours,
	Obj.	You.	Thee.	You.

		Singular.			Plural.
		Mas.	Fem.	Neut.	
3d person.	Nom.	He,	She,	It,	They,
	Poss.	His,	Her or Hers,	Its,	Their or theirs,
	Obj.	Him.	Her.	It.	Them.

	Sing.	Plu.	Sing.	Plu.	Sing.	Plu.
Nominative.	Boy,	Boys,	Pen,	Pens,	Man,	Men,
Possessive.	Boy's,	Boys',	Pen's,	Pens',	Man's,	Men's,
Objective.	Boy,	Boys.	Pen,	Pens.	Man,	Men.

Teacher. "I would like to have you write sentences, for your next lesson, containing these forms of the pronoun, in the order in which they stand in the columns. Construct one such for each pronoun, and when you have written the sentences you may write the parsings of each pronoun, as far as you are able, according to the programme which I gave you last. How many think they can do it?"

Few express assent.

Teacher. "Who can give me a sentence, now, containing the pronoun 'we' properly used?"

Many hands up.

Teacher. "Well, Sarah, you may try."

Sarah. "We study grammar."

Teacher. "Very well. Now, who will give a sentence containing 'them' properly used? James, will you?"

James. "I lost my books this morning, and found them again."

Teacher. "Very well, James. I think you will find no difficulty in writing these sentences. I would rather you would make sentences of your own than borrow them from this book or any other."

CLASSES OF NOUNS.

133. Recitation of Lesson previously assigned.

134. Preliminary Drill. — *Teacher.* "Pupils, you have learned the modifications of nouns,—person, number, gender, and case. I will now give you the classes of nouns. 'Mary is a cheerful girl'; 'John is a studious boy.' The nouns 'boy' and 'girl' apply to whole classes of individuals, while 'Mary' and 'John' are names of particular persons in those classes. In order that we may know where to use capital letters, we must understand this classification of nouns. Those nouns which are common to a whole class of persons or things are called common nouns; as, boy, city, mountain. Those names which are peculiar to individuals, as John, Boston, Alps, are called proper nouns. Now, pupils, how many can tell to which class the noun 'girl' belongs? As many as can may raise the hand."

Hands up.

Teacher. "Susan."

Susan. "Common."

Teacher. "Why? James."

James. "Because it applies to a class of persons."

Teacher. "Very well. Now, what kind of noun is 'Susan Smith'? All together."

Class. "Proper."

Teacher. "Why?"

Class. "Because it is the name of a single girl."

Teacher. "Right. It is her property, and no one can change it without her consent. What class does the noun 'man' belong to? Mary."

Mary. "Common."

Teacher. "Can you name some proper nouns included under the class 'man'? Henry."

Henry. "Abraham Lincoln, U. S. Grant, Horace Greeley."

Teacher. "That's enough, Henry. I think you are all able now to distinguish the classes of nouns. If so, we are ready to complete our programme for parsing nouns. I will place the full programme on the blackboard, where you can all see it."

(The teacher will place it on the board thus: *Species? Class? (Subclass?) Person? Number? Gender? Case? Construction? Rule?*)

Teacher. "I will ask Henry to rise and parse 'John' in the sentence, 'John instructs Mary.'"

Henry. "*John* is a noun, proper, third, singular, masculine, nominative, subject of the verb 'instructs,' Rule 15."

Teacher. "Very good. Charles, you may now parse 'Mary.'"

Charles. "*Mary* is a noun, proper, third, singular, feminine, objective case, object of the verb 'instructs,' Rule 17."

Teacher. "Susan, you may parse 'horse,' in the sentence, 'The horse eats corn.'"

Susan. "*Horse* is a noun, common, third, singular, masculine, nominative, subject of the verb 'eats,' Rule 15."

Teacher. "Right. James, you may parse 'corn,' in the same sentence."

James. "*Corn* is a noun, common, third, singular, neuter, objective, object of the verb 'eats,' Rule 17."

Teacher. "Very good. I will ask you at your next recitation to parse the words I shall indicate in the following sentences."

1. Ella lost *her grammar.*
2. *Mary's* father bought a blue *dress* for her.
3. *My father's* house is on the hill.
4. Buy your *goods* at the *people's* store.
5. No good boy will rob a *bird's nest.*
6. The *pupil's delight* is in study.
7. The *sailor's life* is full of danger.
8. Mary bought some *apples,* and gave *them* to *her* sister.

CLASSES OF PRONOUNS.

135. Examination of Papers.—Grading of books in neatness, on a scale of 1—5. This grading may be deferred till recess or intermission.

136. Preliminary Drill.—*Teacher.* "Before our programme for parsing pronouns can be completed, you will learn something of the classes of pronouns. There are three classes, which I will try to show you by examples. You may answer in concert; what person does 'I' always stand for?"

Class. "First person."
Teacher. "Right. 'He'?"
Class. "Third."
Teacher. "'You'?"
Class. "Second person."
Teacher. "Very good. Does 'you' ever stand for the first person? Mary."
Mary. "It does not."
Teacher. "No; and you will notice that 'I' never stands for any person but the first; 'you' always stands for the second person. Because 'I,' 'thou,' 'you,' 'he,' 'she,' 'it,' always stand each for the same grammatical person, the first, second, or third, they are called personal pronouns. I will now give you the second class. In the sentence, 'I *who* saw it can explain the matter,' in what person is 'I'? James."
James. 'First person."
Teacher. "In what person, then, is 'who'? Susan."
Susan. "First person."
Teacher. "In what person is 'who' in the sentence, You who ate the apples can tell how it tasted'? Henry."
Henry. "Second person."
Teacher. "'He who studies will learn.' 'Who' stands in place of what word? Jane."
Jane. "He."
Teacher. "It is, then, in what person?"
Jane. "Third."
Teacher. "You see, pupils, that some pronouns do not always represent the same grammatical person; they are 'who,' 'which,' and 'that,' and sometimes 'as.' These are called *relative pronouns*.

"The third class of pronouns is used for asking questions, and are called interrogative pronouns; as, 'What shall I do?' 'Who said so?' I will now give you the full programme for parsing the pronoun."

Species? Class? (Sub-class?) Antecedent? Agreement? Person? Number? Gender? Rule? Case? Construction? Rule?

Teacher. "I would like to have some one rise and parse 'I' in the sentence, 'I who saw it will explain the matter.' Who will try it?"

Hands up.
Teacher. "Julia."

Julia. "*I* is a pronoun, personal, agreeing with its antecedent, the person speaking, in the first, singular, common, Rule 5, nominative, subject of 'will explain,' Rule 15."

Teacher. "Very good. Charles, you may parse 'who' by the same programme."

Charles. "*Who* is a pronoun, relative, agreeing with its antecedent, 'I,' in first, singular, common, Rule 5, nominative, subject of 'saw,' Rule 15."

Teacher. "I will now parse an interrogative pronoun for you. I wish you to notice particularly the antecedent and the construction. In the sentence, 'Who told you so?' 'who' is a pronoun, interrogative, agreeing with its antecedent, in the answer of the question, in person, number, and gender unknown, Rule 5, nominative, subject of 'told,' Rule 15. I think you can now parse almost any pronoun. For the next recitation you may parse, in your exercise-books, the italicized words in the following sentences:"

1. The boy *who* laughs grows fat.
2. I respect *my* teacher.
3. The scholar *who* studies diligently will grow wise.
4. The apples *which you* gave me were sour.
5. *We* should be kind to every body.
6. *Who* can recite his lesson well?
7. There is the fly *that* bit my nose.
8. The sun gives light and heat, *which* make plants and trees grow.
9. *Who* swam over the river?
10. *Whom* did you call?
11. Those are the same *as* you gave me.

137. Criticism of Written Parsings.—By the pupils' changing books with each other, and reading the parsing of a fellow-pupil as his parsing may be called for.

138. Further Drill in Pronouns.—*Teacher.*—"Pupils, I have one thing more to tell you about relative pronouns. They are related to their antecedents in such a way as to connect sentences. For example: 'Here is the girl *who* lost her book.' There are here two sentences: 'Here is the girl' is one sentence, and 'who lost her book' is another, since both have verbs in them, as every sentence must have a verb in it. The relative introduces the sentence which modifies the antecedent, and thus connects the two sentences. For this reason I would prefer to call it a '*connecting* pronoun'; but you may follow the usage of the grammars, and call it a *relative* pronoun. I will now give you definitions for the three classes of pronouns, which I wish you to memorize for the next recitation.

"1. *A personal pronoun is one that always stands for the same grammatical person.*

"2. *A relative pronoun is one that may stand for any grammatical person, and connects clauses.*

"3. *An interrogative pronoun is one used for asking a question.*

"You may also memorize the declensions of relative pronouns for the next recitation."

139. Declension of the Relative Pronoun.

Nominative,	who,	which,
Possessive,	whose,	whose,
Objective,	whom,	which.

For the next parsing lesson you may take the words in italics in the following sentences:"

1. Where does the *sun* rise?
2. The earth *which* we inhabit is nearly spherical.
3. *My* ink is black: *yours* is blue.
4. *Who* made the earth and the stars?
5. *They who* are temperate in all things will live long.
6. The book *that* lies on the table is *mine*.
7. The team *that* I bought broke my wagon in pieces.
8. We must answer for every idle word *that* we speak.

Teacher. "You will notice on page 42, in the declensions of personal pronouns, that some of them have two possessive forms. The first form is always used *with* the noun. The second is used *without* the noun, and limits the noun understood. For example: In the sentence, 'My ink is black: yours is blue,' 'yours' is a pronoun, personal, agreeing with its antecedent, the person spoken to, in second, singular, common, Rule 5, possessive case, and limits the noun 'ink,' understood, Rule 19. Pupils, you will find another similar construction in your lesson for to-morrow."

PART TWO.

ETYMOLOGY.—THE NOUN.

140. Definition.—A noun is a *name;* as, *James, Boston, book, tree; truth, mind, hope, desire.*

141. When used as a *name,* any *sign, letter, word, phrase,* or *sentence,* may become a noun; as, * is called an asterisk; *A* is a vowel; Let us have no *ifs* and *ands* about it; "*My Wife and I*" is a novel; "*We celebrate this day,*" was printed on their banners.

142. Classes.—*Proper* and *Common.*

143. A proper noun is a name peculiar to an individual, or class of individuals; as, *Charles, New York,* the *Amazon,* the *Germans, Alleghenies.*

144. Two or more words, forming one name, are parsed as one noun; as, *Central Park, John Greenleaf Whittier.*

145. Every proper noun must begin with a *capital* letter.

146. A common noun is a name which belongs to many objects in common; as, *house, farm, cat, animal; industry, pleasure, mercy, goodness.*

147. Common nouns have three special sub-classes: *Abstract, Collective, Verbal.*

148. An abstract noun is the name of some quality; as, *sweetness, generosity, length.*

149. A collective noun is a name, singular in form but plural in meaning; as, *crowd, company, throng, herd, audience, fleet.*

150. A verbal noun is the name of an action or state of being; as, *precedence, existence, declaration, description, substitution.*

ETYMOLOGY—THE NOUN.

151. Participles become *verbal nouns* by prefixing an article or adjective; as, *The giving* of good advice; *Such measuring* of distances is very convenient and accurate.

152. A common noun, with the definite article, is sometimes used as a proper noun; as, *The Park, The Capitol, The Express.*

153. Common nouns begin with capital letters, only when they begin a sentence, or are of marked importance in a sentence.

154. Modifications.—*Person, Number, Gender, Case.*

155. Person is that modification of nouns and pronouns which distinguishes the speaker, the person spoken to, and the person or thing spoken of.

156. There are three grammatical persons: *First, Second,* and *Third.*

157. The **first person** denotes the name of the speaker; as, *I, Darius,* do make a decree; Grant forgiveness to *us, suppliants.*

158. The first person, as applied to nouns, belongs to names of persons only, or things personified.

159. A noun of the first person is found in no other construction than that of apposition with a pronoun of the first person, and in the nominative absolute by subscription.

160. The **second person** denotes the name of the person spoken to; as, I appeal to you, *Mr. Chairman; Sarah,* you may come here.

161. A noun of the second person can have but two constructions; namely, in *apposition* with a pronoun of the second person, or in the *nominative absolute* by direct address.

162. The second person, as applied to nouns, belongs to persons only, or to things personified.

163. The **third person** denotes the name of the person or thing spoken of; as, *Whittier* has written a beautiful *poem* entitled, "*Snow-Bound.*"

164. The third person is often used for the *first;* as, Your *daughter* pleads; hear, O my father. Sometimes, for the *second;* as, The *Lord* cause his face to shine upon us.

H. Gram.—5.

165. The third person is used in all constructions, except the nominative absolute by direct address, by apposition with the first personal pronoun, and by subscription.

166. A predicate noun is usually in the third person, without regard to the person of the subject; as, Thou art the *man;* I am the *physician.*

167. Number is that modification of nouns and pronouns which distinguishes unity and plurality.

168. There are two numbers: *Singular* and *Plural.*

169. The **singular number** denotes but *one;* as, The *horse* runs; The *boy* walks.

170. Some nouns are found only in the singular; as, *Gold, wheat, temperance, drunkenness, poetry, chemistry, integrity, music.*

171. Proper names are found, usually, in the singular only.

172. The **plural number** denotes more than one; as, The *horses* run; The *boys* walk.

173. Some nouns are found in the plural only; as, *Annals, ashes, billiards, bellows, manners, morals, pincers, scissors, snuffers, tongs.*

174. The plural is formed regularly by adding *s* to the singular; as, *Boy, boys.*

175. Nouns in *s, sh, ch,* aspirates, *z, x, o,* or *i,* usually form the plural in *es;* as, *Lens-es, brush-es, birch-es, quiz-es, fox-es, hero-es, alkali-es.*

176. After a consonant, *y* is changed into *ies,* for the plural; as, *Fairy, fairies.*

177. Nouns in *f* or *fe,* usually form the plural by changing the *f* or *fe* into *ves;* as, *Wife, wives; leaf, leaves.* Such nouns as *turf, grief,* etc., form their plurals regularly.

178. Some nouns form the plural irregularly; as, *Man, men; child, children; mouse, mice.*

179. Compounds ending in *ful* or *full,* form the plural regularly; as, *Spoonful, spoonfuls; handful, handfuls.*

180. The nouns, *Caiman, German, Mussulman, talisman, Turkoman,* not being compounds of the noun *man,* form their plurals regularly; as, *Caimans, Germans, Mussulmans, talismans, Turkomans.*

ETYMOLOGY—THE NOUN.

181. Some nouns have two plurals of different significations; as, *Brother*, *brothers* (of the same parents); *brethren* (of the same fraternity). *Die*, *dies* (used in coining); *dice* (used in gaming). *Fish*, *fishes* (individuals); *fish* (the species). *Penny*, *pennies* (coins); *pence* (the species).

182. In compounds, the sign of the plural is commonly added to the important part; as, *Fathers-in-law; fly-traps; courts-martial; Song-Queens.*

183. The best usage annexes the sign of the plural to the *name*, when a *title* and a *name* are used together; as, The Miss *Smiths;* the Miss *Browns.*

184. Some nouns are alike in both numbers; as, *sheep, swine, cattle, species, alms, corps, measles, nuptials.*

185. Foreign nouns adopted into our language, generally retain their original plural. Those marked *r*, in the following list, have also a regular plural.

Automaton,	automata, *r*.	Genus,	genera.
Axis,	axes.	Hypothesis,	hypotheses.
Basis,	bases.	Lamina,	laminæ.
Beau,	beaux, *r*.	Magus,	magi.
Cherub,	cherubim, *r*.	Medium,	media, *r*.
Criterion,	criteria.	Nebula,	nebulæ.
Ellipsis,	ellipses.	Phenomenon,	phenomena.
Encomium,	encomia, *r*.	Radius,	radii.
Erratum,	errata.	Stratum,	strata.
Focus,	foci.	Vertebra,	vertebræ.
Formula,	formulæ, *r*.	Virtuoso,	virtuosi.
Genius,	genii.	Vortex,	vortices, *r*.

186. The plural of letters, marks, signs, and figures, is formed by adding the apostrophe (') and the letter s; as, algebraic notation employs x's, y's, $+$'s, $-$'s; add the 2's and 10's together.

187. In cases of doubt, refer to Webster's or Worcester's Dictionary.

188. Gender is that modification of nouns and pronouns which distinguishes sex.

189. There are four genders: *Masculine, Feminine, Common,* and *Neuter.*

190. Names of males are **masculine**; as, *man, boy, father, son.*

191. Most masculine nouns have a corresponding feminine; some, however, have not; as, *baker, brewer, carpenter, lawyer.*

192. Names used to denote both genders, though applicable, strictly, to males only, are masculine or feminine, according to their use; as, *heir, poet, teacher.*

193. Names of females are **feminine**; as, *woman, girl, mother, daughter.*

194. Some feminine nouns have no corresponding masculine; as, *laundress, seamstress.*

195. Names which apply in common to males and females are **common** in gender; as, *neighbor, friend, parent, child.*

196. Nouns which are names of objects without sex, are *Neuter;* as, *tree, house, goodness, tribe, race, sex.*

197. Collective nouns are neuter when the objects are considered as a unit; as, The *mob* swept everything in *its* way; The *herd* moved *its* huge mass slowly over the prairie; The *sex* is not a unit with regard to *its* own rights.

198. Neuter nouns become masculine or feminine by personification; as, The *Sun* holds *his* fiery course through mid-heaven; The *Moon* shed *her* pale light on that dismal battle scene.

199. In speaking of inferior animals, and of infants, the distinction of sex is not observed; as, The *swallow* builds *its* nest in chimneys; The *child* is in *its* new carriage.

200. The sexes are distinguished by their names in three ways:

201. By *different words;* as, *boy, girl; brother, sister; beau, belle; king, queen; son, daughter; youth, damsel; swain, nymph.*

202. By *different terminations;* as, *actor, actress; bridegroom, bride; hero, heroine; lion, lioness; prince, princess; giant, giantess.*

203. By *prefixes* and *suffixes;* as, land*lord,* land*lady;* grand*father,* grand*mother;* man*servant,* maid*servant;* *male* child, *female* child.

204. Case is that modification of nouns and pronouns which, by means of form or position, indicates their relation to other words, or their independent use.

205. Nouns have three cases: *Nominative, Possessive, Objective.*

206. The **Nominative Case** is that form or position of the noun or pronoun, which is used to indicate the subject of a finite verb.

207. The nominative case is used with nouns in four dependent constructions, and in five *absolute* positions.

208. The subject of a finite verb; as, *Mary* sings; Our *friends* have come.

209. In the *predicate;* as, James became a *lawyer;* They are *masters* of the situation.

210. In *apposition* with a *noun* or *pronoun;* as, I, *John Smith*, do solemnly affirm; Mr. Jones, the *banker*, has gone to Europe.

211. In *apposition* with a *sentence* or phrase; as, Mary gave the old man a cup of water, a *kindness* which he seemed to appreciate; His finding me there, a *providence* I can never forget, saved me from utter ruin.

212. The construction of *apposition* is used to explain or emphasize the leading noun or pronoun of which the appositive is a modifier.

213. Absolute positions.

214. By *direct address;* as, *George*, you may go with me; O *virtue!* when will all men follow thy guidance.

215. By *exclamation;* as, *Nonsense!* it can't be done; *Fiddlesticks!* it isn't worth the powder.

216. By *inscription;* titles of books, captions, signs for business houses, labels; superscriptions and subscriptions are in the nominative absolute by inscription; as, Webster's *Dictionary*, etc.

REMARK.—It is unnecessary to suppose such words are a part of some sentence.

217. By *pleonasm;* as, *Gad*, a troop shall overcome him; The *stars*, they shall shine forever.

218. With a *participle;* as, The *hack* having gone, we were obliged to walk to the railroad.

REMARK.—Though the construction of the nominative absolute with a participle has no grammatical relation with the sentence with which it is connected, it always has a close logical relation, that of an adverb, generally limiting the verb of the sentence.

219. The **Possessive Case** is that form of the noun or pronoun which is used to limit a noun of different signification.

220. The possessive case denotes *possession, origin, kind, authorship*, etc.; as, *Jane's* slate; The *moon's* gentle beams; *Boys'* hats; *Blair's* Rhetoric.

221. The possessive case is used in three constructions:

222. Limiting a noun of different signification; as, *Mary's* book; *Day's* Composition.

223. Limiting a noun of the same signification when it is in apposition; as, Let it be according to his Highness, the *King's* pleasure.

224. Limiting a participle as its subject; as, *John's* being there was taken as evidence of his guilt.

225. Nouns form their possessives in the *singular* by adding an *apostrophe* (') and the letter *s* to the nominative form; in the *plural*, when the nominative ends in *s*, by adding *only* the *apostrophe*; as, singular, The *boy's* hat; plural, *Boys'* hats.

226. Irregular plurals form the possessive in the same manner as the singular; as, The *oxen's* yoke; *Women's* hats.

227. The *s* is frequently omitted when it would occasion several successive sounds of *s*; as, For peace' sake; For conscience' sake.

228. The *apostrophe* and *s* are simply an indication of plurality when added to *letters, figures*, etc.; as, 9's, 11's, x's.

229. In words like *sheep, deer, swine*, etc., which have the singular and plural alike, the *s* is placed *before* the apostrophe in forming the possessive plural; as, sheeps', deers', swines'.

230. The possessive sign ('s) is an abbreviation of the old English genitive ending, *es* or *is*; the sign (') being called an *apostrophe*, because it indicates the omission of the *e* or *i*.

But in the plural, as, boys', the (') is simply a *sign* of the possessive, and *not* a mark of *abbreviation*.

231. Compound words have the sign of possession at the end; as, *President Grant's* Proclamation.

232. When the possessive is followed by a noun in apposition, or by a prepositional phrase, or by a pronominal adjective, the sign is annexed to the word immediately preceding the limited noun; as, That is *Mr. Good the tailor's* goose; The *Secretary of the Treasury's* desire was to pay off the 7-20's; *Every body else's* business but his own.

233. The possessive is often used with the limited noun understood; as, At Mr. Gilchrist's [store], the dry goods merchant; That is a picture of my father's [pictures].

234. In the expression, 'She is a wife of my brother's,' *brother's* is in the possessive by enallage, used for the objective.

235. Some compound words omit both the hyphen and the sign of the possessive; as, *hogshead, Collinsville.*

236. A noun or pronoun limiting a participle used as a noun, is in the possessive case; as, They objected to *Mary's studying* grammar.

237. The **Objective Case** is that *form* or *position* of a noun or pronoun which is used to indicate the object of a transitive verb in the active voice, or of a preposition.

238. This case is used with nouns in five *regular* constructions, and in one by *enallage.*

239. The *object* of a *transitive* verb in the *active* voice; as, The man *held* the *boy.*

240. The *object* of a *preposition;* as, The city *of New York.*

241. The *subject* of an *infinitive;* as, He desired the *army to march* at daylight; Mary wanted *James to go* home.

242. In the *predicate;* as, They supposed him to be the *janitor;* My friends desired me to become a *merchant;* He reported them to be the *men* who are surveying the new railroad route; His father desired him to be called *John.*

243. In the *predicate* with an *infinitive,* whose subject is a sentence or a phrase; as, *That the prisoner was there at the time,* the jury considered [to be] a *link* in the chain of evidence which secured his conviction; We deemed *his being our enemy* [to be] the very *reason* why we should feed him.

244. In *apposition* with another objective; as, That whip belongs to Mr. Smith, the *wagoner;* I have seen the planet *Saturn.*

245. *In apposition with a sentence or phrase;* as, The Professor noticed *that Samuel came in time*, a rare *circumstance* indeed; He amused the children by *relating anecdotes*, an *exercise* which he evidently enjoyed himself.

246. By *enallage* for the Possessive; as, I never thought of *Mary* coming; for, I never thought of *Mary's* coming. There is no harm in *women* studying politics; for, There is no harm in *women's* studying politics.

REMARK.—For the cases in which the objective of pronouns is used for the nominative by enallage, see page 66, Art. 324.

247. Some grammarians claim that nouns denoting *distance, time, weight, measure*, etc., are independent of construction, or if they please, independent *in* their construction; but they have a *dependent* construction, generally as adverbial elements, and are better disposed of by supposing a preposition understood; as, I walked [over or through] a *mile;* Susan practices music [for] an *hour* [on] each day; The herd of cattle weighed [to the amount of] ten *tons;* The potatoes measured [the quantity of] a bushel; He was six feet tall; (He was tall [to the height of] six feet). The awkwardness of supplying such complex prepositions as "to the extent of," or "to the amount of," is not as vicious as the erroneous assumption that these classes of nouns are "independent," or "are put in the objective independent."

248. The objective case, with the preposition *of*, is frequently used for the possessive case, for *euphony*, or to avoid *tautology;* as, The grave *of Washington;* The Young Ladies' Sewing Society's Contribution; better, The Contribution *of* the Young Ladies' Sewing *Society*.

249. Many verbs signifying *to ask, to teach, to give*, etc., are followed by two objects in different senses. Most grammarians call one of these the direct, and the other the indirect, object. I prefer to reject the term "indirect object" altogether, as involving a contradiction, and supply the preposition with one of the objects, making thus an *adverbial element* of what these grammarians call an "*indirect object*." For example: I gave [to] Henry my book; He taught [to] the children grammar; She awarded [to] John the prize; I asked the boy [for] his name; or, I asked [of] the boy his name.

250. When the verb is found in the passive with either object as its subject, the other may be governed by a preposition understood; as, My book was given [to] Henry; Henry was given [with] my book; Grammar was taught [to] the children; The children were taught [in] grammar; The boy was asked [for] his name; His name was asked [of] the boy.

251. Not unfrequently the object of a preposition (understood) after an active transitive verb, is made the grammatical subject of the passive voice; as, He promised [to] me a book; *I was promised a book.* In such cases, it is better to consider the logical subject, 'book,' in this example, as governed by some preposition understood, rather than to demand a reconstruction of the sentence, under the plea of false syntax. The best usage warrants this illogical use of the remote object as the subject of the passive verb. Even those grammarians who give such examples as "false syntax," or "loose construction," use the same false syntax and loose construction repeatedly themselves in their own discussions.

252. *Declension of Nouns.*—Nouns are declined to denote *number* and *case*. Thus:

Singular.	*Nom.*	child,	girl,	lady,	ox,	boy,
	Poss.	child's,	girl's,	lady's,	ox's,	boy's,
	Obj.	child,	girl,	lady,	ox,	boy,
Plural.	*Nom.*	children,	girl's,	ladies,	oxen,	boys,
	Poss.	children's,	girls',	ladies',	oxen's,	boys',
	Obj.	children,	girls,	ladies,	oxen,	boys.

Proper names are declined thus:

Nom.	Mary,	John,	James,
Poss.	Mary's,	John's,	James's,
Obj.	Mary,	John,	James.

THE PRONOUN.

253. Definition.—A pronoun is a word used in the place of a noun; as, The *colonel* rode at the head of *his* regiment, *which* was proud of *him.*

254. That *word, phrase,* or *sentence* for which the pronoun stands, is called the *antecedent;* as, *James* lost *his* penknife; *To have restored the monarchy, which* then seemed probable, would have ruined the nation; *He humbly implored the conqueror's clemency;* to *which* the haughty victor gave no heed.

255. The *antecedent* itself may be another pronoun; as, That is *he* of *whom* you spoke.

256. The *antecedent* precedes its pronoun; except in (1) interrogative sentences, where it follows in the answer to the question; as, *Who* dealt with you? *John;* and (2) in case of the introductory *it;* as, *It* is *they*, where *it* takes *they* as its antecedent, and (3) in hyperbation; as, "*His* father's counsel and mother's tears the *boy* treated with disdain."

257. Classes.—*Personal, Relative, Interrogative.*

258. A **personal** pronoun is one that always stands for the same grammatical person; *I*, always for the *first; Thou* or *you*, always for the *second; He, she*, and *it*, always for the *third*.

259. *Personal pronouns* have the subclasses Simple and Compound.

260. The simple personal pronouns are, *I, thou* or *you, he, she, it;* and their plurals, *we, ye, they*, etc.

261. The reflexive personal pronouns are *myself, thyself, himself, herself, itself;* and their plurals, *ourselves, yourselves, themselves*, etc.

262. A **relative** pronoun is one that may stand for any grammatical person; and connects clauses; as, *I who* speak will lead the way; *You who* know, should speak out; These are *they who* came from afar. In these different examples, the relative, *who*, stands for all the grammatical persons; the *first, second,* and *third*.

263. *Relative pronouns* have the subclasses *Simple, Compound,* and *Double*.

264. The *Simple relatives* are *who, which, that,* and *as*.

265. *Who* is used only for persons, or for inanimate objects personified; as, These are the *men who* make our laws; And thou art Death, *who* dealest thy favors with impartial hand.

266. *Who* is sometimes used with its antecedent understood; as, *Who* steals my purse, steals trash.

267. *Which* is used for brute animals and for inanimate things; as, The *horse which* you bought yesterday ran away with a *wagon which* cost me one hundred dollars.

268. *Which* is sometimes a pronominal adjective; as, He labors earnestly to make me a grammarian, for *which* purpose I myself will labor also.

269. *Which* is also sometimes an *interrogative pronominal adjective;* as, *Which* [one] will you have?

270. *That* and *as* are used for persons, animals, and things; as, Show me the *boy that* loves his studies; Name such *persons as* you please; The *questions that* were discussed will be debated again; Give me such *things as* are most convenient for you.

271. *That* is a pronominal adjective when it precedes its noun expressed or understood; as, *That* boy is lame; *That* is my book.

272. *That* is sometimes a conjunction; as, Many persons hoped *that* the railroad would be constructed on the present survey.

273. The relative *that*, when in the objective case, can not follow its governing word; as, The caravan *that* you *described* to us is coming; The men *that* you spoke *of* are Arabs. We can not say, The men *of that* you spoke are Arabs.

274. *As* is generally an adverb, a conjunction, or a preposition; but is always a *relative pronoun* when used after the words *such, same,* and *as many.* For example: Such *as* desire, may come and welcome; They are the same *as* you saw yesterday; "To as many *as* received him, to them gave he power to become the sons of God." In the first sentence, *as* relates to persons, understood, for its antecedent, and is the subject of *desire.* In the next example, *as* is the object of *saw.*

Many grammarians deny to *as* any relative force in any arrangement. Their mistake seems to be in failing to carry their analytic process far enough. It is obvious even in Dr. Bullions's own example (Bullions's Grammar, page 320), "Bring such books as are wanted," that *as* is a relative pronoun. Bullions has supplied an assumed ellipsis, thus: "Bring such books as [those which] are wanted." He has left '*those*' without construction. What construction must be given it? Evidently 'those' relates to 'books' understood, which is the subject of 'are' understood. We then read it thus: "Bring such books as [those books are which] are wanted." The question now is, Is 'are' attributive or copulative? '*Are*' is surely *copulative*, and must connect some attribute with its subject, 'books.' That attribute is undeniably the relative pronoun 'as,' which thus is in the predicate nominative with the verb 'are,' referring to the same thing as its subject, 'books.'

In his effort to avoid calling 'as' a pronoun, Dr. Bullions has made a bungling sentence, which serves, when thoroughly analyzed, to convict him of error, and to show conclusively the relative nature of 'as'; hence I prefer the original sentence, parsing 'as' as a relative pronoun, the subject of the verb *are wanted*. This gives the sense intended; while his assumption of an ellipsis gives another meaning to the sentence, and even then makes 'as' a relative pronoun.

275. The *Compound relatives* are formed by adding *ever* or *soever* to the simple relatives *who* and *which*, and to the double relative *what;* as, *whoever, whosoever, whichever, whichsoever*, etc.

276. When thus compounded, relatives have a distributive signification, and the antecedent is frequently understood; as, *Whoever* comes first, will be first served; that is, *Any person* who comes first, etc.

277. The *Double relative* is *What*.

278. *What* is generally used for things, but sometimes with persons for its antecedent; as, You may command *whatever* soldiers you can muster; All persons *whatsoever* are forbidden to enter these premises.

279. *What* is sometimes used for other parts of speech; as,

280. An *interrogative pronominal adjective;* *What* evidence can you bring?

281. *What* is so frequently employed for the conjunction *that*, by good speakers, that the usage seems to be warranted; as, We had no idea but *what* he was honest.

282. An *interjection;* as, *What!* must I suffer defeat?

283. *What* is sometimes an expletive; as, I tell you *what*, that's a fine horse.

284. *What* is also sometimes an *adverb;* as, *What* by intrigue and *what* by bribery, he accomplished his object. Here *what* is equivalent to *partly*.

285. The chief characteristic of the *relative, what*, is its *double* use; being equivalent to *that* [thing] *which, all which, the* [thing] *which*, or *those* [things] *which*, etc. For example: You may pay me *whatever* money you have; that is, You may pay me *all the* money *whichever* you have; You may command *whatever* soldiers you can muster; that is, You may command *all the* soldiers *whichever* you can muster; *Whatever* happens, you may rely on me; that is, You may rely on me, *notwithstanding anything whichever* happens. In these sentences, *what* and its equivalent are in italics. It will be seen that the expanded sentences give the equivalent expressions for *what*. Some good grammarians have made an effort to explain away the double nature of *what*. For example, in the sentence, I care not in *what* manner you accomplish it, the sense is this: I care not *concerning the* manner in *which* you accomplish it. Many grammarians make *what* in this sentence a simple demonstrative; but the truth is, it has *three functions*. Since it contains a relative, it possesses the (1) *connective* and (2) *representative* functions of the relative; since it contains the definite article, *the*, or the demonstrative, *that*, it possesses the (3) *distinguishing* power of these words. Here are, then, two functions of *what*, which these grammarians fail to recognize. *Whatsoever* way he turns, ruin stares him in the face; that is, [In] *that* way [into] *whichsoever* he turns, ruin stares him in the face.

All persons *whatsoever* are forbidden to enter these premises; that is, All *those* persons *whosoever* [they may be] are forbidden, etc.

What sometimes contains an expletive construction; as, *Whatever* I do, he declares it to be wrong; equivalent to, He declares it to be wrong, *the thing whichever* I do. Here, *thing*, the antecedent part of *whatever*, is in the nominative absolute by pleonasm.

286. The *relative* should be placed as near as possible to its antecedent, to avoid ambiguity; as, Rehoboam, *who* reigned after the division, was the son of Solomon; rather than, Rehoboam, the son of Solomon, *who* reigned after the division.

287. An **interrogative** pronoun is one used in asking a question; as, *Who* are you? *What* is that?

288. The *Interrogatives* are *Who* and *What*.

289. *Who*, as an interrogative, is used only for persons.

290. *What*, as an interrogative, is used only for things.

In many sentences, *what* may be considered either an interrogative or a double relative; as, I know *what* was wanted. This is equivalent as an interrogative to, I know [the answer of the question] what was wanted; or to a double relative; as, I know *the thing which* was wanted. Again, I heard *what* prevented his coming. This is equivalent to, I heard [the answer of the question] what prevented his coming; or to this, I heard *the thing which* prevented his coming.

The interrogative *who* has been erroneously treated. I know *who* took the book. In this sentence, '*who*' is an interrogative. I do not mean to say I know the *person* who took the book; for he is one of our number whom we *all* know, and to announce that I *know him* would give *no information*. The plain meaning is, I can answer the question, Who took the book?

In the sentence, I learned, many years ago, who was the first President, I do not intend to say that I learned George Washington, who was, etc., but I learned [how to answer the question], Who was the first President?

291. In an early period, *whether* was used as an interrogative pronoun; as, Whether is greater, the gold or the temple? (Matt. xxiii: 17.) But this use is now obsolete.

292. Most grammarians have classed *which* among the *interrogative pronouns;* but it may easily be shown that, in all such cases, it is an *interrogative pronominal adjective*. All grammarians class *which* as the *definite* interrogative; and because it is thus *definite*, it can not, plainly, be an interrogative *pronoun* at all; for the sense is always, *which one of two;* the noun must be invariably understood. For example: Which will you have? Here, as in all such uses of '*which*,' there is a definite person or thing in the mind. Again: Which remains? In the mind of the speaker, there is a definite word limited by '*which*'; as, Which *piece* of goods remains? Which *person* remains? Hence, *which* can not be an interrogative pronoun.

293. Modifications.—*Person, Number, Gender,* and *Case.*

294. Pronouns must agree with their antecedents in *person, number,* and *gender*.

295. The *first* and *second* personal pronouns are of the common gender, when not definitely determined by the antecedent. They are never neuter; but when they refer to inanimate objects personified, those objects are considered as either masculine or feminine.

296. Only the *third* personal pronoun has distinct forms for the genders; *he,* masculine; *she,* feminine; *it,* neuter.

ETYMOLOGY—THE PRONOUN.

297. In interrogative sentences, when the answer is not known, the interrogative pronoun may be said to agree with its antecedent, in *person*, *number*, and *gender*, unknown.

298. Rulers, editors, and others, who speak for a community or a class of persons, use *we* for *I*, by a figure of speech called Enallage. The verb, in such cases, is always plural; as, "We [the editor] were impressed by the speaker's earnestness."

299. *Scripture, solemn style, poetry*, and the *Society of Friends*, employ *thou* instead of *you*. *You* was originally used only in the plural, and is still constructed with only the *plural* form of verbs, but now represents a single person; as, *You are* the very *man*.

300. *It* has several peculiar uses:

301. Though *neuter*, *it* is sometimes used for infants, or for persons whose sex is unknown, and animals; as, The *infant* soon learns to return *its* mother's smile; The *rabbit* ran so fast that the dog could not catch *it*.

302. *It*, as the subject of the verb 'be,' is frequently followed by an antecedent which it represents, but with which it does not agree: in such cases it is an introductory word; as, *It* is *they*; *It* is *John* and *Susan*.

303. *It* is frequently used for an obvious antecedent, definitely understood. For example: The weather; as, *It* is cold; *It* rains; The ground; as, *It* is very muddy; The time; as, *It* is nine o'clock.

304. *It* is sometimes expletive:

305. In the nominative, as introductory to the sentence. For example: *It* is better *to suffer wrong* than to do wrong. *To suffer wrong* is the logical subject of *is;* while 'it' is the apparent or grammatical subject.

306. In the objective; as, I believed *it* to be necessary that I should go home when I did. The apparent or grammatical objective subject of the infinitive 'to be,' is *it;* while the true or logical subject is the sentence, 'That I should go home when I did.'

307. A "euphonic" (?) slang expletive; as, Come, trip *it* as you go; Go *it* while you are young.

308. The speaker, in alluding to others in connection with himself, should generally first mention the person addressed, and himself last; as, You and he and I are playmates. Not, however, You and I made a great mistake; but, more courteously, I and you made a great mistake.

309. Case.—The case of pronouns, like that of nouns, indicates their relation to other words in a sentence, or their independent use, but is generally determined by their form.

310. *Declension of the personal pronouns:*

		Singular.	Plural.
1st Person.	Nom.	I,	We,
	Poss.	My or mine,	Our or ours,
	Obj.	Me,	Us.

		Singular.		Plural.
		Ordinary style.	Solemn style.	
2d Person.	Nom.	You,	Thou,	You or ye,
	Poss.	Your or yours,	Thy or Thine,	Your or yours,
	Obj.	You,	Thee,	You or ye.

		Singular.			Plural.
		Mas.	Fem.	Neut.	
3d Person.	Nom.	He,	She,	It,	They,
	Poss.	His,	Her or hers,	Its,	Their or theirs,
	Obj.	Him,	Her,	It,	Them.

Declension of the relative pronoun.

	Sing. and Plu.	Sing. and Plu.
Nom.	Who,	Which,
Poss.	Whose,	Whose,
Obj.	Whom,	Which.

311. *Peculiarities* of the *Possessive* case of pronouns.

312. *Forms* for the possessive: When the limited noun is understood, the possessive is strengthened in every case, save that of *his* and *its*. Thus: This book is *yours;* that is *hers;* but there are *ours* and *theirs*. 'Yours,' 'hers,' 'ours,' and 'theirs' obviously limit *book*, or *books*, expressed or understood as the subject of the verb.

Several grammarians have fallen into error concerning the construction of 'mine,' 'yours,' etc. For example: In one popular grammar, 'hers,' in the sentence, "That book is *hers*, not *yours*," is parsed as a "*pronoun; possessive;* antecedent '*book*'; *neuter gender*," etc. This ignores the distinctions of gender, and makes 'hers,' which represents the *owner*, agree with 'book' as the antecedent, in the neuter gender. Another 'Normal Grammar' makes 'mine' a noun in the objective case: "John is a friend of *mine*." The word 'mine' limits *friends* understood; and this expression is equivalent to "John is one of my friends." The word 'mine' in this connection evidently limits a plural noun. Whenever it apparently limits a singular noun it is in the possessive by enallage, used for the objective; as, "That nose of yours"; "That wife of mine"; "That husband of hers," etc. See art. 1254.

These constructions are incorrect for several reasons:

313. A noun is a *name*. Of what, then, is 'hers' or 'mine' the name? It is plainly seen the name remains to be supplied.

314. The substitution of a noun in the possessive case shows the pronoun to be in the possessive case; as, Your book is torn; *mine* is not. Your book is torn; *John's* is not. No one can say that '*John's*' is *not* in the possessive case, or that 'mine' does not stand in the same relation.

315. In former times, the forms *mine, thine,* etc., were always used as possessives before vowel sounds; as, Touch not *mine* anointed, and do my prophets no harm. (Ps. cv. 15.)

316. *Mine* is the original form (of which *my* is an apocopated form of more recent date) derived from an ancient genitive, the equivalent of our possessive.

317. That *mine, thine, yours*, etc., are but strengthened forms used for *my, thy, your*, etc., is seen in the very slight distinction between them. For, if *own* is supplied, the shortened form at once takes the place of the longer. That horse is mine. That horse is *my own* [horse]. 'Own' is an *adjective* and 'my' a pronoun in the possessive case, each limiting 'horse'; and should not be parsed as one word.

318. The possessive introductory is sometimes used; as, *Its* being John was the reason why she accepted.

319. The possessive suggestive occurs; as, I never thought of *its* being ten o'clock.

320. The possessive expletive is met with frequently; as, *Its* being really true that her father had failed, she declared impossible.

321. *Peculiarities* of the *Objective* case of pronouns.

322. The objective case of the relative is always placed before the verb which governs it; and frequently before the governing preposition. For example: These are the boys *whom* you *rewarded;* These are the men *that* you spoke *of*.

323. The pronoun *it* is found in the objective introductory, suggestive, and expletive; as, I took *it* to be John who made these remarks; He declared *it* to be ten o'clock when we came home; We thought *it* necessary for us to go.

324. Objective by enallage: This is the use of the *objective* form or case, in constructions which, by rule, would require the nominative or possessive form or case.

325. For the nominative subject of a finite verb; as, *Me* thinks, *Me* seems.

326. For the nominative absolute; as, Ah *me!* Dear *me!* Here, *me* is used for nominative absolute by exclamation.

327. For the nominative in the predicate after an intransitive verb; as, If I were *him;* It is *me;* That's *him,* etc. This use is only warranted in conversational style.

328. *Whom* is used for *who;* as, Solomon, than whom there never was a wiser, declares wisdom more precious than rubies. Expanding 'whom,' and supplying the ellipses, this sentence reads: Solomon, *and* there never was a wiser [man] than *he* [was], declares wisdom [to be] more precious than rubies [are]. In the above sentence, 'whom' is separated into its two elements; the connective, *and,* and the representative, *he*. It is thus shown that the regular form of *whom* should be *who,* and that 'whom' is objective by enallage, after the conjunction *than,* and not governed by *than,* as some grammarians affirm.

329. The objective form or case is sometimes used for the possessive; as, We had no fear of *them* being lost; There is no use of *him* coming so early. 'Them' is in the objective case by *enallage* for *their,* limiting the participle "being lost." 'Him' is in the objective by *enallage* for *his,* limiting the participle 'coming.'

REMARK.—For the objective of *nouns* by enallage, see page 56, Art. 246.

CONSTRUCTIONS OF NOUNS AND PRONOUNS.

330. Nominative Constructions.

1. *Dependent constructions.*
    Subject of a finite verb.   Rule 15.
    In the predicate with a subject nominative.   Rule 14.
    In the predicate with a subject sentence.   Rule 14.
    In the predicate with a subject phrase.   Rule 14.
    In apposition with another nominative.   Rule 13.
    In apposition with an independent sentence.   Art. 211.
    In apposition with a subject sentence.   Art. 211.
    In apposition with a subject phrase.   Art. 211.
    In apposition with a predicate sentence.   Art. 211.
    In apposition with a predicate phrase.   Art. 211.
    Introductory "it."   Art. 302.
    Suggestive "it."   Art. 303.
    Expletive "it."   Art. 304.
    Euphonic "it."   Art. 307.
    In predicate with a participle whose subject is in the possessive case.

   REMARK.—This construction is in violation of Rule 14, but in accordance with Art. 1,247.

    In the predicate with an infinitive whose subject is the same as that of the finite verb it limits.   Rule 16.

2. *Independent nominative constructions.*
    Absolute by direct address.   Art. 214.
    Absolute by exclamation.   Art. 215.
    Absolute by inscription.   Art. 216.
    Absolute by pleonasm.   Art. 217.
    Absolute with a participle.   Art. 218.

331. Possessive Constructions.

1. *Regular*, i. e., *according to some rule.*
    Limiting another noun or pronoun of different signification.   Rule 19.

Limiting another noun or pronoun of similar signification. Rule 13.

Limiting a noun understood.

EXAMPLE.—He stopped at Mr. Stewart's last night. Art. 233.

Limiting a participle as its subject. Art. 224.

EXAMPLE.—*John's* being there was not disputed.

In the predicate as an attribute limiting the subject.

EXAMPLE.—That book is *mine*. Rule 19.

Possessive introductory "it."

EXAMPLE.—Its being they was the reason I came. Art. 302.

Suggestive "it."

EXAMPLE.—Its raining so hard detained us. Art. 303.

Expletive "it."

EXAMPLE.—Its being telegraphed that the bridge was carried away, prevented a terrible accident. Art. 304.

2. *Irregular, in violation of some rule by the figure of enallage.*

Possessive by enallage used for the objective.

EXAMPLE.—That book of *yours* is returned. Art. 234.

Possessive by enallage used for the nominative absolute.

EXAMPLE.—O *my*, what a fuss you are making about nothing.

Possessive sign carried to the end of a limiting prepositional phrase.

EXAMPLES.—Moses was the daughter of Pharaoh's son; When the king of Babylon's army besieged Jerusalem.

Possessive sign transferred from noun understood to limiting adjective. Art. 1,254.

EXAMPLE.—Let each become the other's friend.

332. Objective Constructions.

1. *Regular constructions.*

Object of an active transitive verb. Rule 17.

Object of a preposition. Rule 18.

Subject of an infinitive. Rule 16.
Objective in the predicate with subject objective. R. 14.
Objective in the predicate with subject sentence. R. 14.
Objective in the predicate with subject phrase. R. 14.
In apposition with another objective. Rule 13.
In apposition with a subject sentence. Rule 13.
In apposition with a subject phrase. Rule 13.
In apposition with an objective sentence. Rule 13.
In apposition with an objective phrase. Rule 13.
Introductory "it."

EXAMPLE.—Who could have thought *it* to be Jane and Harvey who were coming? Art. 302.

Objective suggestive "it."

EXAMPLE.—We thought *it* time to begin. Art. 303.

Expletive "it." Art. 304.

EXAMPLE.—We thought *it* to be true that the man had expired.

Apparent object of an intransitive verb of similar signification.

EXAMPLE.—Let me die the *death* of the righteous.

Objective of an intransitive causative verb.

EXAMPLE.—He *ran* the horse all the way to town.

Nouns denoting time, distance, weight, measure, etc., object of a preposition understood.

One of two objects of an active transitive verb, either of which may be used as the object; the other with a preposition becoming an adverbial phrase. Art. 225.

EXAMPLES.—She taught *me grammar*. 1. She taught me [in the subject of] grammar. 2. She taught [to] me grammar.

REMARK.—Either of these objects may be used as the subject of the passive verb.

2. *Irregular constructions; in violation of some rule by the figure of enallage.*

Objective used for the possessive.

EXAMPLE.—I never thought of Mary failing.

For a nominative subject of a finite verb.

EXAMPLE.—Me thinks; Me seems.

For a nominative absolute by exclamation.

EXAMPLE.—Ah me; Dear me.

For a nominative in the predicate after an intransitive verb in conversational style.

EXAMPLE.—It was me; If I were him.

Whom used for who after than.

EXAMPLE.—Satan, than *whom* none sat higher, then arose.

It will be noticed that there are here given fifty-six different relations in which nouns and pronouns are found. Now, if case is relation, there are as many different cases as relations, viz., fifty-six. Why do the grammarians who define case as "the relation which nouns and pronouns hold to other words," give only three cases?

EXAMPLES FOR DRILL IN PARSING NOUNS AND PRONOUNS.

The words italicized are suggested for exercise in construction especially.

333. And *it* were highly to be wished that legislative power would thus direct the law rather to reformation than *severity:* that *it* would seem convinced *that* the work of eradicating crimes is not by making *punishments* familiar, but formidable.—GOLDSMITH.

334.   Their written *words* we linger o'er,
      But in the sun they cast no shade!
      No voice is heard, no sign is made,
      No step is on the conscious floor!—WHITTIER.

335. Parse 'Whittier.'

336. Wherefore ye *needs* must be subject, not only for *wrath's*, but also for conscience' sake.—ROM. xiii. 5.

337. Day dawns upon the mountain's side;
    There, *Scotland,* lay thy bravest *pride,*
    Chiefs, knights, and nobles, many a *one;*
    The sad survivors *all* are gone.—SCOTT.

REMARK.—Parse the nouns understood which the adjectives limit.

338.   *Him* follow'd his next mate,
Both glorying to have 'scap'd the Stygian flood
As *Gods*, and by their own recover'd strength,
Not by the suff'rance of Supernal Power.—MILTON.

339. O blest *retirement*, *friend* to life's decline,
Retreat from care, *that* never must be *mine;*
How blest is *he* who crowns in shades like *these*,
                                                              ∧
A youth of labor with an age of ease.—GOLDSMITH.

340. But wherefore let *we* then our faithful *friends*,
Th' *associates* and *copartners* of our loss,
Lie thus astonished on th' oblivious pool.—MILTON.

341. Old *friends!* The writings of those words has borne
My fancy backward to the gracious *past*,
The generous *past*, when all was possible,
For all was then *untried*.—LOWELL.

342. His *spear*, to equal *which* the tallest *pine*
Hewn on Norwegian hills, to be the mast
Of some great ammiral, were but a *wand*,
He walked with to support uneasy steps
Over the burning marl; not *like* those *steps*
On Heaven's azure; and the torrid clime
Smote on him *sore besides*, *vaulted* with fire.—MILTON.

343. Consider the *lilies* of the field, how they grow.—MATT. vi. 28.

344. *He that* glorieth, let *him* glory in the Lord.—2 COR. x. 17.

345. A *dungeon* horrible on all sides round,
As one great *furnace* flamed; yet from those flames
No *light;* but rather darkness visible
Served only to discover sights of woe,
Regions of sorrow, doleful shades, where peace
And rest can never dwell; hope never comes,
That comes to *all*.—MILTON.

346. *What*, then, are the proper *encouragements* of genius? I answer, *subsistence* and respect, for these are rewards congenial to
                                                      ∧
its nature. Every animal has an *aliment* peculiarly suited to its constitution. The heavy ox seeks nourishment from earth; the light chameleon has been supposed to exist on air; a sparer diet even

than this will satisfy the man of true genius, for he makes a luxurious banquet ^ upon empty applause. *It* is this alone which has inspired all *that* ever ^ was truly great and noble among us. *It* is, as Cicero finely ^ calls *it*, the *echo* of virtue. Avarice is the passion of inferior natures; *money*, the *pay* of the common herd. The author who draws his quill merely to take a purse, no more deserves success than *he* who presents a pistol.—GOLDSMITH.

348. 347. Within our beds a while we heard
The wind *that* round the gables roared,
With now and then a ruder shock,
Which made our very *bedsteads* rock.
We heard the loosened *clapboards* tossed,
The *board-nails* snapping in the frost;
And on us, through the unplastered wall,
Felt the light-sifted *snow-flakes* fall.—WHITTIER.

348. And while he yet talked with them, behold, the messenger came down unto him, and he said, Behold, this evil is of the Lord; *what* should I wait for the Lord any longer?—2 KINGS vi. 33.

349.   Art divine
Has made the *body tutor* to the soul;
Heaven kindly gives our *blood* a moral *flow;*
Bids *it* ascend the glowing cheek, and there
Upbraid that little heart's inglorious aim,
Which stoops to court a character from man;
While o'er us, in tremendous judgment sit
Far more than *man*, with endless praise and blame.—YOUNG.

350. For *what* ^ shall *it* profit a man, if he shall gain the whole world, and lose his own soul?—MARK viii. 37.

351.   *Me* thou thinkest not *slow,*
Who since the morning-hour set out from heav'n,
Where God resides, and ere mid-day arrived
In Eden, . . . *What* if *that light,*
Sent from *her* through the wide transpicuous air
To the terrestrial moon, be as a *star*
Enlight'ning her by day, as *she* by night
This *earth?* reciprocal, if land be there,
^
Field and inhabitants.—MILTON.

352.   Was *it* then too much
    For *me* to trespass on the brutal rights?—YOUNG.

353. He comes with a careless *"How d'ye do?"*
        And seats *himself* in my elbow-chair:
    And my morning paper and pamphlet new
        Fall forthwith under his special care,
    And he wipes his glasses and clears his throat,
    And, *button* by button, unfolds his coat.—WHITTIER.

354. *Me* miserable! *which way* shall I fly
    Infinite *wrath* and infinite despair?—MILTON.

355.   Ah, *me*, they little know
    How dearly I abide that boast so vain,
    Under *what* torments inwardly I groan,
    While they adore me on the throne of Hell!—*Id.*

356. All *hope* excluded thus, behold, instead
    Of us outcast, exiled, his new *delight*,
    Mankind created, and for *him* this *world*.—*Id.*

357. An *angel*, if a *creature* of a day,
    What would *he* be? a *trifle* of no weight;
    Or stand or fall; no *matter which*; *he's* gone.—YOUNG

358. *Who* would not give a trifle to prevent,
    What he would give a thousand worlds to cure?—*Id.*

359. *It* is not always easy to make *one's self* just *what* one wishes
to be.

360. *What*, then, is unbelief? 'Tis an *exploit;*
    A strenuous enterprise; to gain it, man
    Must burst through every bar of common sense,
    Of common shame, magnanimously wrong.
    And *what* rewards the sturdy combatant?
    His *prize, repentance; infamy*, his *crown*.—YOUNG.

361.   '*Chieftains*, forego!
    I hold him first who strikes, my *foe*.
    Madman, forbear your frantic jar!
    What! is the Douglas fallen so far,
    His daughter's hand is deemed the *spoil*
    Of such dishonorable broil!'—SCOTT.

362. In proud disdain of *what* e'en gods adore,
  Dost smile? Poor *wretch!* thy guardian angel weeps.
            —YOUNG.

363. We *nothing* know, but *what* is marvelous;
  Yet *what* is marvelous, we can't believe.
  So weak our *reason*, and so great our *God.*
  What most surprises in the sacred page,
  Or full as strange, or stranger, must be true.—*Id.*

364. Thy false uncle being once perfected how to grant suits,
  How to deny them; *whom* t' advance, and *whom*
  To trash for overtopping; new created
  The creatures *that* were *mine*, I say, or chang'd them,
  Or else new form'd them: having both the key
  Of officer and office, set all *hearts* i' the state
  To *what* tune pleased his ear; *that* now he was
  The *ivy*, which had hid my princely trunk,
  And suck'd my verdure out *on 't.*—SHAKESPEARE.

365. Dryden, though a great and undisputed genius, had the same cast *as* L'Estrange. *Even* his plays discover *him* to be a *party-man*, and the same principle infects his style in subjects of the lightest nature; but the English tongue, *as* it stands at present, is greatly his debtor. He first gave *it* regular harmony, and discovered its latent powers. *It* was his pen *that* formed the Congreves, the Priors, and the Addisons, who succeeded him; and had *it* not been for Dryden, we never should have known a Pope, at least in the meridian luster he now displays. But Dryden's excellencies ^ as a *writer* were not confined to poetry ^ alone. *There* is in his prose writings an *ease* and elegance *that* have never yet been so well united in works of taste or criticism.—GOLDSMITH.

366. *What* ne'er can die, Oh! grant to live; and crown
  The wish, and aim, and labor of the skies;
  Increase, and enter on the joys of heaven.—YOUNG.

367. Life to the last, like hardened felons, lies;
  Nor owns *itself* a *cheat*, till it expires.
  Its little joys go out by one and one,
  And leave poor man, at ^ length, in ^ perfect night;
  Night darker than *what* now involves the pole.—*Id.*

368. But thou, lorn *stream*, whose sullen *tide*
No sedge-crown'd sisters now attend,
Now waft me from the green hill's side,
Whose cold turf hides the buried friend.—COLLINS.

369. 'Up *drawbridge, grooms—what, Warder, ho!*
Let the *portcullis* fall.'—SCOTT.

370.   That man greatly lives,
Whate'er his fate or fame, who greatly dies.—YOUNG.

371. The truth, through such a medium seen, may make
Impression deep, and *fondness* prove thy *friend*.—*Id.*

372.   *What* if the sun
Be center to the world, and other *stars*,
By his attractive virtue and their own
Incited, dance about him various *rounds*?—MILTON.

373. And *what* she did, *whatever* in itself,
Her doing seemed to justify the deed.—*Id.*

374. Let *it* be understood *that* I will pursue this course no longer.

375. *Which* when Beëlzebub perceived, than *whom*,
Satan except, none higher sat, with grave
Aspect he rose, and in his rising seem'd
A *pillar* of state: deep on his front engraven
Deliberation sat, and public care.—*Id.*

376. I tell thee *what*, corporal, I could tear her. —FOWLER.

377. *Whom* the shoe fits, let *him* put *it* on.

378. *Whatever* doing, *what* can we suffer more,
What can we suffer worse?—MILTON.

379. *Me*, through just *right*, and the fix'd laws of Heav'n,
Did first create your *leader*, next free *choice*,
With *what* besides, in council or in fight,
Hath been achieved of merit; yet this loss,
Thus far at least recover'd, hath much more
Establish'd in a safe unenvied throne,
Yielded with full consent.—*Id.*

380. *Who* steals my purse, steals trash; 'tis something, nothing;
 '*Twas mine*, '*t is his*, and has been slave to thousands;
 But he that filches from me my good name,
 Robs me of *that* which not enriches him,
 And makes *me poor* indeed.—SHAKESPEARE.

381.   Darken'd so, yet shone
 Above them all the *Archangel:* but his face
 Deep scars of thunder had intrench'd, and care
 Sat on his faded cheek; but under brows
 Of dauntless courage, and considerate pride
 Waiting revenge; cruel his *eye*, but cast
 Signs of remorse and passion, to behold
 The *fellows* of his crime, the followers rather
 (Far *other* once beheld in bliss), condemned
 Forever now to have their lot in pain.—MILTON.

382. They heard, and were abash'd, and up they sprung
 Upon the wing, as when men went to watch
 On duty, sleeping found by *whom* they dread,
 Rouse and bestir themselves ere well awake.
 Nor did they not perceive the evil plight
 In which they were, or the fierce pains not feel.—*Id.*

383. Say, *Muse*, their *names* then known, *who* first, who last
 Roused from the slumber, on that fiery couch,
 At their great emp'ror's call, as *next* in worth
 Came singly where he stood on that bare strand,
 While the promiscuous crowd stood still aloof.—*Id.*

384. That hat is only *worth* a *dollar*.

385. He had more money than he knew *what* to do with.

386. Knowing that *whatsoever* good thing any man doeth, the same shall he receive of the Lord, whether he be bond or free.—EPH. vi. 8.

387. 'I have nourished a viper in my bosom.'
 'A *viper*—a *fiddlestick*,' said Miss Sharp to the old lady. . .
 . . . . 'I will do nothing here but *what* I am obliged to do.' . . . . . .

'O *you* droll *creature!* Do let *me* hear *you* sing it.'
'*Me?* No, *you*, Miss *Sharp;* my dear Miss *Sharp*, do sing it.'
THACKERAY.

388. '*What* a beautiful, *byoo-ootiful song that* was you sang last *night*, dear Miss *Sharp*. It made *me* cry, almost.—*Id.*

389. And Zedekiah, *King* of Judah, and his *princes*, will I give into the hand of their enemies, and into the hand of them *that* seek their life, and into the hand of the king of *Babylon's* army, *which* are gone up from you.—JER. xxxiv. 21.

390. Moses was the son of Pharaoh's daughter.

391. Burns' centenary dinner occurred on the same day *as* my *birthday*.

392. After hearing my story, and pausing some *minutes*, he slapped his forehead *as if* he had hit upon *something material*, and took his leave, saying he would try *what* could be done.—GOLDSMITH.

393. Who speaks the truth stabs Falsehood to the heart,
 And his mere word makes *despots* tremble more
 Than ever Brutus with his dagger could.—LOWELL.

394. Among them one, an ancient willow, spreads
 Eight balanced limbs, springing at once all round
 His deep-ridged *trunk* with upward *slant* diverse,
 In outline like enormous *beaker*, fit
 For hand of Jotun, where 'mid snow and mist
 He holds unwieldly revel. This *tree*, spared,
 I know not by *what* grace—for in the blood
 Of our New World subduers lingers yet
 Hereditary feud with trees, *they* being
 (*They* and the red man most) our fathers' *foes*—
 Is one of six, a willow *Pleiades*,
 The seventh fallen, *that* lean along the brink
 Where the steep upland dips into the marsh,
 Their *roots*, like molten *metal* cooled in flowing,
 Stiffened in coils and runnels down the bank.—*Id.*

395. All think *it* a miracle *that* he was not killed.

396. A prompt, decisive *man*, no *breath*
 Our father wasted: '*Boys*, a *path!*'

>   Well pleased, (for when did farmer boy
>   Count such a *summons less* than *joy?*)
>   Our *buskins* on our feet we drew;
>   With mittened hands, and caps drawn low,
>   To guard our necks and ears from snow,
>   We cut the solid *whiteness* through.—WHITTIER.

397. They trespass, *authors* to themselves in all,
    Both *what* they judge and *what* they choose.—MILTON.

398. As one who held *herself a part*
    Of all she saw, and let her *heart*
      Against the household bosom lean,
    Upon the motley-braided mat
    Our youngest and our dearest sat,
    Lifting her large, sweet, asking eyes,
      Now bathed within the fadeless green
    And holy peace of Paradise.—WHITTIER.

399.   Yet not for those,
    Nor *what* the potent victor in his rage
    Can *else* inflict, do I repent or change,
    Though changed in outward luster, *that* fix'd mind
    And high disdain from sense of injured merit,
    That with the Mightiest raised me to contend,
    And to the fierce contention brought along
    Innumerable force of Spirits arm'd,
    That durst dislike his reign, and *me* preferring,
    His utmost *pow'r* with adverse pow'r opposed
    In dubious battle on the plains of Heav'n,
    And shook his throne.—MILTON.

400. Belial came last, *than whom* a spirit more lewd
    Fell not from heaven, or more gross to love
    Vice for itself.—*Id.*

401.   And now his heart
    Distends with pride, and hardening in his strength,
    Glories; for never since *created man*
    Met such embodied force, *as, named* with these,
    Could merit more than that small infantry
    Warr'd on by cranes.—*Id.*

ETYMOLOGY—THE PRONOUN.

402. *What* matter where, if I be still the same,
And *what* I should be, *all but less* than *he*
Whom thunder hath made greater?—*Id.*

403. Delightful *task! to rear* the tender thought,—
To teach the young idea how to shoot.—THOMSON.

404. *What* you say you said is not *what* he said you said.

405. John declares *it* to be impossible for him to tell *what* words are double relatives and *what* are interrogative pronominal adjectives.

406. He asked, "What will the next lesson be?"

407. He asked what would be the next lesson.

408. I heard *what* he said.

409. I learned what the *difficulty was* immediately.

410. I know *who* broke the window.

411. He told *me* of *whom* I could get the morning paper.

412. Who can tell *what* he will do next?

413. Bring *what* materials you have.

414. I know *who* was the first President of the United States.

415. *Whatsoever* way he turns, he is sure to be wrong.

416. *Whatever* he says, you attend to my directions.

417. *Rock* of *ages*, cleft for me,
Let *me* hide myself in thee;
Let the water and the blood,
From thy wounded side which flow'd,
Be of sin the double *cure*,
Save from wrath and make *me* pure.—TOPLADY.

418. I care not *what* course others may take, as for *me*, give *me* liberty, or give me death.—HENRY.

419. I don't know *who* he is, do *you?*

420. Do not let *them* know *who* I am.

421. *Whatever* it is, it is not such *as* I can dispose of soon, I fear.

422. *What* men are afraid to do openly, they often make their boast of as having done secretly.

423. Stigmatize *as* laziness in worship *what* really is such, and don't call *it formality* any more.

424. He told me *what* I never heard of before.

425. It was such a discourse *as* I never listened to before.

426. We can hardly estimate *what loss* and *disgrace* such a *deed as* the one I am speaking of must prove to be, to as many *as* are even thought of *as* the *perpetrators* of it.

427. My teacher may rightfully claim to have made *me whatever* I may honestly judge *myself* to have become; and I thankfully acknowledge *myself* to be made as much of *as* such *materials as* I consist of can be.

428. "On my part," says the teacher, "I only claim *him* to be *what* he made *himself* under such training and skill as I was master of, and with such talents as I knew he was in possession of when I first took *him as* a *pupil*."

THE ADJECTIVE—INTRODUCTORY LESSONS.

429. Correction of Sentences in False Syntax.

Attention to the parsing lesson assigned. Mutual criticism by the pupils, after having exchanged exercise-books.

430. Preliminary Drill.—*Teacher*. "Pupils, I wish to introduce to you another class of words, or, as the grammarians would say, part of speech. An adjective is a word which limits the meaning of a noun or pronoun. For example: A sweet apple, A good boy, A tall tree, They are studious. 'Sweet,' 'good,' 'tall,' are adjectives, qualifying the nouns before which they are placed, and limiting their signification. There are three classes of adjectives: *Descriptive, numeral, pronominal.* To-day we will take only the first two. Now, pupils, if I should say 'That is white sugar,' what quality do I ascribe to the sugar? John."

John. "Whiteness."

Teacher. "The name of the quality is a noun, but 'white' is what? Julia."

ETYMOLOGY—THE ADJECTIVE.

Julia. "An adjective."

Teacher. "Right. Descriptive adjectives ascribe some quality or situation to the nouns they limit. Charles, you may point out the adjective in the sentence 'There is a tall tree,' and tell to what class it belongs."

Charles. "'Tall' is an adjective, descriptive."

Teacher. "Mary, why an adjective?"

Mary. "Because it limits the noun 'tree.'"

Teacher. "Why descriptive? James."

James. "Because it describes the tree."

Teacher. "Take this: 'That is a distant farm.' Sarah, what part of speech is 'distant'?"

Sarah. "An adjective."

Teacher. "What kind of an adjective? Charles."

Charles. "Descriptive."

Teacher. "Yes. You will notice this is descriptive, because it denotes the *situation* of the farm. Julia, what is 'near' in the sentence 'He is a near neighbor'?"

Julia. "A descriptive adjective."

Teacher. "Why? Jane."

Jane. "It denotes situation."

Teacher. "Right. Numeral adjectives are such as denote a definite number; as, one, two, first, second, etc. I will give you some sentences and ask you to point out the adjectives, and give the class of each."

1. *We* have a *white* cat and a black dog.
2. The *dark* clouds poured down rain.
3. The *wild* animals *which* you saw have killed their *keeper*.
4. *Our first* parents inhabited the *western* portion of the *Asiatic* continent.
5. *The* warm sun brings out the *green* grass and ripens the *growing grain*.
6. *Jane's little* canary bird, *which* her father bought, sings a beautiful *song*.
7. *Five* years have passed: time tells a *wonderful* story.
8. The *old* man uses the *walking* stick *which* I found.
9. This book is *interesting*.
10. My time is *valuable*.

Teacher. "Susan, you may name the adjectives in the first sentence."

Susan. "'White' and 'black.'"

Teacher. "Why adjectives? Henry."

Henry. "Because they limit the nouns 'cat' and 'dog.'"

Teacher. "In the fifth sentence, what are the adjectives? Jane."

Jane. "'Warm,' 'green,' 'growing.'"

Teacher. "What kind of adjectives are these? John."

John. "Descriptive."

Teacher. "Why? Julia."

Julia. "Because they describe the nouns by ascribing some quality to them."

Teacher. "What kind of adjective is the first one in the seventh sentence? Charles."

Charles. "Numeral."

Teacher. "Why? Sarah."

Sarah. "Because it denotes a definite number."

Teacher. "I will now parse some adjectives and give you the Rule. Take 'white,' in the first sentence. *White* is an adjective, descriptive, limits the noun 'cat,' Rule 1. Articles and adjectives limit nouns. I will also parse 'growing,' in the fifth sentence. *Growing* is an adjective, descriptive, limits the noun 'grain,' Rule 1. Mary, you may rise and parse 'dark,' in the second sentence."

Mary. "*Dark* is an adjective, descriptive, limits the noun 'clouds,' Rule 1."

Teacher. "Very good. Now, James, you may parse 'walking,' in the eighth sentence."

James. "*Walking* is an adjective, descriptive, limits the noun 'stick,' Rule 1."

Teacher. "Very well, James. If you all have followed me closely, I think you will have no difficulty in parsing the words I have italicized in the preceding sentences, for the next recitation. In addition to the adjectives, I will ask you to parse some nouns, pronouns, and articles, so that you may not forget what you have learned in previous lessons."

The teacher will hereafter ask the pupils to mark such words as he may designate in their grammars for parsing, and as will best meet the wants of the class, in reference to the preliminary drill given each day; bearing in mind that occasional examples must be assigned in previous work, lest any principle or point gained shall be lost or forgotten.

PRONOMINAL ADJECTIVES.

431. Recitation—Classes of Adjectives.

Written parsings criticised by the teacher out of school hours perhaps; and graded in any point in which the particular pupil most *needs* encouragement.

432. Preliminary Drill.—*Teacher.* "In the sentence 'This is an old book,' what does 'this' stand for? All together."
Class. "Book."
Teacher. "What part of speech is it, then? Mary."
Mary. "A pronoun."
Teacher. "But wait a little, Mary; what does 'this' relate to?"
Mary. "The noun 'book.'"
Teacher. "Who will read the sentence so as to show this relation? James, will you?"
James. "This book is an old book."
Teacher. "Yes; but it sounds best to omit 'book' in the first part of the sentence. Now, since 'this' relates to the noun 'book,' what part of speech is it? Mary."
Mary. "An adjective."
Teacher. "Right. 'That slate is broken.' What is the construction of 'that'? Susan."
Susan. "An adjective relating to 'slate.'"
Teacher. "Class, what quality does it give to the noun?"
No hands up.
Teacher. "It gives no quality or situation, therefore it is not a descriptive adjective. Since it limits 'slate,' or distinguishes it as a *particular* slate, it is sometimes called a definitive, or limiting, or specifying adjective. But, as you have seen, it frequently stands *for* the noun, so we will call it a pronoun-adjective, or a *pronominal* adjective, according to the grammars. I will give you a list of the pronominal adjectives, that you may have them for future reference."

For this list of pronominal adjectives, see page 88.

Teacher. "I will give you some sentences containing this kind of adjectives."

1. *Such as* I have, give I unto thee.
2. *These* are the same *that* you saw yesterday.
3. *Which* will you do? I will do *neither*.

4. Here come James and John; *each* has a new hat.

5. *All* who study diligently will learn.

6. The true teacher will do *much* for the slowest and *little* for the quickest.

7. *Some* have gone, *others* remain.

8. Only *one* escaped from the burning boat.

9. *Few* attended the convention, but *enough* were present to transact the business.

10. *Several* persons were present.

11. *None* ever returned.

12. He wants only his *own*.

13. The *more* he gets, the *more* he wants.

14. *No* one saw him do it.

15. The old are cautious, the young are venturesome.

16. Mindful of the unhonored dead, Gray wrote his Elegy.

17. The prompt and regular are here; the careless and uncertain are absent.

18. The true friend will sometimes be considered unkind; the false will always flatter and fawn.

19. The new and the untried captivate the unwary; the old and approved better satisfy the prudent.

Teacher. "Class, you will see that the pronominal adjectives in these sentences stand for their nouns, without the article; hence the definition, *A pronominal adjective is one which may, without an article, represent a noun.* I will parse 'such,' in the first sentence. *Such* is an adjective, pronominal, limits the noun *things*, understood. Rule 1. Henry, you may parse 'these,' in the second sentence."

Henry. "*These* is an adjective, pronominal, limits the noun *persons*, understood. Rule 1."

Teacher. "Very good. I will parse 'as,' in the first sentence. *As* is a pronoun, relative, agrees with its antecedent, *things*, understood, in the third, plural, neuter, Rule 5, objective case, object of the verb 'have.' Rule 17. I think you are now prepared for the next recitation. You may parse, in writing, the pronominal adjectives and other words which are italicized in the preceding sentences."

INTERROGATIVE PRONOMINALS.

434. Recitation—Written Parsings.

435. Preliminary Drill.—*Teacher.* "Pupils, you noticed that the words 'which' and 'what' occur in the list of pronominal adjectives. I wish now to show you how to determine when to call them pronouns, and when interrogative pronominal adjectives. Take the sentence 'What tree is that?' Mary, you may point out the noun."

Mary. "Tree."
Teacher. "What limits it? James."
James. "'What' and 'that.'"
Teacher. "Very good. What kind of words are these? Susan."
Susan. "Pronominal adjectives."
Teacher. "Right. And since 'what' is used in asking a question, it is an interrogative. You will have no difficulty with 'which' and 'what' in such examples as these":—

1. *Which* house is it?
2. *Which* woman was it?
3. *What* man is it?

"But what do you say about 'which' in these sentences?"

4. *Which* is the house?
5. *Which* of you convinceth me of sin?

"To what word does 'which,' in the fourth sentence, refer? Henry."
Henry. "House."
Teacher. "Right. Notice, now, pupils, that 'which' stands *before* the noun, either expressed or understood, to which it refers, and in this position is a *pronominal adjective*. In the following sentences, 'which' comes *after* the noun to which it refers, and in this position is a *relative pronoun.*"

6. Where are the birds *which* you killed yesterday?
7. The clouds *which* threatened rain have disappeared.
8. The study *which* I bestow on grammar is nothing but fun.

9. I like to do anything *which* will improve my mind.
10. The *boots which* uncle gave me I gave my brother.

Teacher. "Now, pupils, when is 'which' a relative pronoun? Jane."

Jane. "When it comes *after* the noun to which it relates."

Teacher. "Very good. John, when is 'which' an interrogative pronominal adjective?"

John. "When it comes *before* the noun to which it refers."

Teacher. "Very well. I am glad to see you taking hold of grammar so readily. Your next lesson will be the parsing, in writing, of such words as I marked in the ten sentences of this lesson. First, I will parse 'which,' in the sixth sentence. *Which* is an adjective, pronominal, interrogative, limits the noun 'person,' understood. Rule 1. Julia, I would like to have you parse 'which,' in the second sentence."

Julia. "*Which* is an adjective, pronominal, interrogative, limits the noun 'woman.' Rule 1."

Teacher. "Who will parse 'which,' in the sixth sentence?"

All hands up.

Teacher. "Charles."

Charles. "*Which* is a pronoun, relative, agrees with its antecedent, 'birds,' in the third, plural, common, Rule 5, objective case, object of the transitive verb 'killed.' Rule 17."

THE ADJECTIVE.

436. Definition.—An adjective is a word limiting a noun or pronoun; as, The *beautiful* flower; He is *wealthy*.

REMARK.—To say that "An adjective describes a noun," is undoubtedly erroneous; but to say that "An adjective limits a noun," is but an abbreviated form for this: "The quality or specification expressed by an adjective is designed to limit the meaning of the noun or pronoun to which it relates, or more philosophically (?) still, to describe or specify the object or objects which the noun (or the pronoun representing it,) may present to the consciousness of the speaker and hearer, or of the writer and reader."

437. An adjective in the predicate may limit any phrase or sentence used as a subject of an intransitive or passive verb; as, To be detained so long at a railway station is very *unnecessary* and *vexatious;* That he should leave so suddenly seems very *strange;* That he is considered *honest* is indeed very *fortunate* for him.

438. Adjectives are sometimes compounded; as, That is a beautiful *light-green* color.

439. Other parts of speech are frequently used as adjectives.

440. Nouns; as, The *iron* bridge is completed; We write with *gold* pens.

441. Pronouns; as, I care not *what* course others may take.

442. Adverbs; as, He is the *very* man; We have *enough* men; He left five years *ago*.

443. Prepositions; as, He plunged into the waters *below;* The *under* current does the mischief; He died five years *since*.

444. Adjectives sometimes *seem* to be used as other parts of speech.

445. For nouns; as, The *wicked* shall perish; but the *good* shall live.

446. In the above example, as well as in *all other similar ones*, the noun is understood, and the adjective must be parsed as limiting it.

447. There is one case in which an adjective becomes a noun: She robbed me of my hopes, my heart, my *all*. In this use of 'all,' it is a noun.

448. *One* is sometimes said to be a noun, but is *never* so used. In the following example, '*ones*' is called by some grammarians a noun: There are many whose waking thoughts are wholly employed on their sleeping *ones*. Plainly, '*ones*' limits *thoughts*, understood, which it here represents in the character of a pronominal adjective, the plural sign being transferred from the noun to the adjective.

449. Words commonly used as adjectives, sometimes become adverbs; sometimes, also, prepositions; as, *like* and *worth*.

450. Classes.—*Descriptive, Pronominal, Numeral.*

451. A descriptive adjective is one that signifies quality or situation.

452. Some are derived from proper names; hence, are called by some grammarians, Proper adjectives; as, *American, Grecian,* etc.

453. Some are derived from verbs, and are called participial or verbal adjectives; as, a *telling* speech; a *pressing* emergency; a *predicted* change; a much *to be wished for* consummation.

454. A participial adjective is distinguished from a participle by being placed immediately before the noun which it limits; it then rejects the idea of time, and retains only that of quality.

455. A pronominal adjective is one which may, without an article, represent a noun, including *every* and *no*, which are pronominals used with *one.*

456. These adjectives limit their nouns in any other respect than quality or situation.

457. A List of Pronominals.

this,	either,	enough,	more,	other,
that,	neither,	few,	most,	others,
these,	all,	little,	no,	own,
those,	any,	less,	none,	several,
both,	certain,	least,	one,	some,
each,	divers,	much,	ones,	such,
every,	else,	many,	only,	

and the interrogative pronominals, which and what.

458. A numeral adjective is one which denotes a definite number.

459. Those which denote *how many* are called *cardinals;* as, *five, eight,* a *hundred,* a *million.*

460. Those which denote a definite place in a series, or a definite part of a unit, are called *ordinals;* as, *fourth, tenth, twenty-second.*

461. Some of the *pronominals* are *indefinite* numerals, but should not be parsed as such; as, *certain, either, few, many, several.*

462. Numeral adjectives are frequently used as nouns; as, They came by *hundreds* and *thousands;* I did not see a *tenth* of the persons.

463. Modifications.—*Number—Comparison.*

464. Number is applied to the adjectives *this* and *that,* which have the plurals *these* and *those*. *One* has its plurals, *ones, few, several, many;* each has its plural, *all.*

465. The English language, unlike most others, does not *inflect* its adjectives to denote *person, number,* and *gender.*

466. Adjectives are **compared** to signify different relative degrees, increase or diminution, in quality or relation.

467. There are three degrees of comparison:

468. The *positive,*—the simple form of the adjective; as, *sweet, hot.*

469. The *comparative,* used in comparing TWO objects which differ in degree; as, James is *taller* than John; This apple is *sweeter* than that; To-day is *hotter* than yesterday.

470. The *superlative,* used to express the highest degree when *more* than TWO objects are compared; as, James is the *tallest* one of the company; My apple is the *sweetest* of the three; This seems to be the *hottest* day of the season.

471. Usage, however, the grammarians to the contrary notwithstanding, warrants the superlative in such expressions as, He is the *tallest* of the two; Which is the *tallest,* James or John?

472. Some name a fourth degree below the *positive,* and called DIMINUTIVE; as, *bluish, brackish,* and other words ending in *ish.*

473. *Comparison* is *regular* or *irregular,* or by *adverbs.*

474. *Regular comparison* is made by adding to the *positive, er* for the comparative, and *est* for the superlative. For example:

Positive.	Comparative.	Superlative.
soft,	soft*er*,	soft*est*.
mild,	mild*er*,	mild*est*.
wise,	wis*er*,	wis*est*.

475. Monosyllables, and dissyllables accented on the first syllable, are compared in the regular way; as, *yellow, yellower, yellowest; worthy, worthier, worthiest; crooked, crookeder, crookedest,* etc.

476. But participial adjectives, and adjectives derived from nouns, are compared by means of adverbs; as, *mixed, more mixed,* etc., *golden,* etc.

477. *Irregular comparison:*

Positive.	Comparative.	Superlative.
good,	better,	best.
bad, evil or ill,	worse,	worst.
little,	less, lesser,	least.
much or many,	more,	most.

478. Some adjectives thus compared are *redundant;*

479. Having more than one superlative; as, *fore, former, foremost* or *first; hind, hinder, hindermost* or *hindmost; near, nearer, nearest* or *next,* etc.

480. Some are *defective;*

481. In the positive; as, *nether, nethermost; under, undermost,* etc.

482. In the comparative; as, *end, endmost; eastern, easternmost; front, frontmost; southern, southernmost,* etc.

483. Comparison by use of the adverbs *more* and *most,* and *less* and *least.*

Positive.	Comparative.	Superlative.
beautiful,	*more* beautiful,	*most* beautiful.
beautiful,	*less* beautiful,	*least* beautiful.

484. Adjectives of two or more syllables are usually compared by using these adverbs.

485. Some adjectives are compared both *regularly* and by *adverbs;* as, *worthy, worthier,* and *worthiest; worthy,* MORE *worthy,* MOST *worthy.*

486. These adverbs, though used in comparing the adjective, are parsed as adverbs, *limiting* the adjective, and *not* as a *part* of the adjective.

487. *Compounds, numerals,* and *proper adjectives* can not be compared.

488. It is hypercritically affirmed by most grammarians that such adjectives as *round, straight, perfect,* and *complete,* do not admit of comparison. All usage, however, is against them. It is obvious to any one but a grammarian that '*more perfect,*' '*more complete,*' etc., are abbreviated expressions for "more nearly perfect," "more nearly complete," etc.

489. Peculiarities of construction.

490. *This*, and its plural, *these*, always refer to an object or objects near at hand; while *that*, and its plural, *those*, refer to a more distant object or objects: The hat and shawl have recently changed places; *this* being worn by men; *that* by women. *This*, as in the preceding example, always refers to the thing last mentioned.

491. An adjective is sometimes used by *enallage* in poetry for an adverb; as,

                Some, sailing down the stream,
  Are snatched *immediate* by the quick-eyed trout.—THOMSON.

492. These two forms of expression, *the first two*, and *the two first*, also *the last three* and *the three last*, are warranted by sufficient use.

493. *One, each, else,* and *other* are never nouns, as some grammarians have taught. Their construction is sometimes peculiar and obscure, but, when not expressed, a noun is always *understood* after them. When these words *seem* to stand in the possessive case, they have only taken the sign of the noun which is to be supplied in parsing. For example: Be ye one another's joy. The ellipses being supplied, this sentence reads thus: Be ye one [person] another [person]'s joy. The construction is obvious; 'one' limits 'person,' and 'person' is in apposition with 'ye.' 'Another' limits 'person's,' and 'person's,' as a possessive, limits 'joy'; 'joy' is the predicate with the intransitive verb, 'be.' Take another example: He declared them to be each other's worst enemies; that is, He declared them, each [person] to be [the] other [person]'s worst enemies. Again: Love one another; that is, [You] one [person] love another [person].

These pronominal adjectives *each other* and *one another*, as used above, may be called reciprocal pronominal adjectives. There are reflexive pronouns, but no reciprocal pronouns.

That is my book and nobody else's. In this, 'else's' is a pronominal adjective limiting 'body,' and takes the possessive sign because standing nearest the noun, which is limited by the possessive. 'Nobody' is the possessive noun limiting *book*, understood.

494. The pronominal *one* with its plural *ones*, in most cases, rather seems a pronoun than an adjective. With pronominals, the limited noun can be supplied without marring the sense; not so with the word *one;* for example: Some *one* has said, etc.; Select all the fair *ones*. In this very common use of 'one' and 'ones,' we can not supply the nouns represented by them without displacing 'one' and 'ones.'

In the example, Let *others* say what they please, etc., we can supply the noun *persons*, by transferring the plural sign from 'others' to the noun supplied, but not so with '*ones.*' Following the general usage of *grammarians*, I have nevertheless classed *one* and *ones* among pronominal adjectives.

495. The expressions, *many a, such a,* etc., are parsed as one word, and limit singular nouns, though the adjectives, when used alone, limit plurals; as, *many a* man, *such* a person.

> Full *many a* gem, of purest ray serene,
> The dark, unfathomed caves of ocean bear;
> Full *many a* flower is born to blush unseen,
> And waste its sweetness on the desert air.—GRAY.

THE ARTICLE.

496. Definition.—An article is a word used with a noun to limit or extend its signification; to distinguish the particular from the general.

497. When the article is not used, the expression is general; as, *Man* is mortal; that is, the *race*,—all mankind. But the expression becomes particular when the article is used; as, *The* man, or *a* man, is mortal; meaning a particular man: again, *the* limits or restricts the signification to a *single* man, while *a* or *an* extends the application to *any* man.

498. Classes.—*Definite* and *Indefinite.*

499. The **definite** article is *the;* which distinguishes, in the particular, the definite from the indefinite.

500. *The* generally indicates that its noun is modified in some way, although *the* itself can hardly be said to have any modifying power.

501. *The* is derived from *that*, but is not so definite.

502. The **indefinite** article is *a* or *an;* which refers to the particular indefinitely.

ETYMOLOGY—VERB—PERSON—NUMBER.

503. *A* and *an* are the same, the form being, originally, *an* only; but the *n* has been dropped before words beginning with a consonant sound.

504. The indefinite article is derived from the Latin *unus* or French *un*, but is more indefinite than our word *one*. *A* man is not so definite as *one* man.

505. Some words beginning with a *vowel* nevertheless begin with a *consonant sound;* these take *a* rather than *an;* as, *A* use, *a* unit, *a* one, etc.; having the consonant sound of *y* and *w*.

506. *A* is frequently a contraction for the prepositions *at, in, on, to;* as, He went *a* fishing; They have gone *a* boating, etc.

507. Constructions.

508. The *articles* can not be used alone, but always in connection with a noun, or an adjective having a noun understood which the article limits.

509. Articles sometimes logically limit a phrase; as, *The dry season* bids fair to include *the remaining weeks of summer;* however, grammatically, '*the*' limits only '*weeks*.'

510. *The* is used as an intensive adverb in such expressions as, *The* faster he runs *the* slower he goes. *The* is frequently thus used with adverbs of the comparative degree; as, *The* more openly it is done, *the* better.

VERB—PERSON—NUMBER.

511. Recitation of Written Parsing Lesson.

512. Person and Number.—*Teacher.* "Pupils, how many remember the definition of a verb?"

All hands up.

Teacher. "Mary, you may give it."

Mary. "A verb is a word that signifies action, being, or state of being."

Teacher. "Right. We begin, now, a systematic study of the verb, taking its modifications in order. You will learn, first, about *person* and *number* as applied to verbs. If you saw Jane very intently poring over her grammar lesson, would you say to me 'Jane study her grammar lesson'? All together."

Class. "Jane studies her grammar lesson."

Teacher. "Is it proper to say, 'The boys reads'? Mary."

Mary. "The boys read."

Teacher. "You are right. You see, class, that between the verb and its subject there is a close relation, which determines the form in which the verb must be written."

1. The boy *runs;* The boys *run.*
2. This bird *flies* alone; Those birds *fly* in company.
3. James *has* a new grammar, but we *have* our old ones.

Teacher. "In what number is the noun 'boy,' in the first sentence? James."

James. "Singular."

Teacher. "Right. So the verb, of which 'boy' is the subject, is said to be in the singular number. If the subject is in the plural number, the verb must be in the plural. In what number is the verb 'run,' in the first sentence? Jane."

Jane. "Plural."

Teacher. "Very good. You will observe that the verb generally drops the 's' in forming the plural, but some verbs have a plural differing otherwise from the singular. For example, in the third sentence. Class, in what number is the verb, 'has'? All together."

Class. "Singular."

Teacher. "Why?"

Class. "Because its subject, 'James,' is in the singular."

Teacher. "In what number is the verb 'have,' in the same sentence? Henry."

Henry. "Plural."

Teacher. "Why? Susan."

Susan. "Because its subject, 'we,' is in the plural."

Teacher. "Would you say, 'He study,' or 'He studies'?"

Class. "He studies."

Teacher. "'I studies,' or 'I study'?"

Class. "I study."

Teacher. "In what person is 'I'?"

Class. "First person."

Teacher. "In what person is 'he'?"

Class. "Third person."

ETYMOLOGY—THE VERB—TENSE.

Teacher. "You see that the *person* of the subject also affects the form of the verb. I will refer you, now, to Rule 9, page 182: 'A finite verb must agree with its subject in person and number.' You may give the person and number of the verbs in the following sentences."

4. I *remember* when you visited us we *had* just built our new house.

5. *One who possesses* contentment *is* far *richer* than the Rothschilds.

6. The polar star *guides* the *sailor* on the deep.

7. We *will avoid* all *altercation*.

8. Tornadoes prostrate forests and destroy villages.

9. Idleness leads to crime.

TENSE.

513. *Teacher.* "Pupils, I wish you to learn one thing more, to-day, in reference to the verb. We find that there are three kinds of time: the past, the present, the future. Each kind of time has two *tenses*, as given in this outline.

Present time. { *Present tense,* / *Present perfect tense.* } *Past time.* { *Past tense,* / *Past perfect tense.* }

Future time. { *Future tense,* / *Future perfect tense.* }

"Since all acts are performed in one of these kinds of time, every verb must be in one of these six tenses. I will give you the form of the verb 'study,' in the first, or simple, tenses: *Present*, I study; *Past*, I studied; *Future*, I shall or will study. You may give the verb 'play,' in the same way, all together."

Class. "*Present*, I play; *Past*, I played; *Future*, I shall or will play."

Teacher. "Very good. I will show you how to inflect these verbs in the different persons and numbers. Follow me closely while I give the verb 'play,' as I shall then give you an opportunity to inflect the verb 'study,' yourselves."

Present tense.

Singular. / *Plural.*

Ordinary style.	Solemn style.		
1. I play.		1.	We play.
2. You play.	Thou playest.	2.	You play.
3. He plays.	He playeth.	3.	They play.

Past tense.

Singular. / *Plural.*

Ordinary style.	Solemn style.		
1. I played.		1.	We played.
2. You played.	Thou playedst.	2.	You played.
3. He played.		3.	They played.

Future tense.

Singular. / *Plural.*

Ordinary style.	Solemn style.		
1. I shall or will play.	Thou shalt or wilt play.	1.	We shall or will play.
2. You shall or will play.		2.	You shall or will play.
3. He shall or will play.		3.	They shall or will play.

Teacher. "You may give the verb 'study,' in concert, as I point to this form on the blackboard.

The teacher should put his inflection of the verb "play" on the board, as he gives it.

Present tense.

Singular. / *Plural.*

Ordinary style.	Solemn style.		
1. I study.		1.	We study.
2. You study.	Thou studiest.	2.	You study.
3. He studies.	He studieth.	3.	They study.

Past tense.

Singular. / *Plural.*

Ordinary style.	Solemn style.		
1. I studied.		1.	We studied.
2. You studied.	Thou studiedst.	2.	Ye studied.
3. He studied.		3.	They studied.

ETYMOLOGY—THE VERB—TENSE.

Future tense.

Singular.   *Plural.*

Ordinary style.	*Solemn style.*	
1. I shall or will study.	Thou shalt or wilt study.	1. We shall or will study.
2. You shall or will study.		2. You shall or will study.
3. He shall or will study.		3. They shall or will study.

Teacher. "Pupils, these three tenses in which you have inflected the verb 'study,' have separate signs by which you may distinguish them. I will give these signs in tabular form."

Signs.

Present tense	. . .	(NOW).
Past tense	. . .	(YESTERDAY).
Future tense	. . .	SHALL OR WILL.

Teacher. "You will not always find the signs, *now* and *yesterday*, used with the verbs, but you can always apply them to their respective tenses and make sense; as, *Present*, I study (now); *Past*, I studied (yesterday); *Future*, I shall or will study."

1. The wind *carried* my hat across the street.
2. I *will study* my lesson.
3. The rose *blooms* beautifully, but it soon *will wither.*
4. My oleander blossoms *have* a beautiful straw color.
5. Father *paid* seventy-five cents for my new grammar.

Teacher. "Now, pupils, who can tell me the verb and its tense in the first sentence?"

All hands up.

Teacher. "Mary."

Mary. "'Carried' is a verb in the past tense."

Teacher. "Why? James."

James. "Because we can use 'yesterday' after the verb and make sense."

Teacher. "Susan, you may read the sentence, showing that the use of 'yesterday' makes good sense."

Susan. "The wind carried my hat across the street *yesterday.*"

Teacher. "Well done, Susan. I will give the programme for parsing a verb, as far as we have studied it, and will parse one for you."

The teacher will here place on the blackboard the following partial programme for parsing a verb:

Species? Tense? Person? Number? Construction? Rule?

The teacher will notice that no other sentences are used but such as contain the three tenses explained.

Teacher. "I will parse 'have,' in the fourth sentence. *Have* is a verb, present, third, plural, to agree with its subject, 'blossoms,' Rule 9, *A finite verb must agree with its subject in person and number.* This rule you will find on page 182. Henry, you may rise and parse 'paid,' in the fifth sentence."

Henry. "*Paid* is a verb, past, third, singular, to agree with its subject, 'father,' Rule 9."

Teacher. "Very good. For your next recitation you may parse such words as I have italicized in the following sentences."

1. Mary *looks* quite well now, though she *was* very sick yesterday.
2. We *believe* diligent study *will bring* a rich reward.
3. The men *worked* until another party *relieved* them.
4. Kindness shown to others *will make* us happy.
5. Honesty pays. *Will* you *try* it?

PERFECT TENSES.

514. Recitation — Written Parsings of Verbs — Signs of the Three Tenses given.

515. Drill. — *Teacher.* "Pupils, we will now give attention to the three *perfect* tenses. 'Perfect' is used in the sense of *completed* or *accomplished*. The *simple past* tense, 'I studied,' refers to simple past time, and may be known by taking (yesterday) after it, as, I have shown you already. The *past perfect* tense, 'I had studied,' refers to a past act completed or perfected before some other past time mentioned or implied, and may always be known by the signs *had* or *hadst*. The *simple present* tense, 'I study,' refers to an act which is now going on. (Now) is the sign of this tense, as I told you yesterday. The *present perfect* tense, 'I have studied,' refers to an act completed in a period of present time. This tense you will know by the signs *have, hast, has,* or *hath.* The *future* tense denotes any future time; the *future perfect* tense points out a time before some other future time; its sign is *shall* or *will have.*"

Signs.

Present perfect tense	HAVE, HAST, HAS, *or* HATH.
Past perfect tense	HAD *or* HADST.
Future perfect tense	SHALL HAVE *or* WILL HAVE.

"All verbs in these three tenses are accompanied by their appropriate signs, hence you can readily distinguish them. For example, the verb 'play': *Present perfect,* I have played; *past perfect,* I had played; *future perfect,* I shall or will have played."

Teacher will write on the board the names of the six tenses, in order.

Teacher. "As I point to this form on the board, you may give the verb 'study,' naming each tense. All together."

Class. "*Present,* I study; *present perfect,* I have studied; *past,* I studied; *past perfect,* I had studied; *future,* I shall or will study; *future perfect,* I shall or will have studied."

Teacher. "Very good. I will ask Jane to take the verb 'rest,' and give the first person in the same way."

Jane. "*Present,* I rest. | *Past,* I rested.
Present perfect, I have rested. | *Past perfect,* I had rested.
Future, I shall or will rest.
Future perfect, I shall have rested or will have rested."

Teacher. "Very well. I will now ask you to parse some words in the following sentences for your next recitation. You may also memorize the signs of the six tenses, so that you can write them on the board, at the next recitation, without looking at your books."

1. I *believe* James *has visited* Europe.
2. When I *saw* Henry, he *said* you *had departed.*
3. Before you *will begin* your work, I *shall have finished* mine.
4. We *live* in an age of many privileges.
5. The hunters *will kill* no squirrels to-day.
6. *One who lives* for others *will find* many friends.

Teacher. "You will use the same programme I gave you yesterday. I will parse 'shall have finished.' You will find it in the third sentence. *Shall have finished* is a verb, future perfect, first, singular, to agree with its subject, 'I,' Rule 9. How many think they can parse all the words in italics, for the next parsing lesson?"

One hand not up.

Teacher. "What word, John, do you think you can not parse?"

John. "'Had departed,' in the second sentence."

Teacher. "Who can parse it?"

Hands up.

Teacher. "Julia."

Julia. "*Had departed* is a verb, past perfect, second, singular or plural, to agree with its subject, 'you,' Rule 9."

Teacher. "John, do you understand it now?"

John. "Yes, sir. I had forgotten how to tell the number, but I see it now."

Teacher. "I think no one of you will have any difficulty with this lesson."

MODE.

516. Recitation—Written Parsings.

Criticism of parsings by pupils themselves, papers being previously exchanged.

Teacher. "Pupils, I will now tell you something about *modes*. There are different ways of expressing actions or states of being. The grammarians call these different ways, modes. You may know them by their use or their signs. All those forms of the verb which you have studied thus far, are in the Indicative Mode. This mode is used simply to declare something, or to ask a question; as, 'The boys run'; 'Have you heard the news?'

517. Potential Mode.—The next mode I wish you to learn is the Potential. You will recognize it by its signs, *may*, *can*, or *must; might, could, would*, or *should*. This mode has but four tenses, and is used to express power, possibility, liberty, or necessity. I will take the verb 'study,' and give the four tenses in the potential mode.

Present tense, I may, can, or must study.
Present perfect tense, I may, can, or must have studied.
Past tense, I might, could, would, or should study.
Past perfect tense, I might, could, would, or should have studied.

"How many think they can now tell when any verb is in the potential mode?"

All hands are up.

Teacher. "You may give the verb 'rest,' in the same way or mode in which I gave 'study.' All together."

Class. "*Present*, I may, can, or must rest; *present perfect*, I may, can, or must have rested; *past*, I might, could, would, or should rest; *past perfect*, I might, could, would, or should have rested."

Teacher. "Very good. You will all notice that, in this mode, the signs of the *perfect* tenses are formed by adding *have* to the sign of the present or past. We can now enlarge our programme for parsing verbs."

The teacher will put on the blackboard the following programme:

Species? Mode? Tense? Person? Number? Construction? Rule?

Before parsing, the teacher should drill the class, in concert, in giving the tenses of the potential mode, using different verbs, until all join in promptly, calling on any pupil singly, when he seems to fall below the class average.

1. You *may go* now, but *must return* in one hour.
2. I can read quite well, but John reads better.
3. We *should treat* others as we desire they should treat us.
4. Many say, when old, I *might have improved* my time much better.
5. Who *could have expected* such a result?
6. The man *may have come* to the house, but I *must have been* at the office.
7. We *might accomplish* much more by a little extra effort.
8. He *should have learned* to control himself in youth.
9. Attention to the warnings of his friends *would have prevented* his disgrace.
10. Who *could see* it, who *would suffer* it, without remonstrance?

Teacher. "Mary, you may rise and parse the first verb in the first sentence, following the new programme."

Mary. "*May go* is a verb, potential, present, second, singular or plural, to agree with its subject, 'you,' Rule 9."

Teacher. "Very good. For the next lesson parse, in your exercise-book, such words as I ask you to mark in your grammars."

IMPERATIVE MODE—SUBJUNCTIVE MODE.

518. Criticism of Written Parsings.

Commend neatness, freedom from blots. Give hearty approval of the industry of the dullest pupils.

519. Imperative Mode.—*Teacher.* "The third mode which I shall ask you to study, is called the Imperative Mode. It is used for commanding; as, 'Give me that book'; for exhorting; as, 'Go not in the way of evil'; for entreating; as, 'Pardon me'; for permitting; as, 'Do as you please.' You notice, pupils, that the imperative mode has four uses, and in no one is the subject expressed, but it is always *thou* or *you* or *ye*, understood; hence it is always in the second person. We might say, 'You come to me,' 'You give me the book'; but it sounds best to omit the subject, *you*. You will also notice that it has but one tense, the present. Point out imperatives in the following sentences."

1. *Seek* the lost; *raise* the fallen.
2. *Treat* all your playmates with kindness.
3. *Complain* not of hard lessons, but *overcome* difficulty by hard study.
4. *Prepare* for a useful life; *spread* happiness around you.
5. *Spare* me, stranger; *take* not a life so young.
6. *Forgive* me, father, all the wrong I've done.

520. Subjunctive Mode.—*Teacher.* "You may include the Subjunctive Mode in this lesson. You will know it usually by the signs *if, though, lest, unless*, which precede the verb; as, 'If you *go*, be careful lest you *offend* some one.' The subjunctive mode is used

to express a conditional circumstance, and is found in two tenses, the present and the past. I will give you examples, and you may parse, for the next recitation, the italicized words."

7. If you *venture*, you may regret the step.
8. Though he *wandered* far, he was not lost.
9. Go not, lest thou *perish*.
10. Unless he *return* soon, he may find the door locked.

Teacher. "How many think they can parse verbs in the subjunctive and imperative modes?"

Some hands up.

Teacher. "They are parsed by the same programme as other verbs. Mary, you may parse 'prepare,' in the fourth sentence."

Mary. "*Prepare* is a verb, imperative, present, second, singular, to agree with its subject, 'thou,' understood, Rule 9."

Teacher. "Why imperative? Mary."

Mary. "Because it is used for commanding or entreating."

Teacher. "Very good. John may parse 'wandered,' in the eighth sentence."

John. "*Wandered* is a verb, subjunctive, past, third, singular, to agree with its subject, 'he,' Rule 9."

TRANSIVITY.

521. Written Parsings of Verbs—Criticism.

522. Transivity.—*Teacher.* "Pupils, I will endeavor, now, to gratify your desire to understand the meanings of those two words, *transitive* and *active*, in Rule 17: *The object of a transitive verb, in the active voice, must be in the objective case.* With reference to their use, all verbs are said to be *transitive* or *intransitive*. Is the following sentence complete? 'James drives.' What do you say, Mary?"

Mary. "It is not, for you do not tell what James drives."

Teacher. "Mary is right. You all see that 'drives' is a verb which will not make complete sense with its subject alone. Who will supply a word to complete the sense?"

Hands up.

Teacher. "James."

James. "James drives a horse."

Teacher. "What is the relation of 'horse' to 'drives'? Susan."

Susan. "*Horse* is the object of the verb 'drives.'"

Teacher. "Very well. A transitive verb, then, is one that requires an object to complete its meaning. We may say, 'The boys run,' or 'The birds fly,' and have complete sense; these verbs are intransitive, for, *An intransitive verb is one that does not require an object to complete its meaning.* I wish you to use these definitions in parsing verbs, hereafter. You may determine which are transitive and which intransitive verbs in the following sentences."

1. The sun rises in the east.
2. Charles gave a ripe peach to the sick woman.
3. Lightning purifies the atmosphere.
4. Our cousins have come from the city.
5. Water freezes at 32° Fahrenheit.
6. Water boils at 212° Fahrenheit.
7. I must learn my lesson.

Teacher. "How many can tell whether the verb 'rises' is transitive or intransitive?"

Most hands are up.

Teacher. "John."

John. "*Rises* is an intransitive verb."

Teacher. "Why, Mary?"

Mary. "It does not require an object to complete its meaning."

523. Drill in Voice.—*Teacher.* "If I should say, 'The horse kicked John,' what is it that acts? All together."

Class. "The subject, 'horse.'"

Teacher. "Very good. You notice, when I change it, thus, 'John is kicked by the horse,' the subject of the verb is 'John,' who does not act, but receives the action. In the first sentence, the verb is said to be in the *active voice*, because the subject, 'horse,' acts. In the second sentence, the verb is said to be in the *passive voice*, because the subject, 'John,' received the action; in other words, is passive to the action. Take another example: 'James plows the field.' In what voice is the verb 'plows'? Henry."

Henry. "Active voice."
Teacher. "Why?"
Henry. "Because the subject, 'James,' acts."
Teacher. "Very well. Who will change this sentence so that the verb may be passive?"
Hands up.
Teacher. "Jane."
Jane. "The field is plowed by James."
Teacher. "Very good, Jane. Now, Julia, why is this verb, 'is plowed,' in the passive voice?"
Julia. "Because the subject, 'field,' receives the action."
Teacher. "*Voice*, then, shows the relation between the verb and its subject, the subject acting or receiving the action. The *active voice*, then, is that FORM which verbs take whose subjects act; the *passive voice* is that FORM which verbs take whose subjects receive action.

"All intransitive verbs are in the active voice, only; and even those which do not denote action, are in the active voice, because they are in the same FORM as those verbs whose subjects do act. Transitive verbs have both voices: the *active* and the *passive*. You may apply this means of distinction in determining the voice of verbs in the following sentences."

8. Sarah met her friend in the city.
9. My slate is broken.
10. The seed was sown, and in due time it will ripen into a beautiful harvest.
11. James was seen by me.
12. The letter was written, but I forgot to mail it.
13. The man whom I saw was the President.
14. The book which you gave me was returned.

Teacher. "We will now enlarge our programme for parsing verbs. You may copy it into your books, as I write it on the board.[1] I will parse the verb 'saw,' in the thirteenth sentence, 'The man whom I saw was the President.' *Saw* is a verb, transitive, active, indicative, past, first, singular, to agree with its subject, 'I,' Rule 9."

---

[1] *Species? Transivity? Voice? Mode? Tense? Person? Number? Construction? Rule?*

Mary's hand is up.

Teacher. "What is it, Mary?"

Mary. "I do not see why the verb 'saw' is transitive here."

Teacher. "Class, who will tell Mary why the verb 'saw' is transitive? James, will you?"

James. "Because it takes the object *whom* to complete its meaning."

Teacher. "Now, Mary, you may parse *whom*."

Mary. "*Whom* is a pronoun, relative, agreeing with its antecedent, *man*, in the third, singular, masculine, Rule 5, and is in the objective case, the object of the verb 'saw,' Rule 17."

Teacher. "Very good. Charles may parse the verb in the ninth sentence, 'My slate is broken.'"

Charles. "*Is broken* is a verb, transitive, passive, indicative, present, third, singular, agrees with its subject, 'slate,' Rule 9."

Susan's hand is up.

Teacher. "What is it, Susan?"

Susan. "Why is it transitive?"

Teacher. "All passive verbs are transitive, because their subjects are objects; or, in other words, their subjects receive the action. For the next recitation you may parse the words you have marked."

NOTE.—Before leaving the second section of this lesson, the teacher should satisfy himself that all the pupils can tell the transitivity and the voice of all the verbs in the first seven sentences of the lesson.

INFINITIVE MODE—PARTICIPIAL MODE.

524. Recitation—Examination of Sentences formed by the Class, and Written Parsings.

525. Infinitive Mode.—*Teacher.* "Pupils, the modes which you have studied thus far are called *finite;* that is, they are finited, or limited, in person and number. The two modes which remain have no person and number. They are the Infinitive and the Participial modes. The infinitive has two tenses, the *present* and the *perfect*, and is found in both *voices*. The sign of the *present* infinitive is TO; for example, *to teach, to be taught.* The sign of the *perfect*

ETYMOLOGY—THE VERB—MODE.

infinitive is TO HAVE; for example, *to have taught, to have been taught.* You may point out the infinitives in the following sentences."

1. Strive to make some improvement every day.
2. I gave James permission to go.
3. Mary was anxious to see Susan.
4. We love to walk in the morning air.
5. I am glad to hear of your success.
6. John is said to have gone to sea.
7. We are not willing to be called lazy.
8. It is better to be loved by a dog than hated by it.
9. He is said to have been educated in science and language.
10. To have obeyed our parents, will enable us the better to obey God.

Teacher. "Before studying infinitives further, I will ask your attention to the participial mode.

526. Participial Mode.—"The participial mode is sometimes called, simply, the Participle, as the infinitive mode is frequently called the Infinitive. The participle has three tenses, *present, past,* and *perfect;* and is found in both voices. Only *transitive* verbs have *passive* participles."

Active Voice.

	SIGNS.	EXAMPLES.
Present participle,	ing;	loving, learning, studying.
Past participle,	(having);	loved, learned, studied.
Perfect participle,	having;	having learned, having studied.

Teacher. "The past *active* participle is used only with some auxiliary to form the *perfect tenses* in the active voice; as, he has *learned,* he had *learned.*"

Passive Voice.

	SIGNS.	EXAMPLES.
Present participle,	being;	being loved, being taught.
Past participle,	(being);	loved, taught, studied.
Perfect participle,	having been;	having been loved, having been taught.

Teacher. "By these signs you will know the different participles. The past *passive* participle may take *being* before it without marring the sense; but you will have no difficulty in determining it by the sense of the passage. For example: 'John had *hidden* the ball in his pocket.' Here, *hidden* is the past *active* participle, being used with *had*, to form a perfect tense to the active voice. But, 'I discovered the ball, *hidden* in John's pocket,' makes *hidden* the past *passive* participle; for I can say, 'I discovered the ball, (being) hidden in John's pocket,' without materially disturbing the sense. You may name the participles in the following examples."

1. Do you hear the children's singing?
2. Mary, having studied her lesson, has gone into the fields to play.
3. The painter, reaching to catch his brush, fell from the scaffold.
4. The house now being erected, belongs to the merchant.
5. He shall be like a tree planted by the rivers of water.
6. My purpose having been accomplished, I returned home.
7. Ringing the bell is the janitor's hourly duty.
8. Exercising the mind develops business power.
9. The enemy being conquered, peace was restored.
10. The workman, wearied by the labors of the day, seeks his quiet home.
11. Mary, admired and beloved by all her schoolmates, has left school.
12. Books handsomely bound too often betray their uselessness.
13. I am expecting goods sent by express.
14. Those exercises, thoroughly examined and corrected, have been returned to their owners.

Teacher. "Pupils, you may turn to page 195, where you will find the 20th Rule, which we will now use in parsing *infinitives* and *participles: Infinitives and participles have the construction of nouns, adjectives, or adverbs.* I will put the programme on the blackboard."

The teacher will put on the board the following:

Species? Transivity? Voice? Mode? Tense? Construction? Rule?

Teacher. "You notice, pupils, this is like the programme for parsing verbs, except that *person* and *number* are omitted. I will parse 'planted,' in the fifth sentence: 'He shall be like a tree *planted* by the rivers of water.' *Planted* is a verb, transitive, passive, participial, past, with the construction of an *adjective*, Rule 20, limiting the noun 'tree,' Rule 1. Mary, you may parse 'ringing,' in the seventh sentence: 'Ringing the bell is the janitor's hourly duty.'"

Mary. "*Ringing* is a verb, transitive, active, participial, present, with the construction of a *noun*, Rule 20, the subject of the finite verb *is*, Rule 15."

Teacher. "Well done, Mary. You notice, class, that 'ringing' is parsed as a *verb*, because it retains its verbal nature in governing the noun *bell*, in the objective case, and has the construction of a noun, because it is the *subject* of another verb. I will now parse 'to walk,' in the fourth sentence of the second section of this lesson: 'We love *to walk* in the morning air.' *To walk* is a verb, intransitive, active, infinitive, present, with the construction of a noun, Rule 20, object of the verb 'love,' Rule 17.

"Your greatest difficulty will be in determining the construction; but I think in most cases you will be able to determine whether the infinitive or participle is used most like a noun, an adjective, or an adverb. Has any one a question to ask?"

Charles' hand is up.

Teacher. "Charles."

Charles. "I would like to have one more example in parsing infinitives."

Teacher. "What shall it be, Charles?"

Charles. "*To have obeyed*, in the tenth sentence, 'To have obeyed our parents, will enable us the better to obey God.'"

Teacher. "Who would like to try it?"

Few hands up.

Teacher. "Susan. I fear, boys, the girls will excel you."

Susan. "*To have obeyed* is a verb, transitive, active, infinitive, perfect, construction of a noun, Rule 20, subject of the verb *will enable*, Rule 15."

Teacher. "Well done. For the next recitation, parse the words you have marked in your grammars."

CLASSES OF VERBS.

527. Criticism of Written Parsings of Participles and Infinitives.

528. Classes of Verbs.—*Teacher.* "Pupils, there are two classifications of verbs: First, as to USE, namely, *transitive* and *intransitive*. These you have already studied. Secondly, as to FORM, verbs are either *regular* or *irregular*. Verbs have three *principal parts*, or parts from which all others are formed; they are the *present* and the *past tenses*, and the *past participle*. Take the verb 'play.' Present, play; *past*, played; *past participle*, played. Pupils, how do the *past tense* and *past participle* differ in form from the *present tense?* All together."

Class. "They have *ed* added to the form of the *present tense.*"

Teacher. "Right. 'Play' is, then, a *regular* verb, because every regular verb forms its past tense and past participle by adding *ed* to the present tense.

"But, according to the fourth rule for spelling, words ending in *e* silent, omit the *e* on taking an additional syllable beginning with a vowel. Charles, you may give the principal parts of the verb 'dine.'"

Charles. "*Present tense*, dine; *past tense*, dined; *past participle*, dined."

Teacher. "I will give the principal parts of the verb 'do,' using the signs of these parts. *Present tense*, I do (now); *past tense*, I did (yesterday); *past participle*, (I have) done. Is 'do' a regular verb? All together."

Class. "It is not."

Teacher. "Why? Mary."

Mary. "Because it does *not* form its past tense and past participle by adding *ed* to the present tense."

Teacher. "You will find the *principal parts* of any verb by using the signs which I just gave you. James, you may give the principal parts of 'do,' omitting the signs."

James. "*Present tense*, do; *past tense*, did; *past participle*, done."

Teacher. "Susan, you may give the principal parts of the verb 'run,' using the signs."

Susan. "*Present tense*, I run (now); *past tense*, I ran (yesterday); *past participle*, (I have) run."

Teacher. "Very good. John, you may give the principal parts of the same verb, without the signs."

John. "*Present tense*, run; *past tense*, ran; *past participle*, run."

Teacher. "Very good. You may determine which are regular, and which are irregular verbs, in the following sentences."

1. Having borne the heat and burden of the day, he welcomed the night.
2. Rejoicing in hope, we press gladly forward.
3. Our mowing machine cut James's foot so badly, he can scarcely walk.
4. Water is the universal solvent.
5. I have written a letter to my cousin.
6. Lucy has composed some delightful music.
7. James, having chosen his life-work, is determined to bend all his energies in that direction.
8. A pure heart is God's best gift to man.
9. Numerous expedients have been tried for the relief of that difficulty.
10. He should have come sooner.
11. I may have been mistaken.

Teacher. "We can now complete our programme for parsing verbs."

The teacher will write on the board: *Species? Classes?* { *Regularity? Transivity?* } (*Principal parts?*) *Style? Voice? Mode? Tense? Person? Number? Construction? Rule?*

Teacher. "By the same form, omitting person and number, I will parse 'having borne,' in the sentence, 'Having borne the heat and burden of the day, he welcomed the night.' *Having borne* is a verb, irregular, transitive; bear, bore, borne, active, participial, perfect, with the construction of an adjective, Rule 20, limiting 'he,' Rule 1.

"In parsing *regular* verbs, the principal parts are omitted. James, you may parse 'has composed,' in the sentence, 'Lucy has composed some delightful music.'"

James. "*Has composed* is a verb, regular, transitive, active, indicative, present perfect, third, singular, to agree with its subject, 'Lucy,' Rule 9."

Teacher. "Very well. I will parse one more verb for you. What shall it be? Mary."

Mary. "'Is,' in the eighth sentence."

Teacher. "Very well, then; I will take 'is,' in the sentence, 'A pure heart is God's best gift to man.' *Is* is a verb, irregular, intransitive; be, was, been, active, indicative, present, third, singular, to agree with its subject, 'heart,' Rule 9.

"Pupils, tell me whether 'welcomed' is regular or irregular. All together."

Class. "Regular."

Teacher. "'Press'?"

Class. "Regular."

Teacher. "'Have written'?"

Class. "Irregular."

Teacher. "Henry, you may give the principal parts of the verb 'write,' using the signs."

Henry. "*Present tense*, I write (now); *past tense*, I wrote (yesterday); *past participle*, (I have) written."

Teacher. "Very good. Take the verb 'having chosen.' Regular or irregular? All together."

Some hesitation. John's hand is up.

Teacher. "John."

John. "I think it is regular."

Susan's hand is up.

Teacher. "What do *you* say, Susan?"

Susan. "I think it is irregular."

Teacher. "We will take a vote on it. As many as agree with John may hold up their hands."

Two or three hands are up.

Teacher. "As many as agree with Susan, that 'having chosen' is an irregular verb, may hold up their hands."

Nearly all hands are up.

Teacher. "John, you may give the principal parts of 'having chosen,' using the signs."

John. "*Present tense*, I choose (now); *past tense*, I —— chose (yesterday); *past participle*, I have chosen. I see it now."

Teacher. "I am glad that John, also, agrees with Susan; and now, I think, we all see that *choose* is an irregular verb. Attention to the *signs* will generally bring you out right. Perhaps you will have no difficulty now; but in case of any doubt, you can refer to the dictionary. I will now assign you a parsing lesson."

THE VERB.

529. Definition.—A verb is a word used to assert or assume action; also, being or state of being.

530. The word 'assert' must be taken in a broad sense as including every variety of predication, among which are to affirm, deny, interrogate, command, condition, etc., etc.

531. The name is derived from the Latin, *verbum*, meaning *the word*, because the early grammarians found the *verb* to be the essential word in the sentence.

532. Classes.—As to *Form;* as to *Use.*

533. As to *form*, verbs are *Regular* or *Irregular; Defective* or *Redundant.*

534. A **regular** verb is one which forms its past indicative and past participle by adding *ed* to the present by the rules of spelling; as, call, call*ed*, call*ed;* love, lov*ed*, lov*ed; e* final, in *love*, is dropped on taking an additional syllable beginning with a vowel, according to Rule 4 for spelling.

535. An **irregular** verb does not form its past indicative and past participle by adding *ed* to the present; as, *write, wrote, written; hear, heard, heard.* *Hear*, although *d* is added to form the past indicative, is irregular, because *ed* is not added. For a list of these verbs, see page 145.

536. A **defective** verb is one deficient in some of the modes and tenses. Defective verbs have no participles.

537. List of Defective Verbs:

Present.	Past.	Present.	Past.
Beware,	———.	Quoth,	quoth or quod.
Can,	could.	Shall,	should.
May,	might.	Will,	would.
Must,	must.	Wis,	wist.
Ought,	ought.	Wit,	wot.

538. *Beware* is generally used in the imperative mode; as, Beware of the tempter.

539. *Ought* is changed to *oughtest* in the solemn style.

540. Verbs by some called *impersonal*, and by others *unipersonal*, may be classed among the *defective* verbs, since they are used only in the third person singular; as, *It snows; It blows; It just struck ten*, etc., with the subject 'it.' 'It' in these cases represents some well known antecedent, as the weather, the air, the earth, the clock, etc.

541. A redundant verb is one which has more than one form in the past tense or past participle.

(See List of Redundant Verbs, page 145.)

542. As to *use*, verbs are *Transitive* or *Intransitive*.

543. A transitive verb is one that requires an object to complete its meaning; as, I *see you;* You *have* a *grammar;* The cat *caught* a *mouse.*

544. Transitive verbs are frequently used without an object expressed; as, John *studies* diligently; Mary *recites* well. These verbs, however, are transitive still, since John must study *something* and Mary recite *something.*

545. The object of an active transitive verb is generally placed *after* it, but may come *before;* as, What *side* will you choose? *Him* will I bring speedily; Here's the man *whom* you saw.

546. A transitive verb expresses *action* or *suffering*, and not *being* or a *state of being.*

547. An intransitive verb is one that does *not* require an object to complete its meaning; as, The wind *blows;* The sun *shines;* He *stares* vacantly at the moon.

548. An intransitive verb may govern an object of kindred signification. For example, 'lives,' 'dreamed,' 'are playing,' 'grinned,' etc., govern objects in such sentences as these: He *lives* a noble *life;* He *dreamed* a *dream;* Those men *are playing a game* of chess; *Grinned* horribly a ghastly *smile*, etc. In such cases, however, some preposition may be supplied, which, by poetic license or popular usage, is suppressed: He lives [in, with, or by] a noble life; He dreamed [in or with] a dream; Those men are playing [at] a game of chess; Grinned horribly [with] a ghastly smile, etc. Intransitive causative verbs also govern an object; as, James *flies* his *kite;* that is, he *causes* it to fly.

549. The intransitive verb *be* is sometimes called a *copulative* verb, or the *copula*, because used to connect an *attribute* with the subject of the verb; as, Iron *is* a *metal;* The apple *is sweet*. 'Metal' and 'sweet' are *attributes* belonging to their respective subjects, and joined to them and asserted of them by the copula 'is.'

550. The verb *to be* is the only pure copula, though other intransitive verbs are frequently thus used; as, *appear, become, seem*, etc.

551. The *attribute* may be a *noun, pronoun*, or *adjective;* as, You are the *man;* I am *he;* The rose is *fragrant*.

552. But an *adverb* is never an attribute. 'He is *here.*' In expressions of this kind, the attribute is included in the verb 'is,' and may be expressed; as, He *is*, or He *is existing* here, or He *is sitting* here, or He *is standing* here, etc., etc. So of 'She was *there.*' In such cases the adverb modifies the copula or the attribute included in the verb 'be.'

553. All verbs may be resolved into a *copula* and an *attribute;* as, James *walks;* James *is walking;* The bird *flies;* The bird is *flying*, etc.

554. An intransitive verb expresses action; as, The boy *runs;* or being; as, I *exist;* or state of being; as, The infant *sleeps*.

555. An intransitive verb is sometimes compounded with a preposition, and is thus rendered transitive; as, Here's the boy who was laughed at. This occurs only in the passive voice.

556. *Causative verbs.*—Intransitive verbs are sometimes used in a transitive sense, denoting that the action implied is caused; as, He *trotted* the horse to town.

557. Modifications.—*Style, Voice, Mode, Tense, Person*, and *Number*.

558. Verbs have four styles: *Ordinary, Solemn, Emphatic,* and *Progressive*.

559. The **Ordinary style** is that most used in speaking and writing; as, I *study;* I *shall learn.* (See page 135.)

560. The **Solemn style** is now obsolete except in the Scriptures, in addresses to the Deity, among the Society of Friends, and in poetry; as, Thou *shalt* love the Lord thy God; Our Father who *art* in heaven, etc. (See page 135.)

561. The **Emphatic style** gives emphasis to the verb; as, I *do* study; I *did* follow your advice.

562. This style is made by prefixing the present or past tense of the verb *do* to the ordinary form. (See page 144.) The emphatic style is generally used for interrogation; as, *Do* you *like* grammar?

563. The **Progressive style** represents an action or state of being as continuing; as, I am *studying.* (See page 141.)

564. The style is made by placing the appropriate tense of the verb 'be' before the present active participle.

565. Some grammarians have spoken of *interrogative* and *negative* styles; but these are not styles of the *verb*, but rather of the *sentence:* they need no further mention here.

566. Voice is that modification of the verb which shows the relation between the verb and its subject.

Verbs have two *voices:* the *Active* and the *Passive.*

567. The **Active voice** is that *form* which those verbs take whose subjects act; as, I *run;* I *have studied.*

568. All intransitive verbs are in the active voice because they have the form of verbs whose subjects act.

569. The **Passive voice** is that *form* which those verbs take whose subjects receive action; as, My book *is torn;* The world *was created.*

570. *Transitive* verbs may be used both in the active and in the passive voice: as, James *gave* me a present; A present *was given* me by James.

571. *Intransitive* verbs do not, ordinarily, take the *passive* voice;

but some intransitive verbs which, in the active voice, seem to take an object having a signification similar to that of the verb, may have a passive form; as, A dream *was dreamt;* A game *was played;* That figure *was danced*, etc.

572. Other languages place emphatic words at the beginning of the sentence. Though our language compels an arrangement which does not generally admit of change for this purpose, yet the passive voice is sometimes thus employed. For example: 'God *created* all things,' calls attention particularly to the *creator*, to the *actor*, as having great power; but 'All things *were created* by God' directs the mind particularly to the *origin* of 'things.'

573. The active voice is frequently used with the passive signification; as, Peaches sell readily at two dollars per bushel; Houses to let; Horses to ride.

574. The passive voice is sometimes used to conceal the *actor;* as, The letter was written; The money was stolen.

575. The passive voice is frequently used in verbs of motion for the active; as, The melancholy days *are come*, for *have come;* also in conversation; as, She's come, for She *has come*, etc.; The friends *were gone* before I arrived, for *had gone*. These verbs are passive by enallage.

576. The passive infinitive frequently omits the sign *to* and the auxiliary *be;* as, He ordered the door [to be] *shut*. (1070, 1075.)

The active infinitive in the progressive style also frequently omits the sign *to* and the auxiliary *be* after the active transitive verbs enumerated in Rule 21; as, We saw him [to be] coming.

577. **Mode** is that modification of the verb which indicates the manner or condition of the assertion.

Modes are of two classes: *Finite* and *Infinite*.

578. The *Finite Modes* are those which are finited or limited by *person* and *number*.

They are the *Indicative, Potential, Subjunctive,* and *Imperative*.

579. The **Indicative mode** is that form of assertion by which verbs make a declaration or ask a question; as, I *have studied;* I *do study;* I *am studying;* Do you see? etc.

580. The **Potential mode** implies *possibility, power, liberty,* or *necessity,* etc.; as, He *may go;* He *can do* it; I *might have accomplished* it; It *must be done.*

581. This mode is also used in asking questions; as, *May I accompany* you?

582. The signs of this mode are, *may, can,* or *must; might, could, would,* or *should.*

583. The **Subjunctive mode** indicates doubt, uncertainty, or contingency; as, If you *go,* you will rue it; Though he *knew* the wrong, he did it.

584. The signs of this mode are the conjunctions *if, though, lest,* and *unless;* also the fact of condition without the preceding signs.

585. The verbal sign is frequently omitted when the order of the words is changed; as, *Had I known* you were going, I would have accompanied you, for *If I had known,* etc.

586. The subjunctive sometimes implies a certainty of a negative character; as, If I had known that, I should have gone, implying that *I did not know.*

587. The subjunctive past is often used by enallage for potential past; as, It *were* a happy life to be a thoughtless swain, for, It *would be* a happy life to be, etc.

588. Little space need be given to the discussion of the subjunctive mode, since it is obsolescent, and will probably soon become obsolete. The *verb* in this mode with many reputable authors has the form of the *indicative.* Some grammarians are coming to the opinion that the subjunctive mood should be entirely rejected from present use and discussion.

589. The **Imperative mode** is used for *commanding, exhorting, entreating, permitting,* and *proposing a condition;* as, *Confess* your sins; *Forward, march! Go* in peace; *Admit* that, and your case is lost.

590. The sign of this mode is its use, being generally without a subject expressed. When the subject is expressed, it usually follows the verb; as, Be *ye* one another's joy.

591. The imperative is used in the third person but rarely. In the exclamatory form: Long *live* the king! By poetic license: Dumb *be* the atheist tongue abhorred!—GOOLD BROWN.

592. Tense is that modification of the verb by which the time of an action is indicated, or the assertion is modified. There are two classes of tenses: *Simple* and *Perfect*.

593. The **Simple tenses** are three in number: *Present, Past,* and *Future.*

594. The **Perfect tenses** are: *Present perfect, Past perfect,* and *Future perfect.*

The tenses will be treated under the different modes.

INDICATIVE MODE.

595. The indicative mode has all the tenses, six in number. (See Conjugation, page 135.)

596. The **Present tense** indicates simple present time; as, I *write;* I *do write;* I *am writing.*

597. The *present* tense asserts general truths; as, God is wise.

598. The *historical* present is used for the past; as, Goldsmith *writes* excellent poetry.

599. The present is frequently used as referring to the future; as, When I [shall] *see* him, I will deliver your message.

600. The **Past tense** indicates simple past time; as, *I wrote;* I *did write;* I *was writing.*

REMARK.—This tense is sometimes called the *preterit.*

601. The **Future tense** indicates simple future time; as, I *shall write;* I *shall be writing;* I *will learn.*

602. The **Present perfect tense** indicates a past time completed in the present, or in a period of time not entirely past; as, I *have written;* The letter *has been written* this morning; The redemption of Italy *has been accomplished* in the nineteenth century.

603. The present perfect tense may indicate future time; as, I will come when he *has returned*—enallage for *shall have.*

604. The **Past perfect tense** indicates a definite past time; as, I *had written.*

605. The **Future perfect tense** indicates a definite future time; as, I *shall have returned* by that time.

606. The tenses of the indicative mode have the following *signs,* arranged in tabular form. Those in parentheses are not always found with the verb, but may always be supplied with their proper tenses without marring the sense:

Tenses.	*Signs.*	*Examples.*
Present,	(NOW).	I study (*now*).
Past,	(YESTERDAY).	I studied (*yesterday*).
Future,	SHALL *or* WILL.	I *shall* study, etc.
Present Perfect,	HAVE, HAST, HAS, *or* HATH.	I *have* studied, etc.
Past Perfect,	HAD *or* HADST.	I *had* studied, etc.
Future Perfect,	SHALL HAVE *or* WILL HAVE.	I *shall have* studied.

POTENTIAL MODE.

607. The potential mode has four tenses: *Present, Past, Present Perfect,* and *Past Perfect.* (See Conjugation, p. 136.)

608. The **Present potential** frequently expresses futurity; indeed, it seems more frequently future than present; as, I *may go* (to-morrow); I *can do* it (now); I *must do* it (soon).

609. The **Past potential** refers to past, present, or future time; as, He *could do* it (yesterday); I *might go* (now); I *should see* him (immediately); I *might help* you (to-morrow).

610. The **Present perfect potential** also refers to past, present, or future time, but more definitely than the past tense; as, He *may have done* it; I *must have taken* it (just now); He *may have become* wiser by that time.

611. The **Past perfect potential** refers to past time in such a manner as to express a negation; as, I *could have done* it; that is, I could, but I did not; You should have heard that speech—implying that the person did *not* hear it.

612. The tenses of the potential mode have the following signs expressed or understood. Each tense, therefore, will always be known by its appropriate sign or signs:

Tenses.	Signs.	Examples.
Present.	MAY, CAN, *or* MUST.	You *may study*, etc.
Past,	MIGHT, COULD, WOULD, *or* SHOULD.	You *might study*, etc.
Present Perfect,	MAY, CAN, *or* MUST HAVE.	You *may have studied*, etc.
Past Perfect,	MIGHT, COULD, WOULD, *or* SHOULD HAVE.	You *should have studied*, etc.

SUBJUNCTIVE MODE.

613. The subjunctive mode has three tenses: *Present*, *Past*, and *Past Perfect*. (Conjugation, pages 134, 137, 140.)

614. The **Present subjunctive** frequently implies future time; as, If I *see* him (to-morrow) I will make it right.

615. The **Past subjunctive** refers (1) to a past contingency; also, (2) to a present supposition; as, (*a*) If you *heard* Beecher you were well paid; (*b*) If I *were* you (now) I'd act differently.

616. The **Past perfect subjunctive** expresses a past supposition, equivalent to an indicative negative; as, *Had* I *known* that was broken ice, I would not have ventured on it; that is, I *did not know*, or I would not have ventured, etc.

617. The signs of the tenses of the subjunctive mode are the same as those of corresponding tenses in the indicative mode.

IMPERATIVE MODE.

618. The imperative mode has one tense,—the *Present*.

619. The imperative frequently refers to the future; as, *Come* and *see* me next week.

620. Number and person are applied to finite verbs.

621. Verbs have in reality no *number* and *person*, but chiefly for the sake of euphony assume different forms to agree with their subjects: rather to agree with the ear. (See Conjugation, page 132.)

622. The *two numbers* are applied to all finite verbs; the three *persons* to all except the *imperative* mode, which is used generally in the *second person*, and occasionally in the *third* (see Art. 591); but never in the first person.

623. The *first person*, singular and plural, takes the simple form of the verb; as, I read; We read.

624. The second person singular, solemn style, takes *st*, *est*, or *edst*, suffixed to the simple form of the verb; as, Thou write*st*; Thou read*est*; Thou wak'*st*; Thou hurri*edst*. The verb *be* changes *are* to *art*; as, Thou *art* the man. (See pages 133, 145.)

625. The second person, singular and plural, ordinary style, takes the simple form of the verb; as, You study; You or ye learn.

626. The third person singular, present indicative active, ordinary style, is formed as the plural of nouns; as, He learns; He studies.

627. The third person singular, present indicative active, solemn style, takes *th* or *eth*; as, Give to him that ask*eth*; He that com*eth* after me is mightier than I.

628. In the *perfect tenses* only the auxiliaries are varied for *number* and *person*.

INFINITE MODES—INFINITIVE, PARTICIPIAL.

629. The infinite modes are those which have no limitation of person and number.

630. They are ordinarily called *Infinitives* and *Participles*.

631. Both are *infinite*, because both are unlimited by person and number.

632. Both are *participial*, because both partake of the nature of nouns, adjectives, or adverbs, in addition to that of verbs. For convenience, however, we call one mode **Infinitive** and the other **Participial**.

633. Infinitives.—There are two Infinitives, *Present* and *Perfect*, known by the signs TO and TO HAVE. For example, the verb *write:*

Active.	Passive.
Present, TO write,	TO be written.
Perfect, TO HAVE written,	TO HAVE been written.

634. The sign of the infinitive is omitted after the verbs *bid, dare, feel, hear, let, make, need, please, see,* and others of similar signification; as, Bid him return; He can't make me run; Please come soon.

635. The infinitive may have the construction of a noun; as,
The *subject* of a verb; as, *To run* is cowardly.
The *attribute* of a sentence; as, To save is *to earn.*
The *object* of a verb; as, Jane *loves to study.*
The *object* of a preposition; as, What went ye out *for to see?*

REMARK.—This form of expression is used in the Scriptures; it is otherwise obsolete.

In apposition with a noun; as, This is my *purpose, to practice* economy.

636. The infinitive may also have the construction of an adjective; as, He gave me *permission to go.*

637. The infinitive is also used with the construction of an adverb: Limiting a verb; as, He *returned to make* an apology.

Limiting an adjective; as, He was *eager to depart*.

Limiting an adverb; as, That horse is large *enough to draw* any load.

638. The infinitive, though constructed as a noun, has no case, as many grammarians affirm. Case is a modification which does not belong to verbs.

639. An infinitive, as the subject of an intransitive verb, may be limited by an adjective in the predicate; but otherwise it is limited by adverbs; as, *To see* the sun shine is *delightful;* For us *to win* seemed *impossible*.

640. 'To,' the sign of the infinitive, has, by many grammarians, been erroneously called a preposition. But this, they confess, is to "obviate embarrassment"; or, in other words, it is the most convenient method of evading the difficulties and obscurities of infinitive constructions, and of concealing their own inability to manage them. It would be just as reasonable to make any verb in the indicative or the potential mode the object of its auxiliary. Whether 'to' is a preposition or not, it is very evident that it loses all prepositional force in becoming the sign of the infinitive. To call the infinitive the object of its sign 'to,' destroys its force in the sentence, and creates the necessity of a new rule for the subject of sentences like the following: To steal is base. If 'steal' is the object of 'to,' there is no subject for the verb 'is'; for no word except a double relative can be the object of a preposition and the subject of a verb at the same time; nor can the preposition and its object together be the subject of a verb: and more, this preposition (?) has no antecedent term of relation, therefore shows no relation. A queer preposition!

Rule XX., on page 195, provides for all the constructions of infinitives, and is at the same time *simple*, *rational*, and necessary.

641. The infinitive is not *absolute* in such sentences as the following: *To be* candid with you, I was in fault; but limits the verb 'I confess,' understood, conditionally.

642. The infinitive of the verb 'be' is frequently understood; as,
They elected him [to be] chairman.
We made him [to be] our captain.
He reported you [to be] absent.
I supposed him [to be] an honest man.
I thought it [to be] necessary.

643. The time of infinitives depends on the time of the leading verb; as, They declared him to be honest. 'To be' is present with reference to the time of the declaration. In the sentence, I think myself *to have been* fortunate, the perfect infinitive is past with reference to the leading verb 'think.'

644. When the infinitive is the subject of a verb, and has itself a subject; and when the infinitive and its subject follow a passive verb, the subject of the infinitive is introduced by the expletive 'for.' 'For' in this case is not a preposition, though having that form; but is used expletively in introducing abridged sentences in the same way that 'that' introduces complete sentences in like circumstances. For example: *For* him to steal is base; equivalent to, *That* he should steal is base.

'Him' in the abridged sentence is the subject of 'to steal.' When the abridged sentence is expanded, 'that' takes the place of 'for.'

It is wrong *for* him to cheat; equivalent to, It is wrong *that* he should cheat: -*For* him to cheat is wrong; equivalent to, *That* he should cheat is wrong.

In this case, also, 'that' takes the place of 'for,' when the abridged sentence is expanded; and either sentence takes the place of the expletive 'it,' in the logical arrangement given in the last equivalents.

645. Infinitives are frequently used as logical subjects:—

1. The infinitive is the antecedent of an expletive 'it' in the nominative; as, *It* is impossible for him *to come*.

2. The infinitive is the antecedent of an expletive 'it' in the objective; as, I thought *it* [to be] impossible for us *to win*.

3. The infinitive is the antecedent of an expletive 'its' in the possessive; as, *Its* being difficult *to accomplish*, was the very thing which stimulated us to make the attempt.

REMARK.—The impossibility of giving the possessive form or case to the infinitive 'to accomplish' when substituted for 'its' in the above example, is evidence, so far as it goes, that infinite verbs do not have case, and never ought to have it attributed to them in any position or relation.

646. *Every* infinitive has a subject, either expressed or understood.

647. An infinitive used as a noun; as, To steal is base. As already seen, the subject is 'him' or 'person' understood; For any *person to steal*, is base; equivalent to, That any *person* should *steal*, is base. Also: I desired *to see* you, has the same subject for both the finite and the infinite verb; expanded, I desired that *I should see* you.

648. An infinitive used as an adverb; as, They elected him [to be] President; They elected him [for *him*] *to be* President; equivalent to, They elected him that *he should be* President. In this sentence, 'him' is the object of 'elected'; but a second *him* understood is the subject of the infinitive 'to be,' 'President' being the predicate objective after 'to be,' and 'to be' has the construction of an adverb of purpose limiting 'elected.'

649. An infinite used as an adjective; as, You have my *consent to remain;* equivalent to, You have my consent [for *you*] *to remain;* equivalent to, You have my consent that *you should remain*. 'To remain' is an abridged sentence, equivalent to, 'for you to remain'; of which 'for' is the introductory expletive, and 'you,' the subject of 'to remain.' This is plainly shown by the expansion of the abridged sentence, 'that you should remain,' having 'that' for the introductory expletive, and 'you' the subject of the finite verb 'should remain.' In this example, the infinitive has the construction of an adjective, as it limits the noun 'consent,' describing the kind of consent granted.

650. Abridged sentences in most cases should be expanded before the construction is determined, since by this artifice the true relation of every element is more clearly seen. Taking sentences we have already had, for illustrating other points: They elected him [to be] chairman. We see that 'him' expressed can not be the subject of 'to be,' because the sentence thus expanded reads: They elected that he should be chairman; and this does not give the same meaning. The *subject* of the *infinitive* always becomes the *subject* of the *finite verb* when the abridged sentence is correctly expanded. I thought it [to be] necessary. Here 'it' is, plainly, the subject of 'to be,' since the sentence expanded can be made to read in no other way than, I thought that it was necessary; in which expanded sentence, 'it' is the subject of the finite verb; hence, 'it' is the subject of the infinitive 'to be.' 'To be' is the object of 'thought.'

651. Participles.—Transitive verbs have six *participles;* namely, three active and three passive. They are called, *Present active*, *Past active*, *Perfect active*, *Present passive*, *Past passive*, and *Perfect passive*. Intransitive verbs have only three *participles;* namely, *Present active, Past active,* and *Perfect active.* They are given in the following table, with their appropriate *signs,* and are always read, *Present active, Past active,* etc., and never *Present, Past,* etc.

		Active.
Perfect passive.	ING; as,	sing*ing*, writ*ing*, etc.
Past active.	(having); as,	sung, written, loved, etc.
Perfect active.	HAVING; as,	*having* sung, *having* loved, etc.
		Passive.
Present passive.	BEING; as,	*being* broken, *being* exhausted, etc.
Past passive.	(being); as,	sung, written, loved, etc.
Perfect passive.	HAVING BEEN; as,	*having been* broken, *having been* exhausted, etc.

652. The *present active participle* is always known by its ending in *ing;* and the *present passive* by taking 'being' before it. All the participles, except the past active, are used in the various constructions of noun, adjective, or adverb. The present active participle is used in conjugating the progressive style of the verb. (Page 141.)

653. The past *active* participle is used *only* in connection with an auxiliary to form the perfect tenses of the finite modes in the *active* voice; as, He *has concealed* his true character.

654. The past *passive* participle is used (1) participially, (2) also to form the perfect tenses of the finite modes in the *passive* voice. When used participially, it may take, as a test, 'being' before it, without marring the sense. When 'being' is expressed, the participle is *present* passive.

Past Active Participle: I have always *respected* him.

Past Passive Participle: { He is a man *respected* by all.
{ He has always been *respected*.

655. Whenever the participles are used to form the perfect tenses of finite modes, they are not parsed as participles, but, in connection with their auxiliaries, as finite verbs.

656. Only transitive verbs can have passive participles.

657. A Participle becomes another part of speech:

658. When placed immediately before the noun which it limits it loses its verbal nature and is no longer a participle, but a participial descriptive *adjective;* as, A *convicted* felon; An *educated* man.

659. When preceded by an adjective or an article, it becomes a noun; as, The *dropping* of water; The *parsing* of a word.

660. When a participle which governs an object is deprived of its verbal force by taking an article or an adjective before it, it must take the preposition *of* after it to govern the object; in no other case should the preposition be used after the participle; as, Shedding tears—*The* shedding of tears.

661. The participle may have the construction of a noun, adjective, or adverb, in addition to its verbal force,—that of *assuming* action, being, or state of being.

662. As a *noun:* By *cultivating* cheerfulness we render others [ ] happy.

 1. Object of a verb: The guard prevented our *entering* the prison limits.

 2. Object of a preposition: After *having been reprimanded*, he was dismissed.

 3. Subject of a verb: *Making* others [ ] happy is substantial happiness for ourselves.

 4. As an attribute: Once saving is twice *earning*.

663. As an *adjective:* I saw James *driving* a fine span of horses; Henry, *having written* a fine essay, was highly complimented; He held a whip firmly *clasped* in his hand.

664. As an *adverb:* She came *bounding* up the lane; He rushed along, *stumbling* over the chairs.

665. Participles have no case in our language, though used as the subjects or objects of verbs, and as the objects of prepositions.

666. The time of a participle depends on the time of the leading verb, in the same manner as infinitives. For example: Mary, being encouraged by her teacher, corrected her fault. Here, the *present passive participle* 'being encouraged' is *present*, with reference to the time of the leading verb. Again: James, having been petted and indulged in every whim and caprice, is rapidly becoming an ungovernable boy. 'Having been petted' and 'having been indulged' are *past*, with reference to the time of the leading verb 'is becoming.'

667. Every participle has a subject expressed or understood. This has already been shown to be true with regard to infinitives. For examples: I have witnessed *your dancing;* equivalent to, I have witnessed that [or how] *you dance; Having bought* a fine team, I can enjoy daily drives around the park; equivalent to, [Since] *I have bought* a fine team, etc.; The atrocious crime of being a young man, I shall attempt neither to palliate nor deny. Here, the subject of 'being' is 'ing' understood, with which 'man' is in predication.

668. Many participial abridged sentences should be expanded, before the construction of the participle can safely be determined.

669. Distinguishing Participles.

670. A *participle* is distinguished from a *participial noun* by retaining the idea of time in the assumption of action, being, or state of being.

671. A *participial noun* is distinguished from a *participle* in being limited by the article or the adjective, and, of course, in rejecting the governing of an object.

672. A *participle* is distinguished from a *participial adjective* by retaining the idea of time in the assumption of action, being, or state of being.

673. A *participial adjective* is distinguished from a *participle* by rejecting the idea of time, and thus expressing only that of quality. This is accomplished in our language by placing the participial adjective immediately before the noun limited, or in the predicate with a copula.

674. A participle is distinguished from a finite verb thus:

675. A finite verb asserts; a participle assumes.

676. A finite verb is limited by person and number; a participle is not.

677. A finite verb is an essential element of a sentence; a participle is not.

678. The *past indicative active* is distinguished from the *past passive participle*:

679. By its being possible to change it into the emphatic style and retain the sense; as, He came yesterday; changed, He *did* come yesterday.

680. And by its being impossible to prefix 'being' without destroying the sense.

681. The *past passive participle* is distinguished from the *past indicative active* by its admitting 'being' before it without destroying the sense.

682. Principal Parts.—*Present Indicative Active, Past Indicative Active,* and *Past Participle.*

683. These are called *principal* parts, because from them all other forms of the verb are made.

684. Any verb lacking one or more of these parts is *defective.*

685. The Past *active* participle is used in forming the perfect tenses in the *active voice;* the Past *passive* participle is used in forming all the tenses of the *passive voice.* The *forms* of these two participles are the same.

686. To give the principal parts is to conjugate the verb.

687. The Principal Parts are known by the signs, as given in the following table:

Principal Parts.	*Signs.*	*Examples.*
Present.	(NOW).	(I) write (now).
Past Indicative.	(YESTERDAY).	(I) wrote (yesterday).
Past Participle.	(HAVE).	(I *have*) written.

The verb *be* is the only verb whose *present* or *root* is not found by the above test. The root is found in the present infinitive.

688. Auxiliaries.—These are *helping verbs,* which assist in the inflection of *principal* verbs.

689. The auxiliaries are *be, do, have, shall,* and *will; may, can,* and *must.*

690. *May, can, must,* and *shall* are never used as *principal* verbs, but are *always auxiliary.*

691. *Be, do, have,* and *will* are frequently used as *principal* verbs. (See list, page 145.)

692. All the *auxiliaries* were originally *principal verbs.*

693. Only *be, do,* and *have* have participles, of which that of *do* is not used as an auxiliary; and that of *have*, only in forming the *perfect participle*.

694. Auxiliaries must be used in forming all tenses except the *present* and the *past;* and are used in all tenses in making the *emphatic* and *progressive* styles. (See Inflection, pages 132-145.)

695. As auxiliary verbs, *had*, *should*, and *would* have some peculiar uses.

696. *Had* is used for *would;* as, I *had* rather it had been you than I; equivalent to, I *would* rather, etc. *Had* for *might;* as, You *had* as well return now; equivalent to, You *might* as well, etc.

697. *Would* expresses:

698. A past custom; as, He *would* return again and again to his prison door. In the same manner, *will* expresses present custom; as, He *will* pace the room from morning till night.

699. A desire; as, When I *would* do good, evil is present with me.

700. Intensifies a negation; as, He *would* [have] none of these things.

701. Advice, or reproof, or dislike, or request in a courteous manner; as, I *would* prefer a different course; It *would* seem wrong to do so; *Would* you lend me your knife? *Should* is also used in the first instance; as, I *should* think the other course preferable.

702. All the auxiliaries are *defective*, except *be*, *do*, and *have*.

703. Only *be* and *have* are varied in forming tenses as auxiliary verbs, in the ordinary style.

704. Conjugation, Inflection, and Synopsis.

705. The **conjugation** of a verb is giving the principal parts in order.

706. Inflection is varying the verb through all its *modes* and *tenses;* giving it in its *persons* and *numbers*.

707. Giving the **synopsis** of a verb is giving only one person and number through all the *modes*, *tenses*, and *voices*.

708. The Verb "Be."

PRINCIPAL PARTS.

Present *Be;* Past, *Was;* Past Participle, *Been.*

INFLECTION.

Indicative Mode.

Present tense.

Singular.		Plural.
Ordinary style.	*Solemn style.*	
1. I am.		1. We are.
2. You are.	Thou art.	2. You or ye are.
3. He is.		3. They are.

Past tense.

Singular.		Plural.
Ordinary style.	*Solemn style.*	
1. I was.		1. We were.
2. You were.	Thou wast.[1]	2. You or ye were.
3. He was.		3. They were.

Present perfect tense.

Singular.		Plural.
Ordinary style.	*Solemn style.*	
1. I have been.		1. We have been.
2. You have been.	Thou hast been.	2. You or ye have been.
3. He has been.	He hath been.	3. They have been.

Past perfect tense.

Singular.		Plural.
Ordinary style.	*Solemn style.*	
1. I had been.		1. We had been.
2. You had been.	Thou hadst been.	2. You or ye had been.
3. He had been.		3. They had been.

---

[1] *Be* in the present and *wert* in the past are old forms, not used except in the Scriptures.

Future tense.

Singular.

Ordinary style. | Solemn style.
1. I shall be.
2. You will be. | Thou wilt be.
3. He will be.

Plural.
1. We shall be.
2. You or ye will be.
3. They will be.

Future perfect tense.

Singular.

Ordinary style. | Solemn style.
1. I shall have been.
2. You will have been. | Thou wilt have been.
3. He will have been.

Plural.
1. We shall have been.
2. You or ye will have been.
3. They will have been.

Potential Mode.

Present tense.

Singular.

Ordinary style. | Solemn style.
1. I may be.
2. You may be. | Thou mayst be.
3. He may be.

Plural.
1. We may be.
2. You or ye may be.
3. They may be.

Past tense.

Singular.

Ordinary style. | Solemn style.
1. I might be.
2. You be might. | Thou mightst be.
3. He might be.

Plural.
1. We might be.
2. You or ye might be.
3. They might be.

Present perfect tense.

Singular.

Ordinary style. | Solemn style.
1. I may have been.
2. You may have been. | Thou mayst have been.
3. He may have been.

Plural.
1. We may have been.
2. You or ye may have been.
3. They may have been.

Past perfect tense.

Singular.   *Plural.*

Ordinary style.	*Solemn style.*	
1. I might have been.	Thou mightst have been.	1. We might have been.
2. You might have been.		2. You, ye might have been.
3. He might have been.		3. They might have been.

Subjunctive Mode.

Present tense.

Singular.   *Plural.*

Ordinary style.	*Solemn style.*	
1. If I be.		1. If we be.
2. If you be.	If thou be.	2. If you or ye be.
3. If he be.		3. If they be.

Past tense.

Singular.   *Plural.*

Ordinary style.	*Solemn style.*	
1. If I were.		1. If we were.
2. If you were.	If thou wert.	2. If you or ye were.
3. If he were.		3. If they were.

Past perfect tense.

Singular.   *Plural.*

Ordinary style.	*Solemn style.*	
1. If I had been.		1. If we had been.
2. If you had been.	If thou had been.	2. If you or ye had been.
3. If he had been.		3. If they had been.

Imperative Mode.

Singular.	*Plural.*
2. Be, or Do thou Be.	2. Be, or Do ye or you be.

Infinitive Mode.

Present.	*Perfect.*
To be.	To have been.

Participial Mode.

Present, Being;   *Past*, Been;   *Perfect*, Having been.

REMARK.—Using the conjunction *if*, all the Tenses of the Indicative and Potential Modes may be made conditional or subjunctive.

709. The Regular Transitive Verb "Love."

Principal Parts.

Present, Love; *Past*, Loved; *Past Participle*, Loved.

INFLECTION.

Ordinary and Solemn Styles.

ACTIVE VOICE.

Indicative Mode.

Present tense.

Singular.		Plural.
Ordinary style.	Solemn style.	
1. I love.		1. We love.
2. You love.	Thou lovest.	2. You or ye love.
3. He loves.	He loveth.	3. They love.

Past tense.

Singular.		Plural.
Ordinary style.	Solemn style.	
1. I loved.		1. We loved.
2. You loved.	Thou lovedst.	2. You or ye loved.
3. He loved.		3. They loved.

Present perfect tense.

Singular.		Plural.
Ordinary style.	Solemn style.	
1. I have loved.		1. We have loved.
2. You have loved.	Thou hast loved.	2. You or ye have loved.
3. He has loved.	He hath loved.	3. They have loved.

Past perfect tense.

Singular.		Plural.
Ordinary style.	Solemn style.	
1. I had loved.		1. We had loved.
2. You had loved.	Thou hadst loved.	2. You or ye had loved.
3. He had loved.		3. They had loved.

Future tense.

Singular		Plural
Ordinary style.	*Solemn style.*	
1. I shall love.		1. We shall love.
2. You will love.	Thou wilt love.	2. You or ye will love.
3. He will love.		3. They will love.

Future perfect tense.

Singular		Plural
Ordinary style.	*Solemn style.*	
1. I shall have loved.		1. We shall have loved.
2. You will have loved.	Thou wilt have loved.	2. You or ye will have loved.
3. He will have loved.		3. They will have loved.

Potential Mode.

Present tense.

Singular		Plural
Ordinary style.	*Solemn style.*	
1. I may love.		1. We may love.
2. You may love.	Thou mayest love.	2. You or ye may love.
3. He may love.		3. They may love.

Past tense.

Singular		Plural
Ordinary style.	*Solemn style.*	
1. I might love.		1. We might love.
2. You might love.	Thou mightst love.	2. You or ye might love.
3. He might love.		3. They might love.

Present perfect tense.

Singular		Plural
Ordinary style.	*Solemn style.*	
1. I may have loved.		1. We may have loved.
2. You may have loved.	Thou mayest have loved.	2. You, ye may have loved.
3. He may have loved.		3. They may have loved.

Past perfect tense.

Singular.		Plural.
Ordinary style.	*Solemn style.*	
1. I might have loved.	Thou mightst have loved.	1. We might have loved.
2. You might have loved.		2. You, ye might have loved.
3. He might have loved.		3. They might have loved.

Subjunctive Mode.

Present tense.

Singular.		Plural.
Ordinary style.	*Solemn style.*	
1. If I love.		1. If we love.
2. If you love.	If thou love.	2. If you or ye love.
3. If he love.		3. If they love.

Past tense.

Singular.		Plural.
Ordinary style.	*Solemn style.*	
1. If I loved.		1. If we loved.
2. If you loved.	If thou loved.	2. If you or ye loved.
3. If he loved.		3. If they loved.

Past perfect tense.

Singular.		Plural.
Ordinary style.	*Solemn style.*	
1. If I had loved.		1. If we had loved.
2. If you had loved.	If thou had loved.	2. If you or ye had loved.
3. If he had loved.		3. If they had loved.

Imperative Mode.

Present tense.

Singular.	Plural.
2. Love, or Do thou love.	2. Love, or Do ye or you love.

Infinitive Mode.

Present.	*Perfect.*
To love.	To have loved.

H. Gram.—12.

Participlal Mode.

Present. *Past.* *Perfect.*
Loving. Loved. Having loved.

PASSIVE VOICE.[1]

Indicative Mode.

Present tense.

Singular. *Plural.*

Ordinary style.	Solemn style.	
1. I am loved.		1. We are loved.
2. You are loved.	Thou art loved.	2. You or ye are loved.
3. He is loved.		3. They are loved.

Past tense.

Singular. *Plural.*

Ordinary style.	Solemn style.	
1. I was loved.		1. We were loved.
2. You were loved.	Thou wast loved.	2. You or ye were loved.
3. He was loved.		3. They were loved.

Present perfect tense.

Singular. *Plural.*

Ordinary style.	Solemn style.	
1. I have been loved.	Thou hast been loved.	1. We have been loved.
2. You have been loved.		2. You, ye have been loved.
3. He has been loved.	He hath been loved.	3. They have been loved.

Past perfect tense.

Singular. *Plural.*

Ordinary style.	Solemn style.	
1. I had been loved.		1. We had been loved.
2. You had been loved.	Thou hadst been loved.	2. You, ye had been loved.
3. He had been loved.		3. They had been loved.

---

[1] The passive voice, except the passive participle, is formed by prefixing the appropriate forms of the verb *be* to the *past passive participle.*

Future tense.

Singular. *Plural.*

Ordinary style. | Solemn style.
1. I shall be loved. | Thou wilt be loved. | 1. We shall be loved.
2. You will be loved. | | 2. You or ye will be loved.
3. He will be loved. | | 3. They will be loved.

Future perfect tense.

Singular. *Plural.*

Ordinary style. | Solemn style.
1. I will have been loved. | | 1. We will have been loved.
2. You will have been loved. | Thou wilt have been loved. | 2. You or ye will have been loved.
3. He will have been loved. | | 3. They will have been loved.

Potential Mode.

Present tense.

Singular. *Plural.*

Ordinary style. | Solemn style.
1. I may be loved. | | 1. We may be loved.
2. You may be loved. | Thou mayst be loved. | 2. You or ye may be loved.
3. He may be loved. | | 3. They may be loved.

Past tense.

Singular. *Plural.*

Ordinary style. | Solemn style.
1. I might be loved. | | 1. We might be loved.
2. You might be loved. | Thou mightst be loved. | 2. You or ye might be loved.
3. He might be loved. | | 3. They might be loved.

Present perfect tense.

Singular. *Plural.*

Ordinary style. | Solemn style.
1. I may have been loved. | | 1. We may have been loved.
2. You may have been loved. | Thou mayst have been loved. | 2. You or ye may have been loved.
3. He may have been loved. | | 3. They may have been loved.

Past perfect tense.

Singular. — *Plural.*

Ordinary style.	Solemn style.	
1. I might have been loved.		1. We might have been loved.
2. You might have been loved.	Thou mightst have been loved.	2. You, ye might have been loved.
3. He might have been loved.		3. They might have been loved.

Subjunctive Mode.

SUBJUNCTIVE FORM.

The subjunctive form of the Subjunctive Mode is obsolescent, many of the best writers rejecting it and using only the indicative form.

Present tense.

Singular. — *Plural.*

Ordinary style.	Solemn style.	
1. If I be loved.		1. If we be loved.
2. If you be loved.	If thou be loved.	2. If you, ye be loved.
3. If he be loved.		3. If they be loved.

Past tense.

Singular. — *Plural.*

Ordinary style.	Solemn style.	
1. If I were loved.		1. If we were loved.
2. If you were loved.	If thou wert loved.	2. If you or ye were loved.
3. If he were loved.		3. If they were loved.

Past perfect tense.

Singular. — *Plural.*

Ordinary style.	Solemn style.	
1. If I had been loved.		1. If we had been loved.
2. If you had been loved.	If thou had been loved.	2. If you, ye had been loved.
3. If he had been loved.		3. If they had been loved.

Imperative Mode.

Singular.   *Present tense.*   *Plural.*

2. Be loved, or Be thou loved.   2. Be loved, or Be ye or you loved.

Infinitive Mode.

Present.
To be loved.

Perfect.
To have been loved.

Participial Mode.

Present.
Being loved.

Past.
Loved.

Perfect.
Having been loved.

PROGRESSIVE STYLE.

ACTIVE VOICE.

Indicative Mode.

Present tense.

Singular. — *Plural.*

Ordinary style.   *Solemn style.*
1. I am loving.   1. We are loving.
2. You are loving.   Thou art loving.   2. You or ye are loving.
3. He is loving.   3. They are loving.

Past tense.

Singular. — *Plural.*

Ordinary style.   *Solemn style.*
1. I was loving.   1. We were loving.
2. You were loving. Thou wert loving. 2. You or ye were loving.
3. He was loving.   3. They were loving.

Present perfect tense.

Singular. — *Plural.*

Ordinary style.   *Solemn style.*
1. I have been loving.   Thou hast   1. We have been loving.
2. You have been loving.   been loving.   2. You, ye have been loving.
3. He has been loving.   He hath   3. They have been loving.
                            been loving.

Past perfect tense.

Singular.

Ordinary style.	Solemn style.
1. I had been loving.	
2. You had been loving.	Thou hadst been loving.
3. He had been loving.	

Plural.

1. We had been loving.
2. You, ye had been loving.
3. They had been loving.

Future tense.

Singular.

Ordinary style.	Solemn style.
1. I shall be loving.	
2. You will be loving.	Thou wilt be loving.
3. He will be loving.	

Plural.

1. We shall be loving.
2. You or ye will be loving.
3. They will be long.

Future perfect tense.

Singular.

Ordinary style.	Solemn style.
1. I shall have been loving.	
2. You will have been loving.	Thou wilt have been loving.
3. He will have been loving.	

Plural.

1. We shall have been loving.
2. You or ye will have been loving.
3. They will have been loving.

Potential Mode.

Present tense.

Singular.

Ordinary style.	Solemn style.
1. I may be loving.	
2. You may be loving.	Thou mayest be loving.
3. He may be loving.	

Plural.

1. We may be loving.
2. You or ye may be loving.
3. They may be loving.

Past tense.

Singular.

Ordinary style.	Solemn style.
1. I might be loving.	
2. You might be loving.	Thou mightst be loving.
3. He might be loving.	

Plural.

1. We might be loving.
2. You or ye might be loving.
3. They might be loving.

Present perfect tense.

Singular.

Ordinary style.	Solemn style.
1. I may have been loving.	Thou mayst have been loving.
2. You may have been loving.	
3. He may have been loving.	

Plural.

1. We may have been loving.
2. You or ye may have been loving.
3. They may have been loving.

Past perfect tense.

Singular.

Ordinary style.	Solemn style.
1. I might have been loving.	
2. You might have been loving.	Thou mightst have been loving.
3. He might have been loving.	

Plural.

1. We might have been loving.
2. You or ye might have been loving.
3. They might have been loving.

Subjunctive Mode.

Present tense.

Singular.

Ordinary style.	Solemn style.
1. If I be loving.	
2. If you be loving.	If thou be loving.
3. If he be, loving.	

Plural.

1. If we be loving.
2. If you or ye be loving.
3. If they be loving.

Past tense.

Singular.

Ordinary style.	Solemn style.
1. If I were loving.	
2. If you were loving.	If thou wert loving.
3. If he were loving.	

Plural.

1. If we were loving.
2. If you or ye were loving.
3. If they were loving.

Past perfect tense.

Singular.

Ordinary style.	Solemn style.
1. If I had been loving.	
2. If you had been loving.	If thou had been loving.
3. If he had been loving.	

Plural.

1. If we had been loving.
2. If you or ye had been loving.
3. If they had been loving.

Imperative Mode.

Present tense.

Singular.
2. Be loving, or Do thou be loving.

Plural.
2. Be loving, or Do ye or you be loving.

Infinitive Mode.

Present.
To be loving.

Perfect.
To have been loving.

Participial Mode.

Present.
Being loving.

Past.
—— ——

Perfect.
Having been loving.

EMPHATIC STYLE.

ACTIVE VOICE.

Indicative Mode.

Present tense.

Singular.

Ordinary style.	*Solemn style.*
1. I do love.	
2. You do love.	Thou dost love.
3. He does love.	He doth love.

Plural.
1. We do love.
2. You or ye do love.
3. They do love.

Past tense.

Singular.

Ordinary style.	*Solemn style.*
1. I did love.	
2. You did love.	Thou didst love.
3. He did love.	

Plural.
1. We did love.
2. You or ye did love.
3. They did love.

Subjunctive Mode.

Present tense.

Singular.

Ordinary style.	*Solemn style.*
1. If I do love.	
2. If you do love.	If thou dost love.
3. If he does love.	If he doth love.

Plural.
1. If we do love.
2. If you or ye do love.
3. If they do love.

Past tense.

Singular.		Plural.
Ordinary style.	*Solemn style.*	
1. If I did love.		1. If we did love.
2. If you did love.	If thou didst love.	2. If you or ye did love.
3. If he did love.		3. If they did love.

Imperative Mode.

Singular.	Present tense.	Plural.
2. Do thou love.		2. Do ye love.

710. List of Irregular and Redundant Verbs.

Present.	Past.	Past Partic.	Present.	Past.	Past Partic.
Abide, *r.*	abode,	abode.	Bleed,	bled,	bled.
Am *or* be,	was,	been.	Blend, *r.*	blent,	blent.
Arise,	arose,	arisen.	Bless, *r.*	blessed,	blessed.
Awake, *r.*	awoke,	awoke.	Blow, *r.*	blew,	blown.
Bear,	bore *or* bare,	born.	Break,	broke,	broken.
			Breed,	bred,	bred.
Bear,	bore *or* bare,	borne.	Bring,	brought,	brought.
			Build, *r.*	built,	built.
Beat,	beat,	beaten *or* beat.	Burn, *r.*	burnt,	burnt.
			Burst, *r.*	burst,	burst.
Begin,	began *or* begun,	begun.	Buy,	bought,	bought.
			Cast,	cast,	cast.
Behold,	beheld,	beheld.	Catch, *r.*	caught,	caught.
Belay, *r.*	belaid,	belaid.	Chide,	chid,	chidden *or* chid.
Bend, *r.*	bent,	bent.			
Bereave, *r.*	bereft,	bereft.	Choose,	chose,	chosen.
Beseech, *r.*	besought,	besought.	Cleave, *r.*	clave,	clave.
Beset,	beset,	beset.	Cleave,	cleft *or* clove,	cleft *or* cloven.
Bet, *r.*	bet,	bet.			
Betide, *r.*	betid,	betid.	Climb, *r.*	clomb,	clomb.
Bid,	bid *or* bade,	bidden *or* bid.	Cling,	clung,	clung.
			Clothe, *r.*	clad,	clad.
Bide, *r.*	bode,	bode.	Come,	came,	come.
Bind,	bound,	bound.	Cost,	cost,	cost.
Bite,	bit,	bitten *or* bit.	Creep, *r.*	crept,	crept.
			Crow, *r.*	crew,	crowed.

H. Gram.—13.

Present.	Past.	Past Partic.	Present.	Past.	Past Partic.
Curse, *r.*	cursed,	cursed.	Hang, *r.*	hung,	hung.
Cut,	cut,	cut.	Have,	had,	had.
Dare, *r.*	durst,	dared.	Hear,	heard,	heard.
Deal, *r.*	dealt,	dealt.	Heat, *r.*	hĕat,	hĕat.
Dig, *r.*	dug,	dug.	Heave, *r.*	hove,	hoven.
Dive, *r.*	dove,	dove.	Hew, *r.*	hewed,	hewn.
Do,	did,	done.	Hide,	hid,	hidden.
Draw,	drew,	drawn.	Hit,	hit,	hit.
Dream, *r.*	drĕamt,	drĕamt.	Hold,	held,	held.
Dress, *r.*	drest,	drest.	Hurt,	hurt,	hurt.
Drink,	drank,	drunk *or* drank.	Keep,	kept,	kept.
			Kneel, *r.*	knelt,	knelt.
Drive,	drove,	driven.	Knit, *r.*	knit,	knit.
Dwell, *r.*	dwelt,	dwelt.	Know,	knew,	known.
Eat,	ĕat *or* ate,	ĕat *or* eaten.	Lade, *r.*	laded,	laden.
			Lay, *r.*	laid,	laid.
Engrave, *r.*	engraved,	engraven.	Lead,	led,	led.
Fall,	fell,	fallen.	Lean, *r.*	lĕant,	lĕant.
Feed,	fed,	fed.	Leap, *r.*	lĕaped,	lĕaped.
Feel,	felt,	felt.	Learn, *r.*	learned,	learned.
Fight,	fought,	fought.	Leave,	left,	left.
Find,	found,	found.	Lend,	lent,	lent.
Flee,	fled,	fled.	Let,	let,	let.
Fling,	flung,	flung.	Lie,	lay,	lain.
Fly,	flew,	flown.	Lift, *r.*	lift,	lift.
Forbear,	forbore,	forborne.	Light, *r.*	lit,	lit.
Forget,	forgot,	forgotten.	Lose,	lost,	lost.
Forsake,	forsook,	forsaken.	Make,	made,	made.
Freeze, *r.*	froze,	frozen.	Mean, *r.*	mĕant,	mĕant.
Freight, *r.*	freighted,	fraught.	Meet,	met,	met.
Geld, *r.*	gelt,	gelt.	Melt, *r.*	melted,	molten.
Get,	got,	gotten.	Mow, *r.*	mowed,	mown.
Gild, *r.*	gilt,	gilt.	Mulct, *r.*	mulct,	mulct.
Gird, *r.*	girt,	girt.	Pass, *r.*	past,	past.
Give,	gave,	given.	Pay, *r.*	paid,	paid.
Go,	went,	gone.	Pen, *r.*	pent,	pent.
Grave, *r.*	graved,	graven.	Plead, *r.*	pled,	pled.
Grind, *r.*	ground,	ground.	Prove, *r.*	proved,	proven.
Grow,	grew,	grown.	Put,	put,	put.

Present.	Past.	Past Partic.	Present.	Past.	Past Partic.
Quit, *r.*	quit,	quit.	Sling,	slung,	slung.
Rap, *r.*	rapt,	rapt.	Slink,	slunk,	slunk.
Read,	rĕad,	rĕad.	Slit, *r.*	slit,	slit.
Reave, *r.*	reft,	reft.	Smell, *r.*	smelt,	smelt.
Rend,	rent,	rent.	Smite,	smote,	smitten.
Rid,	rid,	rid.	Sow, *r.*	sowed,	sown.
Ride,	rode,	rode *or* ridden.	Speak,	spoke *or* spake,	spoken *or* spoke.
Ring,	rang,	rung.	Speed, *r.*	sped,	sped.
Rise,	rose,	risen.	Spell, *r.*	spelt,	spelt.
Rive, *r.*	rived,	riven.	Spend,	spent,	spent.
Roast, *r.*	roast,	roast.	Spill, *r.*	spilt,	spilt.
Run,	ran,	run.	Spin,	spun,	spun.
Saw, *r.*	sawed,	sawn.	Spit,	spat,	spit.
Say,	said,	said.	Split, *r.*	split,	split.
See,	saw,	seen.	Spoil, *r.*	spoilt,	spoilt.
Seek,	sought,	sought.	Spread,	spread,	spread.
Seethe, *r.*	sod,	sodden.	Spring,	sprang,	sprung.
Sell,	sold,	sold.	Stand,	stood,	stood.
Send,	sent,	sent.	Stave, *r.*	stove,	stove.
Set,	set,	set.	Stay, *r.*	staid,	staid.
Shake, *r.*	shook,	shaken.	Steal,	stole,	stolen.
Shape, *r.*	shaped,	shapen.	Stick,	stuck,	stuck.
Shave, *r.*	shaved,	shaven.	Sting,	stung,	stung.
Shear, *r.*	sheared,	shorn.	Stink,	stunk,	stunk.
Shed, *r.*	shed,	shed.	Strew,	strewed,	strown *or* strewn.
Shine, *r.*	shone	shone.			
Shoe,	shod,	shod.	Stride,	strode,	stridden.
Shoot,	shot,	shot.	Strike,	struck,	struck *or* stricken.
Show, *r.*	showed,	shown.			
Shred,	shred,	shred.	String, *r.*	strung,	strung.
Shrink,	shrunk,	shrunk.	Strive, *r.*	strove,	striven.
Shut,	shut,	shut.	Strow, *r.*	strowed,	strown.
Sing,	sang,	sung.	Swear,	swore,	sworn.
Sink,	sank,	sunk.	Sweat, *r.*	swet *or* sweat,	swet *or* sweat.
Sit,	sat,	sat.			
Slay,	slew,	slain.	Sweep, *r.*	swept,	swept.
Sleep, *r.*	slept,	slept.	Swell, *r.*	swelled,	swollen.
Slide,	slid,	slidden.	Swim,	swam,	swum.

Present.	Past.	Past Partic.	Present.	Past.	Past Partic.
Swing,	swung,	swung.	Wear,	wore,	worn.
Take,	took,	taken.	Weave, *r.*	wove,	woven.
Teach,	taught,	taught.	Wed, *r.*	wed,	wed.
Tear,	tore,	torn.	Weep, *r.*	wept,	wept.
Tell,	told,	told.	Wet, *r.*	wet,	wet.
Think,	thought,	thought.	Whet, *r.*	whet,	whet.
Thrive, *r.*	throve,	thriven.	Win,	won,	won.
Throw, *r.*	threw,	thrown.	Wind, *r.*	wound,	wound.
Thrust,	thrust,	thrust.	Wont,	wont,	wont.
Tread,	trod,	trodden *or* trod.	Work, *r.*	wrought,	wrought.
			Wreathe, *r.*	wreathed,	wreathen.
Wake, *r.*	woke,	woke.	Wring, *r.*	wrung,	wrung.
Wax, *r.*	waxed,	waxen.	Write,	wrote,	written.

Those verbs, in the preceding list, which are marked with an *r*, have also a regular conjugation.

The pupil will consult a dictionary to determine whether the regular or irregular form is most used.

THE ADVERB.

711. Definition.—An adverb is a word which limits a verb, adjective, or other adverb; as, He runs *swiftly;* That rose is *very* beautiful; You read *remarkably* well.

712. An adverb may limit a prepositional phrase used adverbially; as, He threw the stone ALMOST *across the river;* Our class have gone NEARLY *through arithmetic.*

713. Many adverbs are condensed expressions representing a phrase; as, The rain falls *gently;* equivalent to, *in a gentle manner.* The last is an *adverbial phrase.*

714. In grammatical drill, all *adverbial phrases* should be fully analyzed and parsed word by word; as, They walked *hand in hand;* equivalent to, They walked [with] *hand* in *hand.* It is a mere shift to parse any expression as an adverbial phrase; sometimes, an artifice to conceal ignorance.

715. Classes.—Adverbs are classified on two bases; first, as to their *Signification;* second, as to their *Function.*

716. As to *signification*, adverbs are divided into the following classes: adverbs of *Time, Place, Degree, Manner,* and *Illation.*

717. Adverbs of time are subdivided as follows:
(1) Of time *when;* as, Yesterday, lately, formerly, ago, etc.
(2) Of time *how long;* as, Suddenly, slowly, eternally, etc.
(3) Of time *how often;* as, Frequently, repeatedly, daily, etc.

718. Adverbs of place are subdivided as follows:
(1) Of place *in which;* as, There, around, within.
(2) Of place *to which;* as, Hither, thither, up, down, back, forth, etc.
(3) Of place *from which;* as, Hence, thence, away, out, etc.
(4) Of place *through which;* as, Midway, overland, etc.

719. Adverbs of degree are subdivided as follows:
(1) Of excess or abundance; as, Much, very, greatly, etc.
(2) Of equality or sufficiency; as, Adequately, enough, sufficiently.

720. Of deficiency or abatement; as, Little, hardly, scarcely, almost.

721. Adverbs of manner are subdivided as follows:
(1) Of quality; as, Well, wisely, justly.
(2) Of method; as, Thus, somehow.
(3) Of certainty; as, Verily, truly, surely, indeed.
(4) Of doubt; as, Perchance, mayhap.

722. Of affirmation; as, Yea, yes, aye, amen.

723. Of negation; as, No, not, nowise.

724. Adverbs of illation are subdivided as follows:
(1) Of cause;
(2) Of reason;
(3) Of purpose;
(4) Of condition;
} as, Then, hence, therefore, wherefore, etc.

REMARK.—While single words, as adverbs, are used in all these different classes of illation almost indiscriminately, phrases and clauses, as adverbial adjuncts, are used with much greater precision.

725. As to *function*, adverbs are divided into two classes: *Modifying* and *Conjunctive*.

726. A modifying adverb is one which limits words or phrases without having any *connecting* power.

727. A conjunctive adverb is one which introduces a subordinate sentence and modifies its verb; as, We will know the truth *when* he returns.

The common disposition of conjunctive adverbs which makes them modify two verbs, is faulty, and should be abandoned.

In the sentence, I shall go *when* he arrives, 'go' is modified by the sentence 'when he arrives' as an adverb of time, while 'when' is its introductory connective. Now, if 'when' has any adverbial power, it must modify 'arrives.'

This disposition of the conjunctive adverb is plainly more simple and logical than to make the subordinate sentence ('he arrives') a modifier of that part of the conjunctive adverb ('when') which modifies the preceding verb ('shall go').

728. The words most frequently used as conjunctive adverbs are *when, where, while, whence, whither, so, as, because, till, until, since, therefore, hence,* etc.

729. Formation.—Adverbs are either primitives or derivatives.

730. The *primitives*, as, *Yes, no, here, there,* etc., are few in number.

731. Many adverbs are formed by compounding other words; as, *To-morrow, indeed, hereby,* etc.

732. Most adverbs of quality are derived from adjectives by adding *ly;* as, *Bright, bright-ly, glad, glad-ly.*

733. Many adverbs having the prefix *a* are contractions representing a preposition and its object; as, *Alive,* formerly written *On life; Anew,* formerly, *Of new; Abroad,* equivalent to, *On board.*

734. In a few words, the prefix *a* is the article; as, *A while,* equivalent to, *A time.*

735. The prefix *al,* a contraction of *all,* is often used; as, *always, alone,* etc.

736. Modification—Comparison.

737. Adverbs expressing quality, and some others, are compared like adjectives; as, *often, oftener, oftenest; soon, sooner, soonest; far, farther, farthest.*

738. Many adverbs ending in *ly* are compared by the use of the adverbs *more* and *most;* as, *gladly, more gladly, most gladly.*

739. A few are compared irregularly; as, *well, better, best; badly* or *ill, worse, worst; little, less, least;* etc.

740. Peculiarities of Adverbs.

741. Many words used as adverbs are sometimes used as other parts of speech; thus, *But* is used (1) As an adverb; as, He sighed *but* once. (2) As a preposition; as, None *but* the brave deserve the fair. (3) As a conjunction; as, He called, *but* no one answered.

742. Sometimes adverbs are used apparently as the adjuncts of nouns and pronouns; as, I alone am responsible; God only is good; really, the adverb limits some other word expressed or understood; as, God [of all beings] only is wise; I am alone responsible. 'Alone' is here to equivalent to 'exclusively.'

743. A few adverbs are used independently; as, Yes, no, amen, etc. In such cases, these words are equivalent to a whole sentence. Did he go? No. 'No' is parsed as an adverb of negation, qualifying the verb *did go* understood, in the answer of the question.

744. *The* is sometimes used adverbially; as in the sentence, *The* faster he runs *the* slower he goes.

745. The adverb 'as' is not unfrequently used to introduce abridged sentences where the conjunction 'that' would be used to introduce the corresponding complete sentence; as, They make their boast of crimes *as* having done them secretly; They make their boast of crimes *that* they have done them secretly.

746. 'As' is used also as a preposition; as, I like him *as* a teacher; also as a relative pronoun; Such *as* I have, I give unto thee.

Adverbs of the second and third classes must be parsed as to their signification. Example: He went *to bathe.* 'To bathe' is an adverb of purpose, and limits 'went.'

THE PREPOSITION.

747. Definition.—A preposition is a word which expresses the relation between elements of thought. *Explanation:* The latter element, when the object of the relation expressed by the preposition, is called the object of the preposition, and is generally a noun or pronoun; the former element is called the antecedent term of the relation.

748. Classes—As to *Use*—As to *Formation.*

749. As to *use*, prepositions may be divided into numerous classes. The following are some of the most distinctive: those representing relations of *Place, Time, Agent* or *Instrument,* and *Cause.*

750. Prepositions showing the relations of *place,* are subdivided into two classes:

751. Of rest in or by a place; as, *In, within, besides.*

752. Of motion to or from; as, *Into, toward, from.*

753. Prepositions showing the relations of *time* are subdivided into two classes:

754. Of time definite; as, *At:* He came *at* noon.

755. Of time indefinite; as, *Before, after,* etc.

756. Prepositions showing miscellaneous relations, such as aversion, substitution, opposition, etc., are not easily classified on logical bases.

757. As to *formation,* prepositions are divided into three classes: *Simple, Compound,* and *Complex.*

REMARK.—In this classification, *simple* means consisting of a single word; *compound* means compounded of *two prepositions;* as, *Out of, from between,* etc.; and *complex* refers to prepositions compounded of a preposition and some other part or parts of speech; as, *On account of, to the extent of,* etc.

758. Alphabetical List of Prepositions.

759. *Simple Prepositions:*

a,	athwart,	in,	save,
abaft,	before,	into,	saving,
aboard,	behind,	like,	till,
about,	below,	mauger,	to,
above,	beneath,	near,	touching,
across,	beside,	next,	toward,
adown,	besides,	nigh,	towards,
after,	between,	notwithstanding,	under,
against,	betwixt,	of,	underneath,
along,	beyond,	off,	unlike,
amid,	but,	on,	until,
amidst,	by,	opposite,	unto,
among,	concerning,	over,	up,
amongst,	despite,	past,	upon,
anear,	during,	pending,	versus,
around,	ere,	per,	via,
as,	except,	respecting,	with,
aslant,	excepting,	round,	within,
astride,	far,	since,	without.
at,	from,		

760. *Compound prepositions:*

aboard of,	but for,	from off,	out of,
as for,	from among,	from under,	over against.
as to,	from between,		

761. *Complex prepositions:*

according to,	in place of,	with respect to,
contrary to,	in respect to,	in the relation of,
devoid of,	on account of,	in the character of,
in consideration of,	previous to,	to the extent of, etc.
instead of,	in spite of,	regardless of.

REMARK.—Many words in the above list are used as other parts of speech.

762. Peculiarities of Prepositions.

763. *For* is used to introduce abridged infinitive clauses; as, For us to venture would be madness; For him to assist me would be impossible: equivalent to, That he should assist me would be impossible. The expanded form of such sentences with the finite verb, instead of the infinitive, is introduced by the conjunction *that*.

764. *A* is used as a preposition in such expressions as, He went *a* fishing; She has gone *a* riding.

765. In such passive forms as *cast up, thrown off, sneered at*, etc., the participles 'up,' 'off,' 'at,' etc., are considered as parts of the verb. Prepositions are often thus used to form the passive voice with *intransitive* verbs; as, She *was laughed at;* The farm *has been taken possession of* by the sheriff.

766. *Save* and *except* were formerly verbs in the imperative mode, but should not now be so construed.

THE CONJUNCTION.

767. Definition.—A conjunction is a word used to connect words, phrases, and sentences; as, John *and* Mary will go; The army was reduced by famine *and* by disease; Cromwell fought *and* Charles bled; Cicero was an orator, *but* Virgil was a poet.

768. Classes.—Conjunctions are classified on two bases; first, as to *Rank;* second, as to *Signification*.

769. As to *rank*, conjunctions are *Co-ordinate* and *Subordinate*.

770. A **co-ordinate** conjunction connects sentences or elements of *equal* rank; as, Henry went, *but* George staid away; James is a studious *and* intelligent boy.

771. A **subordinate** conjunction connects elements of *unequal* rank; as, He fled *because* his life was in danger; I will come *if* possible.

772. As to *signification*, conjunctions are *Copulative* and *Disjunctive*.

ETYMOLOGY—THE CONJUNCTION.

773. A **copulative** conjunction simply *connects* the meaning of phrases or sentences; as, The moon shines *and* the wind blows.

774. A **disjunctive** conjunction connects words, phrases, or sentences, yet indicates alternative, adversative, or antithetic meaning; as, He will go *or* stay; The shop was burned, *but* the house was saved.

REMARK.—These classes may be divided into various subclasses; as, Correlative, Introductory, Final, Causal, Temporal, Illative, Concessive, etc.

775. List of Conjunctions.

776. *Co-ordinate Conjunctions.*

again,	but,	moreover,	otherwise,
also,	either,	nay,	so,
although,	else,	neither,	still,
and,	further,	nor,	though,
besides,	furthermore,	now,	yet.
both,	likewise,	or,	

777. *Subordinate Conjunctions.*

after,	howsoever,	provided,	thus,
as,	howbeit,	since,	unless,
as well as,	if,	than,	when,
because,	inasmuch as,	then,	while,
except,	in case,	that,	whilst,
for,	but,	therefore,	wherefore.
however,	notwithstanding,		

778. Conjunctions are often used to introduce independent sentences; as, *And* they said there is no hope: Jer. xviii. 12; *Therefore* thus saith the Lord: *id.* xviii. 13.

779. *That* is often used to introduce a sentence which is the subject of a finite verb; as, That they should be mistaken is not improbable. In such cases, *that* is a conjunction in *form* only, being really an introductory expletive.

See Rule 24.

780. *Correlative* conjunctions are used in pairs; as,

both—and,	though, or al-	as—so,	nor—nor,
either—or,	though—yet, or	if—then,	so—that,
neither—nor,	nevertheless.	or—or,	so—as.
whether—or,	as—as,		

781. *And* sometimes unifies the two elements of a fact; as, To indulge in idleness and make a business of it is not the road to ruin—it is ruin.

THE INTERJECTION.

782. Definition.—An interjection is a word uttered as the expression of an emotion; as, O Absalom! *Pshaw!* what a blunder!

783. REMARK 1.—Interjections are most frequently used in conversation. They seldom occur in ordinary prose or poetry, except when the writer is addressing an individual or an object personified. They have no grammatical connection with any other word in a sentence.

784. REMARK 2.—*O* is the sign of the *vocative* or *nominative absolute by direct address*. *O* is common to most languages.

785. REMARK 3.—As to *signification*, the classes of interjections are as numerous as the emotions of the human soul.

786. List of Interjections.

ah,	hurra,	hail,	lo,
aha,	huzza,	bravo,	behold,
alas,	hist,	tush,	come,
O,	ho,	pooh,	away,
oh,	hush,	pshaw,	what,
ha,	heigh-ho,	fie,	strange, etc.
hark,	heyday,	avaunt,	

NOTE.—Some of these are used as other parts of speech, particularly as verbs in the imperative mode.

DRILL IN VARIOUS CONSTRUCTIONS.

APPOSITION AND PREDICATE NOMINATIVE.

787. Recitation—Lesson previously assigned.

788. Apposition.—*Teacher.* "Pupils, I wish to give you, to-day, another construction of nouns and pronouns. For example, in the sentence, 'Mr. Jones, the farmer, was elected to the legislature,' the noun 'farmer' is used to explain the noun 'Jones,' and is parsed thus: *Farmer* is a noun, common, third, singular, masculine, nominative, in apposition with 'Mr. Jones,' Rule 13, *A noun or personal pronoun limiting another noun or pronoun, signifying the same person or thing, is in the same case, by apposition.*

"You have learned that nouns are limited by *adjectives*, also by nouns and pronouns in the *possessive case.* This new construction of limitation is called, simply, *apposition*, and may limit a noun or pronoun in any case. In the example, 'This belongs to John, *him* whom you saw yesterday,' the pronoun 'him' is used to explain the noun 'John,' and is parsed thus: *Him* is a pronoun, personal, agreeing with its antecedent, 'John,' in the third, singular, masculine, Rule 5, objective case, in apposition with 'John,' Rule 13. You will notice that there can be no other construction for this word."

1. Adolphus, the heroic lad, saved his drowning brother, Augustine.
2. Johann Strauss, the musical composer, was at the Boston Jubilee.
3. Charles Santley, the great baritone, sings in Mendelssohn's Oratorio, "Elijah."
4. Winter, the hoary-headed sage, retreats before the youthful Spring.
5. We hail thee, Columbia, the land of the free.
6. He has just gone to my friend, the attorney's, office.
7. Mr. Jones, the banker's team, ran away and broke his carriage.

8. Where did that come from? From Mr. Carpenter's, my neighbor across the street.

Teacher. "You will notice, by the sixth, seventh, and eighth sentences, that in cases of a possessive in apposition, the sign is used only with that possessive which immediately precedes the noun limited. In the sentence, 'He has just gone to my *friend*, the attorney's, office,' the noun 'friend' is in the possessive case, limiting 'office,' while 'attorney's' is in apposition with 'friend,' and takes the *sign*, because nearest to the limited noun. 'Where did that come from? From Mr. Carpenter's, my neighbor across the street.' We mean in this, 'From Mr. Carpenter's *house*.' 'Mr. Carpenter's,' then, is in the possessive, limiting 'house,' and has the sign, because nearest the governed noun. 'Neighbor' is in apposition with 'Mr. Carpenter's.'

"I wish you to parse the nouns in apposition, in the preceding sentences. This will be a part of your next lesson. How many think they can do it?"

Some are doubtful.

Teacher. "Jane, you may try the first one now. Which is it?"

Jane. "Heroic."

Hands are up.

Teacher. "What is it, Henry?"

Henry. "*Heroic* is an adjective; *lad* is the word."

Teacher. "Very well. Jane, you may parse 'lad.'"

Jane. "*Lad* is a noun, common, third, singular, masculine, nominative, in apposition with 'Adolphus,' Rule 13."

Teacher. "Very well, Jane. Julia, you may parse 'Augustine,' in the same sentence."

Julia. "*Augustine* is a noun, proper, third, singular, masculine, objective, in apposition with 'brother,' Rule 13."

789. Predicate Nominative.—*Teacher.* "Pupils, there is one other construction that you may study to-day. Who will parse 'bucket,' in the following sentence?"

1. Jane draws a *bucket* of water from the well.

All hands are up.

Teacher. "Charles."

Charles. "*Bucket* is a noun, common, third, singular, neuter, objective, object of the transitive verb 'draws,' Rule 17, *The object of a transitive verb in the active voice must be in the objective case.*"

Teacher. "Very good. Mary, you may parse 'statesman' in the next sentence."

2. The diligent student became a wise *statesman*.

Mary. "*Statesman* is a noun, common, third, singular, masculine,——I don't know what case, unless it is the objective; but I think 'became' is an intransitive verb."

Teacher. "Yes; *became* is intransitive, and can not take an object. According to our rule, only TRANSITIVE *verbs in the* ACTIVE *voice* require the objective case to limit them. Before I explain this I will ask James to parse 'Fanny,' in the third sentence."

3. The girl was named *Fanny*.

James. "*Fanny* is a noun, proper, third, singular, feminine—— This verb is transitive, but it is in the *passive voice*, so it can not govern the objective case."

Teacher. "Right. You have now before you the two forms of the verb, which can not govern an object. They are followed immediately by words which refer to the same thing as the subject. 'Fanny' and 'girl' refer to the same person or thing; 'student' and 'statesman,' in the second sentence, are the same person. These words, 'statesman' and 'Fanny,' are said to be *Predicate Nominatives*, or nominatives in the predicate, because they are predicated or asserted of their subjects. You may now turn to page 187. All watch closely, while Susan reads the 14th Rule."

Susan (reading). "*The predicate noun or pronoun with an intransitive or passive verb, referring to the same thing as its subject, must be in the same case.*"

Teacher. "I will now parse the word 'Fanny,' in the third sentence. *Fanny* is a noun, proper, third, singular, feminine, being in the predicate with the passive verb 'was named,' and referring to the same thing as 'girl,' the subject of the verb, Rule 14.

"Mary, you may now try again to parse the word 'statesman,' in the sentence, 'The diligent student became a wise *statesman*.'"

Mary. "*Statesman* is a noun, common, third, singular, masculine, nominative, being in the predicate with the intransitive verb 'became,' and referring to the same thing as 'student,' the subject of the verb, Rule 14."

Teacher. "Well done, Mary. I will now assign some words in the following sentences, for your next parsing lesson."

1. The convention was generally considered a failure.
2. London is the largest city in Europe.
3. The speaker was called an enthusiast.
4. William has been a farmer, but is now a merchant.
5. James will be the neatest writer in the class.

Teacher. "These words, in connection with those assigned in *Apposition*, will be sufficient for your next recitation. How many think they can parse all the words of this lesson?"

All hands up but one.

Teacher. "What is it, Jane?"

Jane. "I would like one more example; 'writer,' in the last sentence."

Teacher. "Who will try it?"

Hands up.

Teacher. "Henry."

Henry. "*Writer* is a noun, common, third, singular, masculine, nominative, being in the predicate with 'will be,' and referring to the same thing as 'James,' the subject of the verb, Rule 14."

SUBJECT OF THE INFINITIVE—PREDICATE OBJECTIVE.

790. Recitation—Correction of False Syntax, and Written Parsings.

791. Drill on the Subject of the Infinitive.—*Teacher.* "Pupils, I have a new construction for the subject of a verb. You will give me your close attention, won't you? In the sentence, 'He wished that the *boys should depart*,' what are the case and construction of the noun 'boys'? All together."

Class. "Nominative, subject of the verb 'should depart.'"

Teacher. "Right: *nominative*, subject of the *finite* verb 'should depart.' Let me change, or abridge the sentence, thus: 'He wished the *boys to depart*.' You see very plainly he did not wish the *boys*, but their *action*, as expressed in the verb 'to depart.' Since this is the case, 'boys' is as much the subject of the verb 'depart,' now as before when the verb was finite. But observe that the *case* of the noun has changed, as well as the *mode* of the verb. In the sentence with the infinitive, 'He wished the boys *to depart*,' 'boys' is in the *objective* case, subject of the infinitive 'to depart.' You will see this more clearly if a pronoun be substituted for the noun 'boys.' Thus: 'He wished *them* to depart.' Here the objective form must be used; for we could not say, 'He wished *they* to depart.' We have, then, Rule 16. You will find it on page 189. Julia, you may read the first part of the Rule."

Julia (reading). "*The subject of the infinitive is commonly in the objective case.*"

Teacher. "It is *always* so, when the subject is *expressed*, and is different from the subject of the leading, finite verb. For example, '*He* desired *me* to go.' *He* and *me* represent very different persons. But if the subject of the infinitive is the *same* as the *subject of the finite verb*, on which the infinitive depends, then the subject of the infinitive is not again expressed, but is in the *nominative* case. For example: 'He purposed *to run* in the races.' The subject of the infinitive 'to run,' is 'he,' the subject of the leading verb 'purposed.'"

1. Let him enter my presence.
2. Permit the birds to come and sing for us, though they do eat the cherries.
3. Do you not see the creature move?
4. Let others speak your praises.
5. A moment ago I saw James go through the gate.
6. I wish to visit New York City this year.
7. The farmer prepares to harvest his grain, not now with grain-cradles, but by horse-power.
8. Did you see her play on the piano?
9. I felt the slimy creature touch me.
10. James, I desire you to help me harvest to-morrow.

Teacher. "I will parse 'him,' in the sentence, 'Let him enter my presence.' *Him* is a pronoun, personal, agreeing with its antecedent, the person spoken of, in the third, singular, masculine, Rule 5, objective, the subject of the infinitive 'enter,' Rule 16; the *sign* TO being omitted, according to Rule 21, *The active verbs, bid, dare, feel, hear, let, make, need, see, and some others of similar signification, take* the *infinitive after them without the sign* TO.' How many think they can now parse the subjects of infinitives?"

Susan seems doubtful.

Teacher. "Susan, you may try one. Take 'birds,' in the second sentence, remembering that there are two infinitives here, 'to come' and 'to sing.'"

Susan. "*Birds* is a noun, common, third, plural, objective, subject of the infinitives 'to come' and 'to sing,' Rule 16."

Teacher. "Well done, Susan. Notice, class, that the sign TO is omitted in several of the preceding sentences, according to Rule 21. The subject of the infinitive in the sixth and seventh sentences is in the nominative case, as I have explained to you."

792. Drill on the Predicate Objective.—1. James is a good *scholar*.

2. His father desired *him* to be an obedient *boy*.

3. They wish *her* to be named *Mary*.

Teacher. "In studying the Predicate Objective, you will first bring to mind two principles you have already studied. I will ask John to rise and parse 'scholar' in the sentence, 'James is a good *scholar*.'"

John. "*Scholar* is a noun, common, third, singular, masculine, *being in the predicate with the intransitive verb 'is,'* and referring to the same thing as the subject, 'James,' Rule 14."

Teacher. "Sarah, you may parse 'him,' in the sentence, 'His father desired *him* to be an obedient boy.'"

Sarah. "*Him* is a pronoun, personal, agreeing with its antecedent, the person spoken of, in the third, singular, masculine, Rule 5, *objective case, subject of the infinitive* 'to be,' Rule 16."

Teacher. "The Rule which John just used says: '*The predicate noun or pronoun with an intransitive or passive verb, referring to the same thing as its subject, must be in the same case.*' So 'scholar' was parsed as in the same case with 'James,' because referring to the same thing. Since 'to be' is intransitive, the noun 'boy' must be in the objective case, because the subject 'him,' referring to the same thing, is in the objective.

"I will parse 'Mary,' in the sentence, 'They wish her to be named Mary.' *Mary* is a noun, proper, third, singular, feminine, objective, in the predicate with the passive verb 'to be named,' referring to the same thing as 'her,' subject of the verb, Rule 14. Charles, you may parse 'boy,' in the sentence, 'His father desired him to be an obedient boy.'"

Charles. "*Boy* is a noun, common, third, singular, masculine, objective, in the predicate with the intransitive verb 'to be,' referring to the same thing as 'him,' the objective subject of the verb, Rule 14."

Teacher. "Very well. For the next recitation you may parse the words I will now indicate."

4. Astronomers suppose the stars to be suns, and these to be centers of planetary systems.

5. If you wish your work to become a pleasure, give it your best time and efforts.

6. We believe Mary to be a kind girl at home.

7. His friends wished him to become a physician.

8. James desired his favorite pony to be called "Tom Thumb."

9. We thought you to be them who promised not to disturb us.

10. They declared me to be him who frightened them.

DOUBLE RELATIVE.

793. Recitation—Written Parsings.

794. Drill in the Double Relative.—*Teacher.* "Pupils, who will give me the interrogative pronouns?"

All hands up.

Teacher. "Charles."

Charles. "*Who*, *which*, and *what.*"

Teacher. "Right. *Who* and *which*, as you remember, are *relatives* when not used interrogatively. You have not yet learned the relative character of *what*. All the words you have parsed thus far have had but one construction. But the pronoun 'what' has two constructions, and for this reason is called a *Double Relative*. I will try to explain this to you by the use of examples."

1. Pay me *what* thou owest.
2. She was frightened by *what* she saw.
3. The multitude were pleased with *what* was said.
4. *What* the majority may accept will be approved.

Teacher. "You will notice very carefully the form of parsing *double relatives.* I will parse 'what,' in the first sentence, 'Pay me *what* thou owest.' But first I will give the equivalent expression, containing 'what,' separated into its parts. 'Pay me *that* [thing] *which* thou owest.' *That* is an adjective, limiting 'thing,' understood; but ordinarily we omit 'that,' and parse the noun 'thing,' to which 'that' relates, and which has the case and construction needed in this relation. Thus: *What* is a pronoun, relative, double, equivalent to *thing which.* *Thing,* the antecedent part, is a noun, common, third, singular, neuter, objective, object of the verb 'pay,' Rule 17. *Which,* the relative part, is a pronoun, relative, agreeing with its antecedent 'thing,' in third, singular, neuter, Rule 5, objective, object of the verb 'owest,' Rule 17.

"Julia, you may parse 'what,' in the fourth sentence, 'What the majority may accept will be approved,' first reading the sentence with 'what' analyzed."

Julia. "'*That* [thing] *which* the majority may accept will be approved.' *What* is a pronoun, relative, double, equivalent to *thing which.* *Thing,* the antecedent part, is a noun, common, third, singular, neuter, nominative, subject of the verb 'will be approved,' Rule 15. *Which,* the relative part, is a pronoun, relative, agreeing with its antecedent 'thing,' in the third, singular, neuter, Rule 5, objective, object of the transitive verb 'may accept,' Rule 17."

Teacher. "Julia, you have done very well. The class may parse, for the next recitation, all the *double relatives* in the first four sentences of this lesson.

"I wish now to guard you against a possible error. Take the sentence, 'He asked me what was said.' Here, 'what' is *not* a *double relative,* but an interrogative pronoun. The sense is this: He asked me— What was said?

"In the following sentences, 'what' is an interrogative pronoun, *not* a double relative. You can distinguish between 'what' as a *double relative,* and as an *interrogative,* by use of the sign *ever.* *Ever* may be used with the *double relative* without marring the sense, but *can not* be so used with the *interrogative* 'what.' You can say, 'Pay me *whatever* thou owest'; but the sense is marred by saying, 'No man can tell *whatever* will be in the future.'"

1. No man can tell *what* will be in the future.
2. Who knows *what* was paid for that property?
3. I know *what* you want.
4. I can tell *what* is needed there.
5. I know *what* was the occasion of the accident.

Teacher. "In addition to what I have already assigned, you may parse the words I will now ask you to mark."

NOMINATIVE ABSOLUTE.

795. Recitation — Parsing Double Relatives and Interrogatives.

796. Nominative Independent or Absolute. — *Teacher.* "In the sentence, 'James, you may go to school,' what is the construction of 'James'? Who can tell?"

No hands up.

Teacher. "We have had no such construction in any previous lesson. 'James' is not a part of the sentence, but is simply the name of the person to whom the sentence is addressed. For this reason 'James' is said to be *independent*, or *absolute*, and is in the nominative case. I will parse it. *James* is a noun, proper, third, singular, masculine, nominative absolute by *direct address*, according to Rule 22: *A noun or pronoun, independent of sentential structure, is in the nominative absolute.* I will give further examples."

1. The work being completed, we received full pay.
2. My stars! Jane, you frightened me.
3. The moon and the stars, they are His handiwork.
4. The distance to the sun having been computed, other measurements were easily made.
5. O Lord, thou art my rock.
6. The enemy, they shall be overwhelmed.

7. My eyes! that was a blinding flash of lightning.
8. The ground being prepared, the farmer sows his grain.
9. Cincinnati, Ohio.
10. "McGuffey's Fifth Reader."

Teacher. "These sentences contain five constructions of the nominative absolute. I will give them, with other examples, as I wish you afterward to select the same constructions in the preceding sentences."

1. With a *participle;* as, The *company having arrived,* we all sat down to tea.
2. By *exclamation;* as, O *mercy!* what shall I do?
3. By *direct address;* as, *Friends,* I beseech you, hear me.
4. By *pleonasm;* as, The *tyrants,* they shall be slain.
5. By *inscription;* as, Boston, Mass.; "Home, sweet home."

Teacher. "How many think they can now find the similar constructions in the previous sentences?"

All hands are up.

Teacher. "If you have any doubt about a particular construction, you can compare it with the examples given above to illustrate the absolute constructions.

"*Company* is in the nominative absolute with the *participle* 'having arrived.'

"*Mercy* is in the nominative absolute by *exclamation.*

"*Friends* is in the nominative absolute by *direct address.*

"*Tyrants* is in the nominative absolute by *pleonasm.*

"Words or phrases which stand alone, as the *inscriptions of letters,* the *titles of books,* the *captions of music,* etc., are in the nominative absolute by inscription.

"The construction by *pleonasm* is proper only when special emphasis is to be given to the noun so used. Jane, you may now try to parse 'work,' in the first sentence, 'The *work* being completed, we received full pay.'"

Jane. "*Work* is a noun, common, third, singular, neuter, in the nominative absolute *with the participle* 'being completed,' Rule 22."

Teacher. "Very good. Henry, you may parse 'moon,' in the sentence, 'The *moon* and the stars, they are His handiwork.'"

Henry. "*Moon* is a noun, common, third, singular, neuter, in the nominative absolute by *pleonasm,* Rule 22."

PART THREE.

SYNTAX.

797. Rule I.—Articles limit nouns; adjectives, nouns and pronouns; as, *The* river; A *white* hat; I *miserable* am undone.

REMARK.—The word *limit* simply signifies *to modify the meaning of*.

798. Articles—*Position.*—The article is always placed before the noun it limits.

799. When an adjective is used with the noun, the article usually precedes the adjective; as, *A* beautiful picture.

800. The article follows the adjectives *all, such, many, both,* and *what;* also any adjective preceded by the adverbs *too, as, so, how;* as, How *great an* opportunity was presented to *all the* soldiers; What *a* fool he was to squander so *large an* inheritance; Toward *such a* one too great *an* enmity was displayed.

801. Use.—Common nouns in the singular number require *a* or *an* when used *indefinitely;* as, *A* man.

802. Common nouns, either singular or plural, require *the* when used *definitely;* as, *The* house; *The* trees.

803. The article is omitted before:

804. Proper names, and titles used merely as titles; as, *Carnot* is president of the French republic; They called him *Squire*.

805. When proper names are applied to a class of nouns, the article is used; as, Charles II. was *a* Stuart.

806. Names of mountain ranges, rivers, islands, etc., excepting names of lakes, take the article; as, *The* Alps, *The* Amazon, *The* Azores.

807. Names of the arts, sciences, virtues, vices, passions, and abstract names; as, *Geology* unfolds the records of the past ages; *Charity* is not puffed up; *Hope* deferred maketh the heart sick.

808. Names of months, days of the week, holidays, festivals, etc., unless used definitely; as, When *March*, just ready to depart, begins to soften into *April; Friday* is called hangman's day.

809. Names so obviously definite as not to require it; as, *Gentlemen* at large are those who have no especial occupation.

810. When two or more adjectives refer to the same noun, the article is used with the first only; as, *A* red and white ribbon: but when the adjectives refer to different nouns, the article is used with each; as, *A* black and *a* white hat.

811. When two or more nouns are connected by *and*, the article is commonly used with the first only; as, *The* boys and girls study together; but when they are connected disjunctively, the article is used with each; as, *The* boys or *the* girls will go.

812. When two or more nouns limit another noun in apposition, the article is used with the first noun only; as, Jones, *the* painter and glazier. But when the epithets refer to *different* persons, the article is used with each; as Jones, *the* painter and *the* glazier.

813. In comparisons where both words refer to the same person or thing, the article is used with the first only; as, He is *a* better preacher than orator. When they refer to different persons, it is used with both; as, The mother is *a* better nurse than *a* daughter [would be].

814. The article *a* is used before *few, hundred, thousand,* etc., with nouns in the plural; as, *A* few men; *A* hundred dollars.

In such cases 'a' can be parsed as giving a collective sense to the plural expression.

815. *A* before *few* and *little* gives an affirmative meaning to an expression: as, *A* few have complied. When *a* is omitted such sentences become negative: as, Few have complied. *A* is also used after *many*, to denote plurality; as, Many *a* mile.

816. The article *the* is used before a common noun in the singular, to denote a class; as, *The* elm; *The* vine; *The* article, where the classes are designated instead of individuals.

817. Adjectives—*Position.*—The adjective is placed before its noun, excepting:

818. When in the predicate: as, The apple is *sweet.*

819. When other words depend on it; as, A cause *worthy* to be defended will not lack defenders.

820. When the adjective denotes the result of a verb's action; as, Vice makes men *miserable.*

REMARK.—This is really a case of predication; as, Vice makes men [to be] miserable.

821. When limiting pronouns; as, I *wretched* know not where to fly.

822. When a verb comes between the noun and the adjective; as, The vessel rides *buoyant* on the deep. In such cases the adjective is generally the attribute of the sentence.

823. In many instances the adjective may either precede or follow the noun; as, A *wise* and *prudent* statesman; or, A statesman *wise* and *prudent.*

824. In the arrangement of two or more adjectives limiting the same noun, if preceding it, the most generic (or most unchangeable) must be placed nearest the noun, and the most specific farthest from it; but when the limiting adjectives follow the noun, the order may be reversed; as, That nice young man; not, That young nice man; That magnificent old cathedral; An interrogative pronominal adjective; That beautiful, accomplished, intelligent young lady; again, My young friend, so beautiful, accomplished, and intelligent; or, My friend, so young, intelligent, accomplished, and beautiful, is dead.

825. Numeral and pronominal adjectives precede other adjectives which modify the same noun; as, The *ten* great religions; *That* noble character.

826. The numerals, *one, two, three, four,* etc., when used with *first* or *last,* may be placed either *before* or *after* them; as, The *two first* lines; The *last two* lines. When the numerals represent large numbers, the words *first* and *last* are placed *before* them; as, The *first fifty* pages.

REMARK.—In the use of adjectives, that order should be adopted which is the most natural, expressive, and euphonious.

H. Gram.—15.

827. Construction.—Adjectives limit nouns and pronouns, and those denoting number must agree with the word limited; as, *This* book; *These* books; *That* man; *Those* men; *One* ox; *Five* oxen.

828. Use.—When an adjective limits two or more nouns connected by *and*, it is used with the first, and understood with the rest; as, *Great zeal* and *energy* were displayed in the undertaking.

829. The adjective in the predicate limits its noun in the subject; as, God is *good;* The column stands *firm.*

REMARK.—Most intransitive verbs take an adjective in the predicate; as, The *apple* tastes *sour;* The *river* runs *deep;* The *fog* hangs *low* and *thick;* The clouds look *beautiful* (not *beautifully*). In expressions where an intransitive verb is used with a predicate adjective, the verb and adjective are equivalent to the verb *to be*, with an adjunct and an adjective; as, The apple tastes *sour;* equivalent to, The apple *is sour in its taste.*

830. An adjective sometimes limits another adjective; as, A *deep blue* color; A *light brown* tint.

831. An adjective and another word sometimes form a compound adjective; as, A *bright-eyed* child.

832. In the so-called independent or indefinite use of the adjective, a noun is understood in the abridged phrase, and the adjective is plainly an attribute or predicate adjective. For example, in the sentence To be *good* is to be *happy*, 'good' and 'happy' limit the noun *person* understood. The sentence with the ellipses supplied may read thus: [For a person] to be good is [for him] to be happy; or, expanded: That a person is good, is that he is happy.

833. When the conjunction *than* is used to express comparison between two or more objects, the comparative of the adjective is used; as, Henry is *taller than* James; He is taller *than* any of his comrades. The comparative is also used when the amount or degree of difference is stated; as, This load is *heavier* by ten pounds; and by some speakers and writers when *two* objects are compared without *than;* as, This pen is the *better* of the two.

834. The superlative is used when a comparison is made between two or more objects *without* the conjunction *than;* as, Susan is the *most studious* of the two; He is the *best* boy in school; Of the two epic poets, Homer and Virgil, Homer was the *most* original.

835. The latter term of the comparison must *exclude* the former when the *comparative* is used; as, The United States is *more powerful* than any *other* republic.

836. The latter term of comparison must *include* the former when the superlative is used; as, Texas is the *largest* State in the Union; not, The largest State of all others.

837. When the pronominals *this* and *that* are used in comparison or contrast, *this* refers to the circumstance last mentioned, *that* to the circumstance first mentioned; as, Intemperance and idleness are inseparable; *this* effeminates the body, *that* destroys both body and soul. *Former, latter, the one, the other*, are similarly used.

838. The reciprocals *each* and *other* refer to two objects only; as, They exhorted *each other* to be steadfast; equivalent to, They each [person] exhorted the other [person] to be steadfast. But *one another* refers to two objects or *more than two;* as, They envied *one another;* equivalent to, They one [person] envied the other [person or persons].

839. The pronominals *each, either, neither*, and *one* always take a verb in the singular number; as, *Each denies* the fact; *Neither reads* well; If any *one* of you thinks differently, he may raise his hand.

840. *Either* properly refers to *one of two*, but according to good authority may mean *one of several;* as, If, from a point within a triangle, two straight lines are drawn to the extremities of *either* side, etc.

841. Misuse.—The following errors frequently occur in the use of adjectives:

842. *In position;* as, A *new* pair of boots; A *black* lady's glove; A *rattan* gentleman's cane.

843. In the use of adverbs for adjectives; as, They escaped *safely;* She looks *beautifully* this evening.

844. In the use of adjectives for adverbs; as, He reads *good;* The winds blew *wild.*

845. In double *comparatives* and *superlatives;* as, He is *more wiser* than they; That is the *most funniest* blunder.

REMARK I.—The double comparative *lesser* is sanctioned by good authority; as, *Lesser* Asia.

REMARK 2.—Many adjectives which do not logically admit of comparison are nevertheless compared according to good usage; as, This orange is *rounder* than that; That is the *most perfect* specimen. These are abbreviated expressions used instead of the more verbose logical forms; for example: That is the *most perfect* specimen, is equivalent to, That is the *most nearly perfect* specimen, etc.; This orange is rounder than that, is equivalent to, This orange is *more nearly round* than that.

846. In the use of *them* for *those;* as, Give me *them* apples; *Them's* my sentiments.

847. In the use of *this here* and *that there;* as, *This here* knife; *That there* pencil.

848. In using the plural of *this* and *that* for the singular; as, *These* kind of books; *Those* sort of men.

849. Exercises for Drill in False Syntax.—Correct the errors and give the principles violated; parse the words in italics.

850. Articles.—That was *a* awful accident. An harbor was soon found. He carried an *ewer*. The boy drove a horse and ox. Look at the person not *act*. He bought the *old* and *new* book. He gave me a *large* and *small knife*. The general owned an old and new house. We traveled to the north and south. *A* noble and a generous *man scorns* such trifles. The *patience* and love are *slow* to anger. *The* Lake *Superior* is a large body of water. She is a better scholar *than* a *reader*. Errors of *the* past *generations* have been corrected. Napoleon assumed the *title* of an *emperor*. All is lost but the *honor*. Henry was a good *sort* of *a* man. Nothing delayed *finishing* of the work. He is called the Mr. *President*. In the building *roads* there is much labor. Conferring of *degrees*. The Bishop *Atkinson*.

851. Adjectives.—These sort of pens *are* first *rate*. *Those kind* of pears are the same *as* we have. He traveled *fifty* mile a *day*. Give me two pair of shoes. Those are nice *molasses*. I bought *five* bushel of *apples*. He chopped ten *cord* of wood. College students often haze *each other*. Cæsar and Pompey envied one *another*. Peaches are more preferable than plums. She appeared splendidly. She sings *very* sweet. A *new* pair of gloves. The Bible is more precious than *any* book. Of all *other* vices, *lying* is the meanest. The latter of the three is the better. The last of the two was the best. He is an old intelligent *man*. They built a *red, large, brick* house. An old, magnificent cathedral. A *stone*, irregular, *ruined* abbey. Such *another* man was never seen. Give *me* them *books*. Where are *them* boys? Each may enter in their turn. No *scholar* will be allowed to leave their *seat*. He *acted* wise and prudent. Let every boy mind their own business. That is a hat of mine. She is a wife of hisen. They passed an irrevocable, final decree. My teacher gave me a birthday splendid present. What is the matter of that nose of yourn?

852. Rule II.—Adverbs limit verbs, adjectives, and other adverbs; as, John writes *smoothly;* That is a *remarkably* interesting book; They conversed *very* intelligently.

853. Position.—The adverb is placed in that position in which it will best convey the intended meaning and render the sentence euphonious.

854. It is usually placed *before* adjectives; as, An *uncommonly* dark night.

855. It is usually placed *after* simple forms of the verb; as, William reads *rapidly.*

856. When compound tenses are used, the adverb is usually placed after the auxiliary; as, He was *certainly* mistaken.

857. *Never* precedes the verb which it limits; *often, always,* and *sometimes* may either precede or follow.

858. The limitation of *only* depends upon the position which it occupies; hence care should be taken to locate it so that all ambiguity will be avoided. Thus, in the sentence, He occupied the throne *only* for a year, 'only' is incorrectly used, since it conveys the impression that he occupied the throne and nothing else, whereas the sense intended is, He occupied the throne for one year *only.*

859. Use.—A few adverbs *apparently* limit nouns and pronouns; as, We *alone* [of all persons] have done this thing; 'alone' really limits some adjective expressed or understood. Not *only* the *soldiers* perished, but *also* the *officers.* 'Not only' and 'but also' are correlative disjunctive conjunctions.

860. Adverbs frequently limit prepositional phrases; as, The stone struck just *beneath the window;* He threw the stone almost *over the river.*

861. Adverbs also limit sentences; as, *Verily,* I say unto you.

862. Adverbs are sometimes used as adjectives; as, The *above* title; Food *enough.*

863. Some adverbs are used as nouns; as, Not till *then.*

864. *Yes, no, amen,* etc., represent entire sentences; as, Will he come? Yes. Here 'yes' is equivalent to the sentence, He will come.

865. Conjunctive adverbs are generally said to unite clauses, and to limit a verb in each; as, He will *start when* the train *arrives.* Here 'when' is a conjunctive adverb, and according to this view limits both 'start' and 'arrives.' But a better disposition of conjunctive adverbs is this: Consider the clause which the conjunctive adverb introduces as a modifier of the verb in the leading clause, and the conjunctive adverb as the introductory of the subordinate clause, also a modifier of its verb.

866. Two negatives make an affirmative; as, *Nor* did they *not* improve the opportunity; that is, They *did* improve it. The repetition of an independent negative strengthens the negation; as, *Not* one, *no, not* one.

867. An adverb often limits a verb understood; as, I'll *away* to the wars; *Truly* [I say] he was a genius.

868. The adverbs *once, hence, thence,* and *whence,* become nouns when a preposition is placed before them; as, I will come *at once;* From *whence* comest thou? equivalent to, From *what place* comest thou?

869. *There* is used as an expletive to introduce sentences; as, *There* was a man named John.

870. There is much diversity of opinion as to the use of *never* and *ever.* In such expressions as, Charm he *never* so wisely, or, *ever* so wisely, either is correct, since both express the same idea. *Never* applies to time and *ever* to degree; as, Seldom or *never;* Grant them *ever* so little.

871. Errors in the use of Adverbs.

872. Adjectives should not be used for adverbs; as, She smiles *sweet;* The ship sails *slow;* He reads *bad.*

873. The wrong use of negatives should be avoided; as, He don't know *nothing* about it; I can't do *nothing* for you; *Nor* is he *not un*prepared.

874. The use of *no* for *not* should be carefully avoided; as, I care not whether he comes or *no*.

875. The adverb should not be misplaced in a sentence; as, The prisoner *immediately* was confined; He spoke of the dangers and hardships of the journey, *eloquently*.

876. The adverb *like* should not be used for the conjunction *as;* as, She looks very much *like* her brother does: correct, She looks *as* her brother does; or, *like* her brother. In the latter case, 'like' is best parsed as a preposition, taking 'brother' for its object. Many, however, prefer to consider it an adjective with the preposition *to*, understood, after it, taking 'brother' for its object. But in the sentence, He walks *like* his father does, if 'does' is retained, *like* must be changed to *as*. But the better form of expression is, He walks *like* his father; considering 'like' as a preposition, taking 'father' for its object. But many prefer to consider 'like' an adverb, in the sense of *similarly;* then 'father' is the object of *to* or *unto*, understood.

877. Exercises.—Correct the errors and give the principles violated; parse the words in italics.

His *voice* sounds *harshly*. They passed by quiet. The *end* will be never reached. He imprudently *acted* in *that* affair. He argued the case before the jury and the *assembled throngs* of people *eloquently*. *Seldom* or ever was the *like* seen *before*. This apple *feels* softly. Do you know *whether* this is *him* or not? Nobody said nothing about *it*. We arrived *home* safely. *They* did not like neither his appearance nor his *address*. He told *me very sad* how he had been wronged. The army marched *triumphant* through the pass. The *stricken* hero fell unconsciously *on* the field. I wish my book was just like his is. I wish I could write just like you can.

878. Rule III.—Conjunctions connect words, phrases, and sentences; as, Birds *and* insects fly in the air; In my experience *and* in yours there are many points in common; You may go, *but* I will stay.

879. Position.—Conjunctions are usually placed between the elements which they connect, but subordinate conjunctions often introduce sentences and precede both; as, *If* this be true, there is an end of argument.

880. Use.—Co-ordinate elements are connected by co-ordinate conjunctions; as, The war is over, *and* peace smiles once more upon the land. An *inferior* element is connected with a *superior* by a subordinate conjunction; as, The city surrendered *because* there was no hope of relief.

881. Words, phrases, and clauses having the same relations to another word, are united by co-ordinate conjunctions; as,

882. Nouns and pronouns in the same case; as, *Jane* and *Mary* ate an *apple* and an *orange;* They sent an invitation for *you* and *me*.

883. Adjectives limiting the same noun or pronoun; as, A *wise* and *upright* judge.

884. Prepositional phrases; as, The poor boy received the gift *with joy* and [with] *thankfulness*.

885. Verbs; as, They *fought* and *fell*.

886. Adverbs; as, The chieftain harangued them *briefly* and *eloquently*.

887. Adverbs with prepositional phrases; as, He acquitted himself *heroically*, yet not *with entire success*.

888. Dependent clauses; as, *That the one should escape* and *the other be taken*, is rather strange.

889. The conjunction *may be understood* in many of the preceding examples.

890. When two or more terms refer jointly to a subsequent term, it must be equally applicable to each of them; as, He wrote notes *on* and an appendix *to* the work, instead of, He wrote notes and an appendix *to* the work. Better: He wrote notes on the work and an appendix to it.

891. In the use of correlative conjunctions, care should be taken that the second member of the pair corresponds to the first; as, *Neither* the boat *nor* the train arrived in time; *Whether* he will go *or* stay is uncertain; The weather was *so* cold *that* many of the soldiers perished.

REMARK.—For a list of corresponding conjunctions, see page 156.

892. In expressing comparison, *than* is used after *comparatives*, *else*, *other*, and *rather*, but not after *different*.

893. There is usually an ellipsis after *than;* as, You are older than he [is]; This tree is taller than that one [is tall].

894. *Than* is not a preposition, save in the sense of *except* or *beside.*

895. Two or more conjunctions frequently come together; as, *And if* he disbelieves you, convince him of his error.

896. Exercises.—Correct the errors and give the principles violated; parse the words italicized.

Education always *has* and always will be requisite to success. He is *more skillful* but not so powerful *as* his adversary. These *principles* always have and always *ought to be* held in reverence. James is as *studious* and even more so than John. We were *afraid lest* he was lost. No one *denies* but *what* he did the deed. It was nothing else but deceit. He wrote a thesis *discussing* and commenting on the *affair.* As far as I can remember, this is *none other* than he. No sum is so small *but* that it should be saved. This piece is not *so* good as *that.* They neither desired or opposed the change. His speech was *different* than and superior *to* the *other.* Neither the man or the horse was found. You are two *year* older than *him.*

897. Rule IV.—Prepositions show the relation of their objects to other words; as, Each *in* his narrow *cell* forever *laid.*

REMARK.—This rule is applied in parsing prepositions, and has no exceptions.

898. Explanations.—The subsequent term of the relation expressed by a preposition is called the object of the preposition; as, Byron the poet died in *Greece.*

899. The word limited by the preposition and its object is called the antecedent term of the relation; as, The vessel *sailed* from London.

900. Position.—The preposition comes before its object, excepting in:

901. Interrogative sentences; as, Whom did he send *for?*

902. Relative clauses; as, He bought an ax to chop wood *with;* It is a circumstance *which* I never heard *of* before.

903. Use.—Care should be taken to select that preposition which exactly expresses the meaning designed to be conveyed; as, He departed *in* anger, not *with* anger; It is different *from* this, not *to* this.

904. *To* before an infinitive is not a preposition, but is merely the sign of the infinitive; as, *To learn to die* is the great business of life.

905. *For* before the objective subject of an infinitive is merely an introductory expletive; as, *For* us to learn to die is the great business of life. In such expressions, *for* expresses no relation, and can not therefore be a preposition.

906. Two prepositions sometimes come together; as, He came *from between* the seas. They are then parsed as a compound preposition.

907. One or more prepositions are frequently joined with a noun to express a relation; as, *On account of* your remissness the plan failed; He comes *in the character of* a business man.

908. This is equivalent to, He came *as* a business man; hence 'as' is a preposition in the last example.

909. Exercises.—Correct the errors and give the principles violated; parse the words in italics.

The soldiers were perishing for *thirst*. The children *went* in the house. I differ from *you* in that opinion. He jumped on to the *wagon*. She was accused for *equivocation*. The regiment passed *from* Ohio to *Indiana*. The boys went, *but* the girls staid to *home*. The teacher compared this *book* to *that*. The father divided the peaches *between* his five *sons*. It was partitioned *among* the two. Henry and John differ *widely* with each *other*. There is no occasion of such violence. He has no desire for *to go*. Their conduct does not conform with their *profession*. He *turned* away with *anger* from the scene. We had no faith with respect to such professions of regard. Good morning; will you walk *in?* *Whatever* business he entered, he thought *himself* sure of success. She works better than *him*.

910. Rule V.—A pronoun must agree with its antecedent in *person*, *number*, and *gender;* as, A bishop hath *his* office, and therefore *he* can not meddle with another office, *which* alone requireth a whole man.

911. Position.—The personal and the relative pronoun represent the preceding noun standing nearest with which they do not disagree; as, Socrates, amid all the revolutions of state, the commotions of society, and the acerbity of Xantippe, maintained *his* placidity of temper and *his* devotion to philosophy.

912. The *relative* pronoun must be placed as near as possible to its antecedent, otherwise obscurity, ambiguity, or nonsense is the result.

913. Use.—In using the pronoun the same style should be preserved in the same connection. For instance, in this example: *You* are the very man I was looking for; I don't want *thee* to leave me again; a member of the Friends' society would say, *Thee* is the very man I was looking for; I don't want *thee* to leave me again. Many members of the same society would say, more correctly, *Thou* art the very man I was looking for; I don't want *thee* to leave me again. Except with the Friends, the correct form would be, *You* are the very man I was looking for; I don't want *you* to leave me again.

914. *It*, though neuter, is used for brute animals and young children; as, The child resembles *its* father; Before I purchase a horse, I wish to be sure that *it* has no vicious habits.

915. *It*, the subject of *is*, may introduce an antecedent of any person, number, or gender in the predicate; as, *It* is the men whom you were expecting; Was *it* you that broke the window? *It* in the last sentence is parsed as representing its antecedent 'you,' but not agreeing with it, according to the authority of this article.

916. When the antecedent is an inanimate object *personified*, the pronoun must agree with it in the figurative sense; as, Time, my lord, hath a wallet at *his* back, wherein *he* puts alms for oblivion.—SHAKESPEARE.

> Then Ceremony leads *her* bigots forth,
> Prepared to fight for shadows of no worth.—COWPER.

917. When the antecedent is a noun used *metaphorically*, the pronoun agrees with it in its literal sense; as, Christ himself being the chief corner-stone on *which* all the building fitly framed together groweth into a holy temple unto the Lord.—BIBLE.

918. When the antecedent is a noun used by *metonymy* for one having different properties, the pronoun agrees with it sometimes in its literal, sometimes in its figurative, sense; as,

> Is Heaven tremendous in *its* frowns? Most sure;
> And in *its* favors formidable, too.—YOUNG.

> Man's glory Heaven vouchsafes to call *her* own.—*Id.*

919. When the antecedent is a noun used by *synecdoche* for more or less than it really signifies, the pronoun agrees with it in its figurative sense; as, My Life, my Love, to *thee* I fly.

920. When the antecedent is a *sentence*, a *phrase*, or a *word* used merely as a word, the pronoun agrees with it in the third, singular, neuter; as, I wrote to her but I regret *it;* His being there was *itself* no evidence of his guilt; His name was *John; it* was the same as his father's.

921. When the antecedent is a singular noun limited by the phrase *many a*, the pronoun may agree with it in the singular or represent it in the plural; as,

> Full many a flower is born to blush unseen,
> And waste *its* sweetness on the desert air.—GRAY.

Many an hour have we spent together: *they* were the happiest of my life.

922. As the English language has no pronoun of the common gender in the third singular, the masculine pronoun is often used as including both genders; as, I wish every pupil to close *his* book; Wisely foreseeing, no doubt, that the more palatable *each* had rendered them to *his* own taste, the more *he* would be affected by their approaching loss.

923. Exercises.—Correct errors and give the principles violated; parse the words in italics.

My *friend*, I look to thee for aid, and *hope you* will not disappoint me. Was it you that called me? Every *one* of the children was at school this *morning*, and *it* would have rejoiced you *to see* how happy *they* looked. Our Father *which art* in heaven. The people which I have chosen *are gone astray*. The *moon* looked down in all *its* quiet beauty. It was them that committed the deed. I heard the *news* but I could not believe *them*. There you will find two gentlemen, *one* of *which* I wish *to see*. Taste *these* molasses; I believe you will like *them*. The *tribes* of Israel *whom* God in ancient times especially *favored*, are now scattered. They will obey *his* commands *that* loves God. The feast was in honor of Bacchus, *who* is the *name* of the God of wine. *He* is christian *which* does as he would be done *by*. The friend has gone to the city that has been visiting *us*. There is a certain *grace* about her manners *which one* can scarcely describe. There are the *man* and the horse *which* I wished you to notice.

924. Rule VI.—A pronoun having for its antecedent a collective noun, conveying the idea of plurality, must agree with it in the plural number; as,

> Then shall the race of men confess
> With *their* united voice.

925. A pronoun having for its antecedent a collective noun conveying the idea of unity agrees with it in the singular number according to Rule V; as, He sees a nation groaning under *its* heavy yoke.

926. Rule VII.—A pronoun having two or more antecedents connected by *and*, must agree with them in the plural number; as, Milton and Shakespeare have expressions peculiar to *themselves*.

927. When two singular antecedents connected by *and* are antithetically distinguished, the pronoun agrees with them in the singular number; as, John, and not James, was praised for *his* bravery.

928. When the antecedents are preceded by *each*, *every*, or *no*, or are singular and connected by *as well as*, the pronoun agrees with them in the singular; as, It is sad, but nevertheless true, that every town and city in our land has *its* liquor shops; The rich man as well as the poor has *his* needs.

929. When singular antecedents connected by *and* are in apposition, the pronoun agrees with them in the singular; as,

> The scorn and wonder of our days,
> Whose ruling passion was the love of praise,
> Though wondering senators hung on all *he* spoke,
> The club must hail *him* master of the joke.—POPE.

930. When the antecedents connected by *and* denote one person or thing, the pronoun agrees with them in the singular; as, My Lord and Master, *thou* wilt not cast me off; That coach and four is *its* master's sole remaining property.

931. Exercises.—Correct errors and give the principles violated; parse the words in italics.

The honest man and the knave, too, have their friends.

> And let each heart and voice proclaim
> The goodness of their God.

Every officer and private soldier returned to their homes. Every drove and flock by themselves. I think a minister, as well as a political speaker, should never read *their* discourses. Wealth and honor will be obtained by him who strives for *it*. This horse and wagon is for sale: who wants to buy *them?*

932. Rule VIII.—A pronoun having two or more singular antecedents connected by *or* or *nor*, must agree with them in the singular number; as, In this instance neither honesty nor purity was *its* own reward.

933. Exercises.—Correct errors and give the principles violated; parse the words in italics.

Neither *you* nor I *can blame ourselves*. In my estimation either Brown, Bullion, or Harvey, with all *their* disagreements, *are* preferable to Pinneo. One may as well act malice or hatred as feel them. Either *I* or *my* brother must relinquish *our* claims. If a *child* or a savage may wish *to express* a general conception, *they* will be limited by *their* present *vocabulary*. I *should think* that John or Henry either would exert *themselves to be* present. Neither faith, *hope*, nor charity make *their* homes in *his* heart.

934. Rule IX.—A finite verb must agree with its subject in person and number; as, I *love;* You *love;* He *loves.*

REMARK.—All verbs are finite when used in the indicative, potential, subjunctive, and imperative modes. All verbs are infinite when used in the infinitive and participial modes.

935. Position.—A finite verb follows its subject; except in

936. Interrogative sentences; as, Who is he?

Explanation.—Here the verb is intransitive, and not only precedes its subject, but follows its predicate nominative. Which is the subject and which the predicate in interrogative sentences, can be determined more clearly in all cases by answering the question; as, Who is he? He is my brother. 'Brother,' the antecedent in the answer, fills the place of 'who' in the question, and determines its construction and case.

937. Hyperbaton; as, Silver and gold have I none; Sad was she.

938. Imperative sentences; as, Come, thou fount of every blessing; Go, bind thou up those dangling apricots.

939. Use.—Every finite verb must have a subject, expressed or understood, with which it must agree in person and number.

940. Verbs in the imperative mode generally agree with *thou, ye,* or *you,* understood; as, Give [thou] some support to the budding twigs; Go [ye] immediately.

941. The adjuncts of a subject do not change the person and number of its verb; as, Magnus, with his accomplices, *was put* to death; One of those boys *is* sick; Six hours' work *is* necessary to accomplish it.

942. An infinitive, a participle, a phrase, or a sentence, is often the subject of a finite verb: such a subject requires the verb in the third, singular; as, To live *is* Christ, to die *is* gain; Doing nothing *is* doing ill; Why he acted as he did *is* not known; A rolling stone gathers no moss, *is* a proverb.

943. When two nominatives precede an intransitive or passive verb, that which stands nearest the verb is the subject, and the other is the attribute; as, He ascertained *what* the *lesson* was from his roommate.

944. Peculiarities of certain verbs in agreement.

945. The verb *ought* being defective, rejects the *s* in the third, singular, present; as, He *ought* not to go there.

946. The verb *need*, in the sense of *ought*, also rejects the *s* in the third, singular, present; as, He *need* not expect me to come. But in the sense of *require* it retains the *s* in the third, singular, present; as, He *needs* aid.

947. Exercises.—Correct errors and give the principles violated; parse the words in italics.
They *was present.* He *need* not do it. He needs not *do* it. The conditions *seems* reasonable. So *much* of ability and merit are seldom found. His sins *has weakened* his mind. It is useless for *you to deny* it. There is principles in man *which causes* him to offend. These things *happeneth* to all men. *What makes* the matter plainer *is, that* his eyes were bloodshot and heavy, and his hands were stained with blood. The diversity of the cases *are* very apparent. Why *was n't* you there? *To be* wise and prudent were his greatest desire. All [ ] *is* well *that* ends well. That we should study and improve our time *admit* of no dispute.

948. Rule X.—A finite verb having for its subject a collective noun, conveying the idea of plurality, must agree with it in the plural number; as, The nobility *were* there.

949. It is sometimes difficult to determine whether the collective noun should express the idea of unity or of plurality; in such cases present usage generally requires a plural verb.

950. A collective noun conveying the idea of unity is a singular noun, and the agreement of the verb with such a subject comes under Rule IX; as, The crowd *has dispersed;* The crowds *have dispersed.*

951. Exercises.—Correct errors and give the principles violated; parse the words in italics.

The seventh regiment *were called* out. The *fleet* is all arrived in port. These *kind* of habits *are* dangerous. The committee *were* quite full. The *amount* of expenditures and disbursements far exceed our calculations. The *council* was quarreling over the *motion*. The House of Representatives *are a body* separate from the Senate. The *society* of these places are always changing.

952. Rule XI.—A finite verb having two or more subjects connected by *and*, must agree with them in the plural number; as, Even Phidias and Michael Angelo *study* the nature of the rough block they have to hew; Sun and moon *are* both confounded; Tardiness, greediness, and vainglory *have* never *been* the sources of his inspiration.

953. Exceptions.—When the subjects connected by *and* denote one person or thing, the verb should be singular; as, Jesus, my strength and righteousness, my savior and my king, *hears* me when I call.

954. When the subjects are preceded by *each, every,* or *no,* or are singular and connected by *as well as,* the verb should be singular; as, Each sect and party *has* a set of opinions peculiar to itself; Every man, woman, and child *was* numbered; Now, no slave, no master, *exists* in our land; Religion, as well as culture, *is* essential to a perfect man.

955. When the verb stands between its subjects, it agrees with the first, and is understood with the rest; as,

> The mountains in their places stand,
> The sea, the sky.—WILLIS.

956. Two or more subject phrases connected by *and*, expressing unity of thought or action, take a singular verb; as, To rise and retire early *is* essential to a student's highest success.

957. Two co-ordinate verbal constructions, if both finite, or if both infinite, must be connected by a co-ordinate conjunction; but if one is finite and the other infinite, the conjunction is excluded; as, James rose early *and* went to market; Mary, *coming* in *and observing* the large company, was much embarrassed; The migratory birds, *deceived* by the early spring, *came* too early, so that many of them perished.

958. Exercises.—Correct errors and give the principles violated; parse the words in italics.

Was you and John there? Each boy and girl in *their* turn *receive* the money to which they *are entitled*. Not only John, but *Henry* and and James *are coming*. *To understand* the condition of the writers, as well as to examine the meaning of the sacred scriptures, *are processes* necessary to the *theologian*. No person but *children were* at the picnic. After every boy and girl in the room *learn* their lessons, we will sing. Not a house, not a tree *appear*. *Economy*, not mean *savings*, bring wealth. To be honest, and never *to play* the hypocrite, *are*, I think, necessary *to* a true *Christian*.

959. Rule XII.—A finite verb having two or more singular subjects connected by *or* or *nor*, must agree with them in the singular number; as, There *is* no speech nor language where their voice is not heard.

960. When the subjects are of different persons or numbers, the verb must agree with the one which immediately precedes it, and be understood with the rest; as, Neither the mother nor the children *are* able to work; Either John or I *am* to go.

961. When the subjects connected by *or* or *nor* are in apposition, the verb should agree with the principal word; as, The sign of equality, or two short parallel horizontal lines, *is used* in such cases.

962. Exercises.—Correct errors and give the principles violated; parse the words in italics.

Neither *John* nor *James* are remarkable for *their* talent. Neither animate nor inanimate nature *teach* the *immortality* of the soul. *Either* the girls or *their* brother *have purchased* the property. Too *much* sense or *nonsense* are apt to become *tiresome*. Either you or I *are to blame.* One *turnout*, or, in other words, a *barouche and four*, were all that *remained* of the season.

963. Rule XIII.—A noun or personal pronoun limiting another noun or pronoun, signifying the same person or thing, is in the same case by apposition; as, Cromwell, the *Protector*, was a patriot; I saw Johnson, the *farmer's*, wagon; That shaft was aimed at us, *citizens* of the republic.

964. *Position.*—The noun or pronoun in apposition usually stands after the limited noun or pronoun, but sometimes, especially in poetry, it is placed before; as, *Daughter* of morn, *Aurora* tints the east! Sometimes it is difficult to distinguish which is the principal term and which the appositive; as, Longfellow the poet.

965. Use.—A noun, pronoun, phrase, or sentence, may be the basis of an appositive.

966. A single word; as, The *Emperor* William.

967. Two or more words; as, *Virtue and liberty*, harbingers of prosperity, go hand in hand.

968. A phrase; as, *By telling stories*, a practice of which he was fond, he became popular with the children.

969. A sentence; as, *The world gave liberally to Chicago*, an instance of generosity which will never be forgotten.

970. A noun is used distributively in apposition with a plural; as, The soldiers dispersed, *each* [soldier] to his tent.

971. A plural is used appositively with several singular nouns; as, Peace, prosperity, happiness, *all* [these things] were sacrificed.

REMARK.—In the last two examples the nouns *soldier* and *things* are supplied in parsing, since pronominal adjectives do not have case.

972. A title is parsed in apposition with a proper noun; as, Colonel Thompson; Squire Jones; Mr. Brown; Miss Drake.

973. A proper and a common name are often associated in apposition; as, The Ohio river; Cape Horn; Mount Olympus; The Desert Sahara.

974. In such expressions as, The Emperor of Germany's prime minister, Bismarck, the sign of the possessive is affixed to the last word of the complex noun; but in parsing the separate words, the sign should be transferred to its true place, thus making the possessive *Emperor's*, and leaving 'Germany' in the objective case, the object of the preposition *of*.

975. When two or more possessives are in apposition, the sign is used only with the one which immediately precedes the noun limited, and indicates the relation of the others; as, He stopped at Mr. Smith's [house] the merchant last night.

REMARK.—In the expression, Shakespeare, as a dramatic poet, has no equal, *as* is a preposition, being equivalent to the complex preposition, *in the relation of*, or *in the character of*, though some grammarians consider *as* in this connection a conjunction, and *poet* in apposition with *Shakespeare*.

976. Exercises.—Correct the errors and give the principles violated; parse the words in italics.

It was sent by my *brother*, *he* who wrote the letter. It was my cousin John, *him* who commanded the Chesapeake. I sent a present to my *friends*, they *who* we met at the fair. We are given to death, *us* and *ours*. The stranger *prayed* for his enemies, *they who* he had reason to curse. You had better do that *yourself;* not ask me! *That* he was in such company was *itself* presumptive *evidence* of his guilt. Let *him* come and bring it *himself*.

977. Rule XIV.—The predicate noun or pronoun, with an intransitive or passive verb referring to the same thing as its subject, must be in the same case; as, Plato was a *philosopher;* The stranger seemed to be an honest *man;* I thought him to be *you;* We declared it to be *them*.

978. Position.—The predicate noun or pronoun usually follows the verb, but may come before it in the following cases:

979. In interrogative sentences; as, *Who* are you?

REMARK.—It is always safe to answer the question before deciding which is the subject and which the predicate word in interrogative sentences.

980. When there is a rhetorical or poetical transposition of terms; as, *Feet* was I to the lame.

981. In cases where both the subject and the predicate nominative come before the verb; as, They cared not whose *son he* was.

982. Use.—Any verb may take a predicate nominative except a transitive verb in the active voice.

983. Any word, phrase, or sentence used as a noun may have the construction of a noun in the predicate.

984. The predicate noun or pronoun after a finite verb can be in the nominative case only, but after *infinitives* or *participles* it may be either in the nominative or objective; as, *John* is said to be a good *boy;* They desired *him* to become a *lawyer;* The *gladiator* being an expert *swordsman*, soon dispatched his unwary antagonist; We did not hear of *him* becoming a *soldier.* See Arts. 1228 and 1247. Close attention to the sense of the passage will enable the pupil to decide whether the noun in the predicate is in the nominative or in the objective case.

985. Exercises.—Correct the errors and give the principles violated; parse the words in italics.

It is me. We *thought* it was her. *If* I had been *him* I would have gone. *Who* did you *say* he was? We knew *it* to be them. They *supposed* it was me. *It* was not me who he was finding fault *with*. *Whom* do you *think* they are? They declared she herself *to be* the author of the *mischief*. Whom do you say that he is? *Had* it been me *I* would have resisted such demands. They thought *it* to be unjust that they should be thus robbed of their property. They declared it to be impossible for him to prevaricate under any circumstances. Let them become one another's joy. We supposed *it* safe to make the investment. His being the *teacher* is no *reason* why we should change our conversation. Its being him is just what's the matter. Is not their conversation being improper the reason for its change? Let each [ ] esteem other [ ] better than *themselves.*

986. Rule XV.—A noun or pronoun which is the subject of a finite verb, must be in the nominative case; as, *Fish* swim; *Birds* fly.

987. Position.—The nominative usually stands before its verb, except:

988. When a question is asked without the use of an interrogative pronoun; as, Shall *man* be more just than *God?*

989. When the verb is in the imperative mode; as, Abide *ye* here.

990. When a wish or emotion is expressed; as, Long live the *king*.

SYNTAX. 189

991. With the introductory expletive *there;* as, There lived a man.

992. When a conjunction denoting supposition is omitted; as, Had *we* known this, we could have saved him.

993. In emphatic sentences; as, Here am *I*.

994. After *say*, *think*, and *reply;* as, Thus saith the *Lord*.

995. Use.—Every nominative unless in the nominative absolute, in apposition, or in the predicate, must be the subject of a finite verb, expressed or understood.

996. A noun and its pronoun must not both be used as the subject of the same verb; as, Byron, *he* was a great poet.

997. The subject must not be omitted when its omission would injure the sense.

998. Exercises.—Correct the errors and give the principles violated; parse the words in italics.
Them are fine apples. These trees are taller than *them*. James and *me* read together. Who is there? Me. You and him *will go*. Us who have escaped *should be* thankful. How *is* thee, my friend? *None* is liked better *than* her. The boys plays *ball*. Nobody thought so *but them*. *Him* being at home we were kindly welcomed. It was *her* who did the mischief. *Whom* do you think he was? Who do you travel *with?* The smoke's *being* dense, we thought there was a great fire. He is taller *than* her. She is not as wise *as* him. If I were *him* I would read *more* and talk less.

999. Rule XVI.—The subject of the infinitive is commonly in the objective case. But when the subject of the infinitive is the same as the subject of the finite verb limited by the infinitive, it is in the nominative case; as, They wished *him to go; John* expected *to buy* the house; It was supposed *to be* his horse.

REMARK.—This rule is given in this form for the sake of brevity. When the subject of the infinitive is any thing else than a noun or pronoun, it is not strictly applicable, since only nouns and pronouns have case.

1000. Explanations.—Every infinitive has a subject expressed or understood, and this may always be supplied and the infinitive phrase expanded into a finite clause; as, I desired *him to go;* equivalent to, I desired *that he should go.* I wished *to go;* equivalent to, I wished *that I could go.*

1001. A noun or pronoun in the objective can not be the object of a preposition and the subject of an infinitive *at the same time.* For example in the sentence, For positive people to be mistaken is nothing very uncommon, 'for' is merely an introductory expletive, being a preposition only in form, and does not govern 'people' as an objective; it has no antecedent term of relation.

1002. After an active verb which admits of two objectives, one of the objects is apparently used both as the object of the finite verb and as the subject of the infinitive; as, I taught *him* to read. No noun or pronoun but a double relative can be found in two constructions at the same time. The only safe way to decide which construction the objective really has, is to expand the infinitive phrase. Thus the above example would read, I taught him, that he should read. If 'him' is considered the direct object of 'taught,' *that he should read,* is an adverbial element modifying the verb 'taught,' and its equivalent infinitive takes another *him* for its subject, and the original sentence with this *him* supplied, becomes: I taught him [for him] to read. But if *to read* is considered the direct object of 'taught,' 'him,' with the preposition 'to,' understood, becomes the adverbial element limiting 'taught,' and the sentence will become: I taught *to read* (equivalent to reading) [to] him. In some cases it is somewhat doubtful whether the objective is the object of the active transitive verb or the subject of the infinitive verb; as, I ordered him to saddle the horse; for, I ordered him that he should saddle the horse, and, I ordered that he should saddle the horse, may either be considered as giving the meaning of the sentence, although the first expression is undoubtedly the preferable equivalent.

1003. Rule XVII.—A noun or pronoun which is the object of a transitive verb in the active voice, must be in the objective case; as, The boy shot a *bird.*

REMARK.—Infinitives, participles, pronominal adjectives, and clauses, when used as the objects of transitive verbs, have no case. The modification of case belongs only to nouns and pronouns.

1004. Position.—The object of a transitive verb is placed after it, excepting in:

1005. Relative clauses; as, He is the one *whom* they sought.

1006. Interrogative sentences; as, *Whom* does the nation honor?

1007. Emphatic expressions; as, *Him* his companions forsook.

1008. Poetic or inverted style; as, *Gold* many hunted—sweat and bled for gold.

1009. Government.—The objective is governed by a transitive verb as the receiver of the action or influence denoted by it.

1010. When the construction is changed from the active to the passive, the object of the active verb becomes the subject of the passive, and the subject of the active the object of a preposition; as, He broke the window; active: The window was broken by him; passive.

1011. Verbs of *teaching, giving, allowing, denying,* and others, *apparently* govern two objectives, one as an immediate and the other a remote object; as, She taught *him French;* He gave *me* an *apple*. Really, however, the *remote* object is governed by a preposition understood; as, He gave an apple *to* me. In changing such expressions from the active to the passive construction, either the *immediate* or the *remote* object may become the subject of the passive verb; as, An *apple* was given [to] me; *I* was given [*with?*] an apple. Logically, the immediate object only can become the *true* subject of the passive verb, since a preposition can not be supplied with it in either voice without marring the sense.

1012. Verbs signifying *to make, choose, name,* etc., *apparently* govern two objectives; as, They made *him emperor*. But verbs belonging to these classes really have an abridged infinitive sentence for their object. In the sentence, He made that log a boat, 'log' is not the object of 'made,' surely, nor is 'boat,' for the idea is really this: He made (accomplished) that the *log* should be (become) a *boat;* in other words, He made the log [to be] a boat. So, also, We elected him [to be] president; He called (denominated) her [to be] Sarah. In these examples it may be seen that the *fact* given by the infinitive and its adjuncts is the direct object of the finite transitive verb of the principal sentence. This becomes more apparent when the infinitive clause is expanded, and the construction changed from the active to the passive form. The first sentence would then read thus: That the log should become a boat, was made [accomplished] by him. The *true object* of the active verb is now the *subject* of the passive, and the *subject* of the active, the *object* of a preposition.

1013. A transitive verb does not permit a preposition to govern its object; as, I will not *allow of* such conduct.

1014. Some *intransitive* verbs govern an objective of kindred signification with the verb; as, He laughed a scornful *laugh;* She danced a *waltz;* They ran a *race.*

REMARK.—Intransitive verbs have the active voice only except (1) in expressions like the above, when they have the passive also; as, That race *was well run* by them; (2) by enallage; as, He *was gone* before sunset.

1015. Intransitive causative verbs govern an objective; as, Henry trots his *pony;* equivalent to, Henry causes his pony to trot.

1016. Exercises.—Correct the errors and give the principles violated; parse the words in italics.
Who did he send? *Whom* was sent by him? *He* they praised, *she* they censured. They chose *John* and *I monitors* for the week. *He*, after a short discussion, they elected *Treasurer*. They invited *she* and her *sister* to dine at *Delmonico's*. Who did he *ask?* Who do you take me to be?

1017. Rule XVIII.—A noun or pronoun which is the object of a preposition, must be in the objective case; as, The book is on the *shelf;* Columbus sailed from *Palos.*

1018. Position.—The object is usually placed *after* the preposition, except:

1019. In interrogative sentences, when it is sometimes placed before; as, *What* did he send *for? Whom* did you write *to?*

1020. When the object is a relative pronoun expressed or understood; as, That is the place *which* I sent him *to;* They cut a rod to divine *with.*

1021. Government.—The preposition is often understood:

1022. When it is used with the first noun of a series, and omitted before the rest; as, He sent a present *to* Henry, Jane, and Susan.

1023. After verbs of giving, teaching, etc.; as, She gave [to] him a coin; I taught them [in] algebra; or, I taught algebra to them. See page 191, art. 1011.

1024. After *near, nigh, like, worthy,* and *unworthy;* as, She is like [to] her father; We sat near [to] the wall; He was not *worthy* the confidence reposed in him. However, the better disposition of these equivocal words *near, nigh, like, worthy,* and *unworthy* is to consider them prepositions.

1025. After verbs and adjectives before nouns denoting time, value, weight, and measure; as, The fair lasted [through] a week; The fish weighs [to the amount of] ten pounds; The fence is five feet high; that is, it is high *to the extent of* five feet.

1026. Before nouns denoting time *when indefinitely;* as, The president arrived *last week.* The preposition is generally used before nouns denoting time *when definitely;* as, We arrived *on* Monday, late *in* the evening.

1027. Use of Prepositional Phrases.

1028. The prepositional phrase should be placed as near the word it limits possible. Violations of this principle lead to many ambiguities; as, He declared that there was treachery in the camp *with fierce indignation;* We saw that all was lost *in a moment;* The commander came to see the vessel sail *in a carriage.*

1029. The practice of connecting two prepositions with one object; as, They came up *to* and turned away *from* the goal, although condemned by grammarians as "splitting particles," is sanctioned by much good usage.

1030. Exercises.—Correct the errors and give the principles violated; parse the words in italics.

The teacher gave you and I that *book.* Who did you go with? We expected better *things of* you and she. Who did *you* send the letter *to?* I will ask whoever I *please.* Between you and I, that is an affair of our *own.* She they inquired *for, me* they neglected. The speed was very slow of the vessel. A package was delivered to the tall gentleman in the black coat marked C. O. D. The miller was eating his dinner *in* his white hat. He threw a dime to the veteran *leaning on* a crutch with one *leg.*

1031. Rule XIX.—A noun or pronoun limiting another noun or pronoun signifying a different person or thing, is in the possessive case; as, *Greeley's* History; *Bacon's* Rebellion; *Our* destiny.

1032. Position.—The noun or pronoun in the possessive is placed immediately before the noun it limits, except when an adjective intervenes; as, Gentlemen's *black* boots.

1033. Government.—The possessive is governed by a noun in any case. The governing noun may be understood; as, He went to St. Peter's [church].

1034. Use.—The *possessive* case, and the *objective* governed by the preposition *of*, are equivalent when *of* denotes possession; as, The governor's house; or, The house *of* the governor.

1035. When several possessives denoting *common* possession limit the same noun, the sign is used with the last only; as, *Mary* and *Alice's* shawl. But when they denote possession *not in common*, the sign is used with each; as, James's and Lucy's hats.

1036. *S*, the sign of the possessive, is omitted when it would bring together several hissing sounds; as, Jesus' sayings; Davies' Surveying; For righteousness' sake; Ulysses' silence.

1037. The sign *'s* is not used with pronouns; as, Hers, Its, etc.

1038. A noun limited by a possessive plural, or by two or more possessives severally, may be singular or plural, as the sense requires; as, The men's *farm;* The women's *hats;* The boys' and girls' *sled*.

1039. The possessive *whosesoever* may be divided by tmesis; as, *Whose* name *soever* it was.

1040. A pronoun limits a pronoun in the possessive when the limiting word is used as an attribute; as, He is *mine* and I am *his*.

1041. Exercises.—Correct the errors and give the principles violated; parse the words in italics.

The soldiers *spirit* was broken. The *mens'* courage failed *when* the crise's came. The ladie's *fans* were lost. The dogs' *ear* was cut off. London and Paris's *drainage* are *very* different. He stopped at Johnson's & Co.'s. He read *Washington*, the patriot, soldier, and statesman's address. This book is his', that one is *your's*. Its value is nothing compared with mine'. *Were* John and Jame's *confession* alike? Were *John's* and *James's* confessions alike? Were William and Mary's *friends* the same? Were *Jacob's* and *Esau's* parents alive? The childrens' *health* was seriously affected. The mens *ways* was low. The boys story was believed. The bishop's of Dublin's palace. The mistake was the teacher, not the pupil's.

1042. Rule XX.—Infinitives and participles have the construction of nouns, adjectives, or adverbs; as, *To drink* is dangerous; The army had orders *to march;* He waited *to state* his case; *Lying* is sinful; The horse *running* away broke the buggy; They came *pleading* for peace.

I. INFINITIVES.

1043. Use of the Infinitive.

1044. As a *noun, adjective,* or *adverb.*

1045. Used in the predicate after the verb *be,* the infinitive may denote:

1046. A simple equivalent; as, To die is *to sleep.*

1047. Possibility or obligation; as, Lead is *to be found* in Missouri; This rule is *to be observed.* In the last two instances, the infinitives have the construction of *adjectives* in the predicate.

1048. Something determined or expected; as, We are *to go* next Tuesday. In this case *to go* has the construction of a noun, being the object of *expecting* or *intending,* understood.

1049. The infinitive after *have* denotes necessity; as, We *have to go;* He *has to do* better. Here the infinitive has the construction of a noun, and is the object of the verb *have.*

1050. The infinitive is used after most verbs to denote purpose; as, He came *to study.* *To study* is an adverbial element of purpose limiting *came;* in other words, it has the construction of an adverb.

1051. The infinitive is used in comparisons after *so, as, too,* and *than;* as, Be so good *as to go;* He knew better *than to resist.* The first sentence expanded reads thus: Be so good *as* it is good to go. Here *to go* is the logical subject of *is,* understood. In the second example, *to resist* has the construction of a noun, being the subject of [*is*]. Supplying the ellipses the sentence reads thus: He knew better than [to think that] to resist (equivalent to, resistance) [is safe]. The elliptical infinitive *to think* has the construction of an adverb limiting *better.*

1052. As a *verb,* the infinitive may have all the modifications of a verb except person and number.

1053. Use of the Infinitive Sign.

1054. When several infinitives come together, the sign *to* is often used with the first and omitted before the others; as, They came *to* see, hear, and judge for themselves.

1055. Nothing should come between the infinitive and its sign *to;* as, John was told *not to go;* rather than, John was told *to not go.*

II. PARTICIPLES.

1056. Use of the Participle.

1057. As a *noun, adjective,* or *adverb.*

1058. Used in the construction of a noun in the nominative, the participle may be either the subject of a finite verb or in the predicate after it; as, *Promising* is not *performing.*

1059. Used in the construction of a noun in the objective, the participle may be the object of an active transitive verb or of a preposition; as, Avoid *defaming* your neighbors; He desisted from *persecuting* his enemies.

1060. When the participle is used as a noun, its subject is frequently expressed in the possessive case; as, Nothing prevented the soldier's returning home. But by enallage the objective is often used for the possessive; as, I did not think of *them* returning so soon. In this sentence, *them,* the objective subject of the participle, is used by enallage for the possessive subject *their.* But often the *possessive* construction gives a meaning *entirely different* from the *objective.* This may be readily seen by comparing the following sentences: There is no harm in *children's* playing by the roadside; There is no harm in *children* playing by the roadside. The first asserts that there is no harm *in the playing* of the children; the second, that there is no harm in the *children themselves.*

1061. When a participle is preceded by an article or an adjective, it becomes a noun, and must be followed by the preposition *of* to govern the noun which was before its object. Thus, Many hands are employed in *printing* dailies; or, Many hands are employed in *the* printing *of* dailies. In these forms of expression, *the* and *of* must be either both used or both omitted. The two constructions, however, are not always exactly equivalent. For example, the sentences,

We experienced great pleasure in *hearing* John; and, We experienced great pleasure in *the* hearing *of* John, have very different meanings. In the use of *the* and *of* the writer must be guided solely by the sense and harmony of the passage.

1062. A participle may become an attribute by the *implied affirmation* of an intransitive verb; as, The vine lies *withering* on the ground; that is, The vine *is withering* in lying on the ground. The participle has all the modifications of a verb except person and number.

1063. The present active participle of many verbs whose passive form does not express continued action, is used with the verb *be* in a passive sense to denote progressive action; as, The fleet *is building;* The house *is refitting.*

1064. Errors in the use of the Participle.

1065. The use of the *past participle* for the past indicative; as, I *seen* him fall; John *done* that mischief.

1066. The use of the *past indicative* instead of the *past participle* in forming the *past perfect* tense; as, We *have saw* much better times; Mary *had wrote* a letter; They *had* just *went* home.

1067. The use of the past indicative active as a past passive participle; as, He sent a letter *wrote* on parchment.

1068. Ambiguity in the reference of the participle should be carefully avoided; as, He guided the man *eyeing* him closely.

1069. Exercises.—Correct the errors and give the principles violated; parse the words in italics.

Infinitives.—We *expected* to have gone. He declared the enemy to evacuate the fort. It is not right for *to do* so. He was seen pass through the meadow. They thought *to have delayed* us. The governor ordered them go home. The teacher *desired* the boy to carefully *study* his lesson.

Participles.—*By* the reading books we *obtain* valuable information. Hazing of fellow *students* is a barbarous practice. I seen *him* laugh. Standing in the field, the house can be seen. He went to catch a horse, carrying a bridle behind him. The boy had went before we *came*. They *had rode* past the spot before we arrived, calling for assistance. There is no necessity of the boy *knowing* these things.

There is little probability *of George* becoming dishonest. The ancients never *thought* of *steam* becoming a motive power. There is no harm in women *studying* politics. Who is afraid of woman's voting? A well wrote letter is a welcome *missive*. They hid the gold stole from the *governor*. We passed through the *meadow* lately mowed. As when the potent *rod* of Moses *waved* over the river *called* up a cloud of locusts that darkened all the land.

1070. Rule XXI.—The active verbs *bid, dare, feel, hear, let, make, need, see,* and some others of similar signification, take the infinitive after them without the sign *to;* as, They *bade* him *stay* a while; I *heard* him *read;* We *let* them *go,* etc.

1071. The sign *to* is almost always used after the passive forms of these verbs, and sometimes after the active; as, They *dared* the enemy *to cross* the line.

1072. The omission of the sign *to* after *need* is confined entirely to *negative expressions;* as, They *need not go;* She need *work no longer;* They need *to go* once more; She needs *to try* again.

1073. The auxiliary *be* of the infinitive is also omitted after some of the above verbs; as, I heard the lesson [be] assigned.

1074. When *have* denotes necessity, the infinitive following it takes the sign *to;* as, He *had to read.* Otherwise the sign may be omitted; as, Would you *have* us *reject* such an offer? The sign *to* should not be supplied in parsing the infinitive after any of these verbs given in Rule XXI. To use the sign *to* after any of these signs of the infinitive would be a violation of the rule; in other words, false syntax.

1075. Exercises.—Correct the errors and give the principles violated; parse the words in italics.

You may let *him* to go. James needs study his lesson a little more. The army *need* not to entrench. They *bade* him to not stay. We made the *culprit* to go. An energetic man will make his *influence* to be felt. We sometimes see the best of men to be persecuted. Would you have me to deny my own act?

1076. Rule XXII.—A noun or pronoun independent of sentential structure, is in the nominative absolute; as, *Susan,* go to school; *Huntsman,* rest.

1077. Cases in which a noun or pronoun may be in the nominative absolute:

1078. *By direct address;* as, *Henry,* shut the door.

1079. *By exclamation;* as, *Stuff* and *nonsense!*

1080. *By inscription;* as, *Blair's Rhetoric; Gibbon's Rome.*

1081. *By pleonasm;* as, The *boy,* O where was he?

1082. *With a participle;* as, The *dog* barking, the wolf slunk away. In this construction the participle may be understood; as, His prestige [being] such, no foe could hope to conquer.

1083. Use of the nominative absolute.

1084. The nominative absolute with the participle generally has a *temporal* or *causal* force, being equivalent to an abridged phrase or clause; as, The *sun rising,* the snow began to melt; equivalent to, Because the sun *was rising,* the snow began to melt.

1085. The nominative absolute by pleonasm is used for *emphasis;* as, *Babylon,* she is fallen.

1086. All titles of books, headings of pages, inscriptions of names on monuments, coins, and signs; also labels on goods or packages, superscriptions, and signatures of letters, are in the nominative absolute by inscription.

1087. The nominative absolute gives *strength* and *vivacity* to thought. Some other part or parts of speech *may* be supplied with every word used in this construction; but supplying the assumed ellipsis only encumbers speech and misleads the pupil from the true construction and full force of the expression involved.

1088. Exercises.—Correct the errors and give the principles violated; parse the words in italics.

Him *being* young, they led him *astray.* And me, what shall I do? Them *having departed,* deliberation was at an end. *Us* asking naught but peace, they refused to *entertain.* O happy us! what prospects cheer our rugged paths!

1089. Rule XXIII.—Interjections have no dependent construction; as, *Alas!* poor Yorick! *O* Jerusalem!

REMARK.—To this rule there are no exceptions.

1090. Position.—The interjection may be placed before or after a sentence, or between its parts; as, *Heyday!* and what's the matter now? He has gone, *alas!* to return no more; The victory is ours, *hurra! hurra!*

1091. Use.—Words not in the nominative absolute following an interjection, do not depend upon it; as, Alas! poor *me*. Here *me* is in the *objective* used by enallage for the *nominative* absolute by exclamation.

1092. When pronouns follow an interjection, those of the *first person* are usually in the *objective*, those of the *second person* in the *nominative;* as, Ah me! O thou!

1093. Rule XXIV.—The expletive words *it, that, there*, are used to introduce sentences; and the expletive *for*, is used to introduce the infinitive with its objective subject; as, *It* is good *for* us to be here; or, *It* is well that we were there; *That* men could be so base seems impossible; *There* was a great tumult among the people; *For* men to kill each other by thousands, is not considered murder.

1094. Examples under Rule XXIV.

It is necessary to explain the causes of such a delay. *It* is impossible *for* such a thing to occur again. *It* is an outrage on society *that* he should boast of his crimes. *For* men to *act* lies is worse than to *speak* them. *It* is unnecessary *for* us to proceed further on our journey.

> *There's* a magical isle up the river of Time
> Where the softest of airs are playing—
> *There's* a clouldless sky and a tropical clime,
> And a song as sweet as a vesper chime,
> And the Junes with the roses are staying.—TAYLOR.

GENERAL REMARK.—Several of these twenty-four rules for the sake of brevity are somewhat illogical; *e. g.*, Rule XVIII., if fully expressed, will run thus: *A noun or pronoun representing the object of the relation expressed by a preposition, must be in the objective case.*

RULES OF SYNTAX.

1. RULES OF LIMITATION.

797. RULE I.[1]—Articles limit nouns; adjectives, nouns and pronouns.

852. RULE II.—Adverbs limit verbs, adjectives, and other adverbs.

2. RULES OF CONNECTION.

878. RULE III.—Conjunctions connect words, phrases, and sentences.

897. RULE IV.—Prepositions show the relations of their objects to other words.

3. RULES OF AGREEMENT.

910. RULE V.—A pronoun must agree with its antecedent in person, number, and gender.

924. RULE VI.—A pronoun having for its antecedent a collective noun, conveying the idea of plurality, must agree with it in the plural number.

926. RULE VII.—A pronoun having two or more antecedents connected by *and*, must agree with them in the plural number.

932. RULE VIII.—A pronoun having two or more singular antecedents connected by *or* or *nor*, must agree with them in the singular number.

---

[1] The number in arabic preceding each rule refers to the corresponding section which begins the discussion of the rule.

934. RULE IX.—A finite verb must agree with its subject in person and number.

948. RULE X.—A finite verb having for its subject a collective noun, conveying the idea of plurality, must agree with it in the plural number.

952. RULE XI.—A finite verb having two or more subjects connected by *and*, must agree with them in the plural number.

959. RULE XII.—A finite verb having two or more singular subjects connected by *or* or *nor*, must agree with them in the singular number.

963. RULE XIII.—A noun or personal pronoun limiting another noun or pronoun, signifying the same person or thing, is in the same case by apposition.

977. RULE XIV.—The predicate noun or pronoun, with an intransitive or passive verb referring to the same thing as its subject, must be in the same case.

4. RULES OF GOVERNMENT.

986. RULE XV.—A noun or pronoun which is the subject of a finite verb, must be in the nominative case.

999. RULE XVI.—The subject of the infinitive is commonly in the objective case. But when the subject of the infinitive is the same as the subject of the finite verb limited by the infinitive, it is in the nominative case.

REMARK.—This rule is given in this form for the sake of brevity. When the subject of the infinitive is anything else than a noun or pronoun, it is not strictly applicable, since only nouns or pronouns have cases.

1003. RULE XVII.—A noun or pronoun which is the object of a transitive verb in the active voice, must be in the objective case.

1017. **Rule XVIII.**—A noun or pronoun which is the object of a preposition, must be in the objective case.

1031. **Rule XIX.**—A noun or pronoun limiting another noun or pronoun, signifying a different person or thing, is in the possessive case.

1042. **Rule XX.**—Infinitives and participles have the construction of nouns, adjectives, or adverbs.

1070. **Rule XXI.**—The active verbs *bid, dare, feel, hear, let, make, need, see,* and some others of similar signification, take the infinitive after them without the sign *to*.

5. RULES OF INDEPENDENT CONSTRUCTION.

1076. **Rule XXII.**—A noun or pronoun independent of sentential structure, is in the nominative absolute.

1089. **Rule XXIII.**—Interjections have no dependent construction.

1093. **Rule XXIV.**—The expletive words *it, that, there,* are used to introduce sentences; and the expletive *for*, is used to introduce the infinitive, with its objective subject.

PART FOUR.

PROSODY.

1095. Prosody treats of figures of Speech, Punctuation, and Versification.

1096. Figures.—A grammatical figure is a deviation from the ordinary use of a word, either in *spelling, formation, construction,* or *application.*

1097. Classes.—Figures of *Orthography, Etymology, Syntax, Rhetoric.*

FIGURES OF ORTHOGRAPHY.

1098. A figure of **Orthography** is a deviation from the true spelling of a word. The principal figures of Orthography are Mimesis and Archaism.

1099. Mimesis is a ludicrous imitation of mispronunciation, or is the misuse of a word; as,

>And he said that he had heard
>That *Hamericans* spoke *Hinglish;*
>But he deemed it quite *habsurd,*
>Yet he felt the deepest *hinterest*
>In the missionary work.—SAXE.

An oat straw will *suction* up a sherry cobbler in four minutes and a half by the watch.—JOSH BILLINGS.

1100. Archaism is the use of obsolete words or phrases in accordance with ancient usage; as,

>Right *jollie* is *ye tailyor*-man
>As *annie* man may be;
>And all *ye daye* upon *ye benche*
>He worketh *merrilie.*—SAXE.

FIGURES OF ETYMOLOGY.

1101. A figure of **Etymology** is a deviation from the ordinary formation of a word. The principal figures of Etymology are Apheresis, Syncope, Apocope, Prosthesis, Paragoge, Diæresis, Synæresis, Tmesis.

1102. Apheresis is the elision of initial letter or letters of a word; as, 'gan, 'neath, 'bove.

1103. Syncope is the elision of letters in the middle of a word; as, e'en, o'er, sp'rits, lab'ring.

1104. Apocope is the elision of the final letter or letters of a word; as, tho', for though; th', for the; t'oher, for the other.

1105. Prosthesis is prefixing a syllable to a word; as, *a*down, *a*going, *a*running, etc.

1106. Paragoge is the annexing of a final syllable; as, dear*y* for dear; John*ny* for John.

1107. Diæresis is the separation of concurrent vowels into different syllables; as, co-operate, orthoëpy.

1108. Synæresis is the joining of two syllables into one; as, seest, for seëst; loved, for lovĕd.

1109. Tmesis is the inserting of a word between parts of a compound; as, Which way soever he turns; To us ward.

FIGURES OF SYNTAX.

1110. A figure of **Syntax** is a deviation from the ordinary construction of a word. The principal figures of Syntax are Ellipsis, Pleonasm, Hyperbaton, Enallage, Syllepsis.

1111. Ellipsis is the omission of a word or words necessary to complete construction, but not necessary to the meaning of a sentence; as,

The large [man] and the small man; One [friend] of my friends; George was prepared. James was not [prepared]; I went the way you directed me; I went [in] the way [in which] you directed me. There may be an ellipsis of any part of speech, and sometimes whole phrases or clauses are omitted.

1112. Asyndeton is the ellipsis of connectives; as,

I came, [and] I saw, [and] I conquered.

1113. Pleonasm is the use of more words than are necessary to the full construction of a sentence; as,

The villain, is he yet alive? *The gold you sent*, it was squandered.

1114. Polysyndeton is the use of superfluous conjunctions; as,

The lion *and* tiger *and* elephant roam in the jungles of Asia.

1115. Epizeuxis is the emphatic repitition of a word; as,

Break, break, break,
On thy cold gray stones, O sea!—TENNYSON.

1116. Anadiplosis is the use of the same word at the end of one clause or sentence, and at the beginning of the next; as,

He *lives!*
Lives! A father's curse can never die.—COLERIDGE.

1117. Anaphora is the repetition of the same word at the beginning of several successive clauses or sentences; as,

Two strangers meeting at a festival;
Two lovers whispering by an orchard wall;
Two lives bound fast in one with golden ease;
Two graves grass-green beside a gray church tower.
　　　　　　　　　　　　　　　TENNYSON.

1118. Hyperbaton is an inversion of the natural order of the words or phrases in a sentence; as,

Deep on his front engraven,
Deliberation sat, *and public care*.—MILTON.

Hail, holy Light, offspring of Heav'n, first-born,
Or of th' Eternal co-eternal beam,
May I express thee unblamed?—*Id.*

He wanders *earth around.*

1119. Enallage is the use of one part of speech or one modification for another; as,

They fall *successive* and *successive* rise; Poor *me!* Solomon, than *whom* there never was a wiser; *M*ethinks; *M*eseems; There is no danger of *him* falling; It is *me.*

1120. Syllepsis is the agreement of one word with another used in a figurative sense; as,

The *word* was made flesh and dwelt among us, and we beheld *his* glory; The *Earth* is decked in *her* robes of green.

FIGURES OF RHETORIC.

1121. A figure of **Rhetoric** is a deviation from the usual application or signification of words. The following are the most important:

Simile,	Personification,	Anti-climax,
Metaphor,	Apostrophe,	Paralepsis,
Allegory,	Vision,	Litotes,
Metonymy,	Exclamation,	Euphemism,
Synecdoche,	Interrogation,	Catachresis,
Hyperbole,	Antithesis,	Antonomasia,
Irony,	Climax,	Paronomasia.

1122. A **Simile** is a simple comparison; as,

The Assyrian came down *like a wolf on the fold.*—BYRON.

They shall mount up *as eagles.*

1123. Metaphor is the use of a word in a sense different from its original meaning. It expresses the similarity between two objects by applying the name, an attribute, or an action of the one to the other; as,

He was a *stay* to his aged parents; To take up arms against a *sea* of troubles; His sword was a *shield* to the helpless; The *roots* of honor; The *veins* of wealth.

1124. An **Allegory** is a series of metaphors so connected as to form a parable or fable; as,

Thou hast brought a *vine* out of Egypt, etc.—PSALM lxxx: 8.

1125. Metonymy is a change of names by which one word is put for another; thus, the *cause* for the *effect*, the *effect* for the *cause*, a *place* for its inhabitants, a *sign* for the *thing signified*, etc.; as,

He purchased *Milton* and *Pollok;* We supposed the measures of the *government;* that is, *of the men* who administered the government; The army smote the *city;* He wielded the *scepter;* that is, *kingly power*.

1126. Synecdoche puts a *part* for the *whole*, or the *whole* for a *part*, a *species* for the *genus*, or the *genus* for a *species*, etc.; as,

No sheltering *roof* was *nigh;* that is, *house;* Men shall not live by by *bread* alone; that is, *food;* All the *world* looked on indifferently; that is, all who knew of the events.

1127. Hyperbole is extravagant assertion, or a magnifying of the ideas to be conveyed, beyond their proper limits; as,

The fugitives outstripped the wind in their flight; She drowned her woes in a flood of tears.

1128. Irony asserts the *contrary* of the meaning intended to be conveyed; as,

These men are certainly *honest;* they would not accept a *bribe* while their fingers are in the *public treasury*.

1129. Personification ascribes life and intelligence to inanimate or unintelligent beings; as,

Hail to thee, *blithe spirit!*
Bird thou never wert.—SHELLEY.

Come, *Inspiration!* from thy hermit seat.—THOMSON.

All *ye beasts* of the field, come to devour, yea, all *ye beasts* in the forest.—Isaiah lvi: 9.

> Then, too, the *Old Year* dieth,
> And the *forests* utter a moan.—Longfellow.

1130. Apostrophe is an abrupt turning from *narration* to direct address; as,

Death is swallowed up in victory; *Oh death! where is thy sting? Oh grave! where is thy victory?*

> You all did love him once, not without cause;
> What cause withholds you then to mourn for him?
> *Oh judgment! thou art fled to brutish beasts,*
> And men have lost their reason.—Shakespeare.

1131. Vision represents the objects of the imagination as present to the senses; as,

I *see* the rural virtues leave the land; The combat *deepens, on* ye brave.

1132. Exclamation is used to express strong emotion; as,

Oh, what a fall was there, my countrymen!—Shakespeare.

Oh, I could weep my spirit from mine eyes!—*Id.*

1133. Interrogation puts in the form of a question what is meant to be a strong affirmation; as,

Hath the Lord said it? and shall he not do it? Hath he spoken it? and shall he not make it good?

1134. Antithesis contrasts things different or entirely opposite in character; as,

Wit exists by *antipathy;* *Humor* by *sympathy.*—Whipple; *Anoint* a villain and he will prick you; *prick* a villain and he will anoint you.—Holland; The *wicked* flee when no man pursueth; but the *righteous* are as bold as a lion.—Proverbs.

> Say first, for *Heav'n* hides nothing from thy view,
> Nor the deep tract of *Hell.*—Milton.

1135. Climax is a succession of particulars, each more important than the preceding one; as,

What a piece of work is man! how noble in reason! how infinite in faculties! in form and moving, how express and admirable! in action, how like an angel! in apprehension, how like a god.—HAMLET.

1136. Anti-climax is a series of participles, each of which is of less importance than the one preceding it; as,

Have not these monsters taken the hunting-grounds of the red men, killed their game, thrown down their wigwams, stolen their hatchets, and broken their pipes?

1137. Paralepsis is a figure by which a speaker pretends to pass by something which he really mentions; as,

I make no mention of the enemy's bad faith and treachery, nor will I notice his unscrupulous attempts to array the friendly powers against us.

1138. Litotes asserts the truth of a proposition by denying the contrary; as,

The boy was no fool; that is, he was smart enough.

1139. Euphemism is the substitution of a delicate or softened expression for one that is harsh or disagreeable; as,

She has gone to her *final resting-place;* Johnson & Co. have *stopped payment;* His accounts were found somewhat confused, for he was guilty of *embezzlement.*

1140. Catachresis is the using of a word to express something at variance with its true meaning; as,

Brass *coppers;* Or *taste* the *smell* of dairy.—THOMSON.

1141. Antonomasia is the use of a proper name, or the name of an office, rank, profession, etc., instead of a common name; as,

He is a *Hoosier;* My friend is a *Benedict;* The *Queen City.*
Some village *Hampden* that with dauntless breast
 The little tyrant of his fields withstood;
Some mute, inglorious *Milton* here may rest,
 Some *Cromwell,* guiltless of his country's blood.—GRAY.

1142. Paronomasia, or *punning*, is a play upon words, in which the same word is used in different senses, or words of similar sound are placed in antithetic relations to each other; as,

> The *case* is, I've no *case* at all,
> And in *brief*, I've never had a *brief*.—SAXE.
>
> To *curb* his emotions, he sat
> On the *curb*-stone the space of a minute.—*Id.*
>
> They went and *told* the sexton, and
> The sexton *tolled* the bell.—HOOD.

PUNCTUATION.

1143. Punctuation is the use of any other characters than letters or figures to aid the reader in determining the thought of the writer.

1144. Punctuation is of four kinds: *Rhetorical, Etymological, for Reference,* and *for the Printer.*

1145. Rhetorical punctuation is that used to determine sentential structure.

1146. The rhetorical points are:

The Period (.)	The Interrogation (?)
The Comma (,)	The Dash (—)
The Semicolon (;)	Parenthesis ( )
The Colon (:)	Brackets [ ]
The Exclamation (!)	Quotation Marks (" "), (' ').

1147. Rules for Rhetorical Punctuation.—Declarative and imperative sentences making complete and detached sense, require *the period;* as, In every human being there is the wish to ameliorate his own condition. Listen while I tell this story.

When only pauses of similar length and strength occur within a sentence, they require the comma; as, Still, however, the contest continued.

In a series of words, all of the same part of speech, the comma should be used where the conjunction is omitted; as, John, Henry,

James, and Anne will please rise. Bones are, in shape, long, short, flat, and irregular.

Dependent phrases or clauses should be set off by the comma; as, Many phrases, which in their natural or usual order do not require to be punctuated, are, when inverted, set off by a comma from the rest of the sentence.—WILSON.

The ellipsis of a verb should be indicated by a comma; as, You seek wealth, I, honor.

Words in apposition are generally set off by the comma, but appositive words forming a compound term, are not separated; as, General George Washington, the father of his country, was a man of prayer.

When pauses of two distinct degrees of length and strength occur within the same sentence, the weaker requires the comma, the stronger the semicolon; as, The judges were removable at his pleasure; the juries were nominated by the sheriffs; and in almost all the counties of England, the sheriffs were nominated by himself.

Before *as, to wit, namely*, and other words of a similar import, when they introduce examples, specifications, or enumerations, a semicolon should be used; as, Please send me the following articles; namely, A barrel of sugar, a hogshead of molasses, and a sack of coffee.

When pauses of three distinct degrees of length and strength occur within the same sentence, the feeblest requires the comma; the stronger, the semicolon; the strongest, the colon; as,

> Be wise to-day; 't is madness to defer;
> Next day the fatal precedent will plead:
> Thus on, till wisdom is pushed out of life.

Before examples, specifications, and enumerations not introduced by the adverbials *as, namely, to wit*, etc.; before quotations and addresses, and before an additional explanatory remark, the colon should be used; as, The pronominal adjectives are the following: this, that, etc., etc.

A rule is well stated by Pope in his essay on criticism:

> In words, as fashions, the same rule will hold;
> Alike fantastic if too new or old;
> Be not the first by whom the new are tried,
> Nor yet the last to lay the old aside.

Hence has resulted a language capable of expressing, by combinations of its own native words, every shade of meaning required even by the teeming brains of that nation of students: a language uniting infinite diversity of forms with entire simplicity of materials.

Interrogation and Exclamation points are used as their names indicate; as, When are you coming? O Absalom! my son! my son!

Dashes are used to denote broken sense; as, O my full heart!— But should I give it vent, etc.

Parenthetical marks include parentheses; as, Is it possible? are there, on earth (let me not call them men) who lodge a soul immortal in their breasts, etc.

Double quotation marks are used to inclose direct quotations; single quotation marks, included or indirect quotations, and quotations involved in others; as,

"Truth crushed to earth, shall rise again;
The eternal years of God's are her's."

"But Error, wounded, writhes in pain,
And dies amidst her worshipers."

"In consequence of this discovery, he was not only forced to relinquish his hopes of the white staff, but was removed from the direction of the finances to the more dignified but less lucrative and important post of lord president. 'I have seen people kicked down stairs before,' said Halifax, 'but my Lord Rochester is the first person that I ever saw kicked up stairs.'" "He privately admonished him 'that if he would but trust to his own merits, glory and regal power would spontaneously fall to his lot.'"

1148. Etymological punctuation is that used in orthography and orthoepy.

The etymological points are:

The Apostrope (')	Accent, Grave (`)
The Caret (∨)	Accent, Acute (´)
The Diæresis (¨)	Accent, Circumflex (^)
The Macron (¯)	The Hyphen (-)
The Breve (˘)	The Period (.)

The Tilde (˜)

1149. The *apostrophe* is used to indicate the omission of a letter; as, Don't, Brown's, O'clock.

1150. The *caret* is used in the correction of an error of omission in the manuscript; as,

$$\textit{Remember} \overset{\textit{me}}{\wedge} \textit{to all my family.}$$

1151. The *diæresis* is used to separate two vowels which would otherwise form a diphthong; as, Zoölogy.

1152. The *macron* and *breve* are used to indicate the quantity of a syllable; as, Rĕpōrt.

1153. The *tilde* is a Spanish mark placed over *n* to give it the sound of *ny;* as, Cañon, pronounced *canyon*. In English it is only used to indicate certain sounds of vowels.

1154. The *accents* are used to denote the accented syllable in a word, also to indicate inflection of the voice in the delivery of a passage.

1155. The *hyphen* is used to connect the parts of a compound word, also to separate a word into its syllables; as, Wood-house, Punc-tu-a-tion.

1156. The *period* is used to denote abbreviation; as, Mr.; N. Y.

1157. Punctuation **for reference** is that used for referring the reader to the margin or appendix.

The points for reference are:

The Asterisk (*)	The Section (§)
The Obelisk or Dagger (†)	The Paragraph (¶)
The Double Dagger (‡)	The Index (☞)
The Parallels (‖)	The Asterism (⁎) or (⁂).

These marks are often doubled. Letters and figures are also used for reference.

1158. Punctuation **for the printer** is that used by the writer to direct the printer as to the kind of type to be used.

For italics. A word to be printed in italics must be underscored with one line in the manuscript; as,

Less suggests *quantity;* fewer suggests *number*.

For small capitals. A word to be printed in small capitals must be underscored with two lines in the manuscript; as,

Special Rules for Punctuation.

For large capitals. A word to be printed in large capitals must be underscored with three lines in the manuscript; as,

The objective Element.

For headings. Words designed for headings should be underscored with four lines; as,

The Pronoun.

PART FIVE.

ANALYSIS.

1159. Analysis is that division of grammar which treats of the separation of the sentence into its elements, and of determining their relations.

1160. A Sentence is an enunciation of thought, including a verb and its subject.

1161. Classes. — Sentences are classified as to *structure*, and as to the *nature of the proposition.*

AS TO STRUCTURE.

1162. A Simple Sentence is one that contains but one proposition, or one verb and its subject.

EXAMPLES.—Horses run. The bird sped swiftly through the air.

1163. A Complete Sentence is one whose verb is finite.

EXAMPLE.—The news *came* yesterday.

1164. An Abridged Sentence is one whose verb is in the infinitive or participial mode.

EXAMPLES.—We expected *him to go.* *Avoiding the sentries,* the prisoner escaped. An infinitive abridged sentence is always subordinate; a participial *may* be subordinate or independent.

1165. A Complex Sentence is one that contains a complete subordinate sentence as a constituent part.

EXAMPLES.—A fortune *which was gained by years of toil* was lost in a moment of folly.

1166. A **Principal Sentence** is the entire complex sentence with all its subordinate sentences.

1167. A **Subordinate Sentence** is one that is used to modify some word or phrase in another sentence.

EXAMPLE.—Such is the report *which was circulated last night.*

1168. A **Compound Sentence** is one that contains two or more simple or complex sentences of equal rank.

EXAMPLES.—They came and desired an interview. They who were first shall be last, and they who were last shall be first.

1169. A **Partial** compound sentence is one in which either or both of the principal elements are compound.

EXAMPLES.—*John* and *James* went to the city. John *went* to the city yesterday and *returned* to-day. *John* and *James went* to the city yesterday and *returned* to-day.

1170. A **Leading Sentence** is the first simple or complex sentence contained in a compound sentence.

1171. A **Co-ordinate Sentence** is any other sentence than the first, and of equal rank with it in a compound sentence.

AS TO THE NATURE OF THE PROPOSITION.

1172. A **Declarative Sentence** is one that makes an assertion.

EXAMPLE.—The ship arrived yesterday.

1173. An **Imperative Sentence** is one whose verb is in the imperative mode.

EXAMPLE.—Go where glory waits thee.

1174. An **Interrogative Sentence** asks a question.

EXAMPLE.—Did James go to the city?

REMARK.—An interrogative sentence may be subordinate in a declarative or imperative sentence.

EXAMPLES.—I know what he said. I know who broke the window. She asked me where he was going. He told me what he had been doing.

1175. An **Element** is any part of a sentence, including words, phrases, and subordinate sentences.

1176. Classes.—Elements are classified *as to relative importance, structure, relation,* and *bases.*

AS TO IMPORTANCE: PRINCIPAL, SUBORDINATE.

1177. Principal Elements are those without which a sentence can not exist. They are the subject and predicate.

1178. The **Subject** is that of which something is asserted.

EXAMPLES.—*Mary* sings. (It) is sweet *to die for one's country.* That *I should do such a thing* is improbable.

REMARK.—The subject may be any word, phrase, or sentence used as a noun.

1179. Such word, phrase, or sentence is sometimes called a Substantive.

1180. The **Predicate** is the assertion made concerning the subject, and consists of an attribute and copula.

EXAMPLE.—This apple *is sweet.* In this sentence 'is sweet' is the predicate, of which 'sweet' is the attribute and 'is' the copula.

1181. The **Attribute** is that property, quality, characteristic, name, or circumstance asserted or assumed of the subject by the verb.

EXAMPLES.—January is *a cold month.* Water is *a liquid.*

EXPLANATION.—The term 'assert' in this definition is used as signifying affirm, deny, command, interrogate, including every form of finite verb.

1182. The **Copula** is that which joins the attribute to the subject and makes the assertion. It is generally some form of the verb *be.*

EXAMPLES.—Iron *is* heavy. Snow *is* white.

REMARK.—The verb *be* is hence called the *copulative verb*, but the attribute and copula are frequently combined in the same verb; as, The boy reads; that is, he is reading. Those verbs which contain both the attribute and copula are called *attributive verbs*.

1183. Subordinate Elements are all other than the principal elements. They are adjective, adverbial, and objective, also connectives.

REMARK.—In infinitive abridgments the subjective element is also subordinate.

1184. Both Principal and Subordinate elements are subdivided *as to structure, relation,* and *base*.

AS TO STRUCTURE.

1185. A Simple Element is one without modifiers, or one considered apart from its modifiers.

EXAMPLE.—The bird sings sweetly. In this sentence 'sweetly' is a simple adverbial element, unmodified. 'Bird' and 'sings' are also simple elements when considered apart from their modifiers 'the' and 'sweetly.'

1186. A Complex Element is a simple element with its modifiers.

EXAMPLES.—The girls play *very merrily*. In this sentence 'very merrily' is a complex adverbial element limiting 'play,' and 'play very merrily' is the complex predicate; 'play' is the simple predicate. The simple element is also called the *base* of a complex element; 'merrily' is the base of the complex element 'very merrily.'

1187. A Compound Element is one comprising two or more simple or complex elements of equal rank connected by co-ordinate conjunctions expressed or understood.

EXAMPLES.—William writes *smoothly and rapidly*. The work was performed *amidst hardships and great dangers*.

AS TO RELATION.

1188. An **Adjective Element** is one that modifies a noun or pronoun.

EXAMPLES.—He bought a *fine* horse. They *all* went home.

1189. An **Adverbial Element** is one that modifies anything else than a noun or pronoun, an active transitive verb as its object, or an infinitive as its objective subject.

1190. An **Objective Element** is one that is used as the object of a transitive verb in the active voice.

EXAMPLES.—Seals eat *fish*. They came desiring *assistance*.

AS TO THE BASE.

1191. An **Element of the First Class** is one whose base is a single word.

EXAMPLE.—*The frightened* stag ran bounding away.

REMARK.—All the elements in this sentence are of the first class.

1192. An **Element of the Second Class** is one whose base consists of a preposition and its object, or an infinitive.

EXAMPLE.—Henry went *to the city*. We expect *to go immediately*.

REMARK.—The subject of the infinitive modifies the infinitive, an element of the second class, as its base. In the sentence, She desired him to go, 'to go' is the base of the objective element, being the direct object of the transitive verb desired. 'To go,' an element of the second class, is limited by 'him,' a simple subjective element of the first class. The subjective element 'him' in this abridged construction is subordinate, not principal. The subjective element is always principal in complete sentences.

1193. An **Element of the Third Class** is one whose base is a subordinate sentence.

EXAMPLES.—This is the guest *whom we have so long expected.* That *he should have resisted such tyrannical exactions* is perfectly natural. He declared *that he never would fail again.*

1194. A Connective is any word that joins words, phrases, or sentences.

1195. Classes.—*Co-ordinate, Subordinate.*

1196. A Co-ordinate Connective is one that joins sentences or elements of equal rank.

EXAMPLE.—George will go *and* bring a bucket of water.

1197. A Subordinate Connective is one that joins elements of unequal rank.

EXAMPLE.—I adopted that course *because* it seemed best. Subordinate connectives involve three parts of speech; viz., *Conjunctions, relative pronouns,* and *conjunctive adverbs.*

DIAGRAMMED ANALYSIS.

1198. Simple Sentences—Elements of the First and Second Classes.

For the verbal analysis of sentences in this section, see page 228.

1. I write.
2. The merchant fulfilled his contract.

$$1. \begin{cases} I \\ write. \end{cases} \quad 2. \begin{cases} \text{merchant} \mid \text{The} \\ \text{fulfilled} \mid \text{contract.} \mid \text{his} \end{cases}$$

3. He threw the stone almost over the river.

$$3. \begin{cases} He \\ threw \end{cases} \begin{cases} \text{stone} \mid \text{the} \\ \underline{\text{over river.}} \mid \text{the} \\ \quad (\text{almost}) \end{cases}$$

1199. Explanation of the Notation used in Diagramming.—Elements of the same rank stand in the same vertical column. Thus the principal elements stated in the first column; subordinate elements of the first degree in the second, and so on.

A bar (|) is used for separating and subordinating an element; as *the* and *contract* in the second sentence. A brace ({) is used for separating, subordinating, and co-ordinating two or more elements; as, *a* and *diligent* in the fourth sentence. A tie (() is used for unifying the parts of a single element, as in the third, fourth, and fifth sentences under Complex Sentences. A vinculum combined with a half brace (⌐) is used to connect a modifier to the anterior part of a simple element, as in the eighth sentence; the same combination (a vinculum and half brace) is used, provided the whole base of a second class element (a preposition and its object,) is modified by an adverbial element. See Example 3.

The first word of a sentence commences with a capital, wherever it may be situated in the diagram.

4. A man less diligent in business would have failed in the enterprise.

```
       ⎡ man { A
       ⎢       { diligent { less
   4.  ⎢                   { in business
       ⎣ would have failed | in enterprise. | the
```

5. Experience give maxims of utility, but rather bitterly sometimes.

```
       ⎡ Experience
   5.  ⎢           ⎧ maxims | of utility,
       ⎣ gives   { but
                   ⎩ bitterly | rather
                              ⌐ sometimes.
```

EXPLANATION.—Words having no dependent construction are inclosed in parentheses. Such are expletives and independent forms. Words supplied to complete constructions are inclosed in brackets.

6. Follow the path to honor.
7. Will he deny the charges?

```
    { [you]          { the              { he
6.  { Follow | path  { to honor.   7.   { Will deny | charges? | the
```

EXPLANATION.—Interrogative sentences are diagrammed as if declarative, save that the interrogation point is placed at the termination. In imperative sentences the subject is supplied in brackets.

8. To read well is most certainly a valuable accomplishment.

$$8. \begin{cases} \text{To read} \mid \text{well} \\ \text{is accomplishment.} \begin{cases} a \\ \text{valuable} \end{cases} \\ \quad \neg \{ \text{certainly} \mid \text{most} \end{cases}$$

1200. Complex Sentences—Elements of the Third Class.

For the verbal analysis of sentences in this section see page 229.

1. A man who is honest will be respected.
2. The ship which sailed yesterday was laden with salt.

$$1. \begin{bmatrix} \text{man} \begin{cases} A \\ \begin{bmatrix} \text{who} \\ \underline{\text{is}} \text{ honest} \end{bmatrix} \end{cases} \\ \text{will be respected.} \end{bmatrix} \qquad 2. \begin{bmatrix} \text{ship} \begin{cases} \text{The} \\ \begin{bmatrix} \text{which} \\ \underline{\text{sailed}} \mid \text{yesterday} \end{bmatrix} \end{cases} \\ \text{was laden} \mid \text{with salt.} \end{bmatrix}$$

EXPLANATION.—A subordinate sentence is preceded by a tie, to prevent it from appearing as two co-ordinate elements. Words having a double use have a line drawn under them. Such are relative pronouns which are used both as connectives and as pronouns; also conjunctive adverbs which are used both as connectives and as modifiers.

3. The hope that better news would come raised their sinking spirits.

$$3. \begin{bmatrix} \text{hope} \begin{cases} \text{The} \\ \begin{bmatrix} \text{(that)} \\ \text{news} \mid \text{better} \\ \text{would come} \end{bmatrix} \end{cases} \\ \text{raised} \mid \text{spirits.} \begin{cases} \text{their} \\ \text{sinking} \end{cases} \end{bmatrix}$$

4. That the way is difficult is evident.
5. His wish is that we should come early.

$$4. \begin{bmatrix} \begin{bmatrix} \text{(That)} \\ \text{way} \mid \text{the} \\ \text{is difficult} \end{bmatrix} \\ \text{is evident.} \end{bmatrix} \qquad 5. \begin{bmatrix} \text{wish} \mid \text{His} \\ \text{is} \begin{bmatrix} \text{(that)} \\ \text{we} \\ \text{should come} \mid \text{early.} \end{bmatrix} \end{bmatrix}$$

6. The joys that cheer us most in life spring from worthy acts and good deeds which we have performed.

6. {
     joys { The; [that; cheer { us; most; in life }
     spring { from acts; and; [from] deeds }
    } | worthy { we; have performed. | which } | good

7. The faithful dog came when he was called.

8. The army crossed the river where the passage was easiest.

7. {
     dog { The; faithful }
     came { he; was called. | when }
    }

8. {
     army | The
     crossed } river | the; [passage | the; was easiest. | where]
    }

1201. Compound Sentences—Compound Elements.

For the verbal analysis of sentences in this section, see page 231.

1. Frankness is certainly commendable, but impudence is very offensive.

1. {
     { Frankness; is commendable; certainly }
     but
     { impudence; is offensive. | very }
    }

EXPLANATION.—A modifier of the copula is connected with its base by a half brace, as in the above diagram, the copulative verb, in such cases, being underlined with a vinculum.

2. The children came with laugh and shout and filled the halls with glee.

2. {
     { children | The
       came { with laugh; (and); [with] shout }
     }
     { and
       [they]
       filled { halls | the; with glee. }
     }
    }

ANALYSIS.

3. They labored diligently and were rewarded with plenty and prosperity.

```
      ⎧ ⎡They
      ⎪ ⎣labored | diligently
      ⎪     and
   3. ⎨ ⎡[they]
      ⎪ ⎣were rewarded ⎧ with plenty
      ⎪                ⎨     and
      ⎩                ⎩ [with] prosperity.
```

1202. Partial Compound Sentences.

1. The fire blazed and sparkled in the great chimney.

```
      ⎧ fire | The
   1. ⎨ blazed
      ⎪ and      ⎫ in chimney. ⎧ the
      ⎩ sparkled ⎭             ⎩ great
```

2. Disease and death reign supreme in war.

```
      ⎧ Disease
      ⎪   and
   2. ⎨ death
      ⎪ reign ⎧ supreme
      ⎩       ⎩ in war.
```

1203. Sentences Containing Double Relatives, Expletives, and Independent Forms.

For the verbal analysis of sentences in this section, see page 232.

1. It was not surely very wise to begin in that manner.

```
      ⎧ (It)
   1. ⎨ to begin | in manner. | that
      ⎩ was wise | very
              ─────────
              ⎤ not
              ⎦ surely
```

2. I will grant *what* you request.
2. I will grant *the thing which* you request.

```
      ⎧ I                    ⎧ the
   2. ⎨ will grant | thing   ⎨ ⎡you
      ⎩                      ⎩ ⎣request. | which
```

EXPLANATION.—Double relatives are separated into their equivalent parts; the antecedent part belongs in the principal sentence, and the relative part in the subordinate sentence. The equivalent of the double relative is leaded in the expanded form.

3. Heaven and earth! must I remember?
4. The will! the will! we will hear Cæsar's will.

$$\left\{\begin{array}{l}\text{(Heaven and earth!)}\\ \left[\begin{array}{l}\text{I}\\ \text{must remember?}\end{array}\right.\end{array}\right.$$
4. $\left\{\begin{array}{l}\text{(The will! the will!)}\\ \left[\begin{array}{l}\text{we}\\ \text{will hear | will. | Cæsar's}\end{array}\right.\end{array}\right.$

5. It is reported by speculators that diamonds have been discovered in Arizona.

$$\left\{\begin{array}{l}\text{(It) (that)}\\ \left[\begin{array}{l}\text{diamonds}\\ \text{have been discovered | in Arizona.}\end{array}\right.\\ \text{is reported | by speculators}\end{array}\right.$$

1204. Second and Third Class Objective Elements.

For the verbal analysis of sentences in this section, see page 233.

1. I expected to go to the city.
2. He said that the work was already completed.

1. $\left\{\begin{array}{l}\text{I}\\ \text{expected | to go | to city. | the}\end{array}\right.$

2. $\left\{\begin{array}{l}\text{He}\qquad\text{(that)}\\ \text{said |}\left[\begin{array}{l}\text{work | the}\\ \text{was completed. | already}\end{array}\right.\end{array}\right.$

5. They desired him to accept doctrines which he disbelieved.

3. $\left\{\begin{array}{l}\text{They}\\ \text{desired | to accept}\end{array}\right.\left\{\begin{array}{l}\text{him}\\ \text{doctrines |}\end{array}\right.\left[\begin{array}{l}\text{he}\\ \text{disbelieved. | which}\end{array}\right.$

4. She wished him to go immediately.

4. $\left\{\begin{array}{l}\text{She}\\ \text{wished | to go}\end{array}\right.\left\{\begin{array}{l}\text{him}\\ \text{immediately.}\end{array}\right.$

5. I learned many years ago who was the first President.

5. $\left\{\begin{array}{l}\text{I}\\ \text{learned}\end{array}\right.\left\{\begin{array}{l}\text{[at] years}\left\{\begin{array}{l}\text{many}\\ \text{ago = gone by}\end{array}\right.\\ \left[\begin{array}{l}\text{who}\\ \text{was President.}\end{array}\right.\left\{\begin{array}{l}\text{the}\\ \text{first}\end{array}\right.\end{array}\right.$

1205. Predicate Constructions.

For the verbal analysis of sentences in this section, see page 234.

1. He was elected governor.
2. She was named Mary.

REMARK.—These sentences may be analyzed in two ways.

1. { He / was elected | [to be] governor. }

This form may be expanded thus:

1. { He / was elected | } { (that) / he / might be | governor. }   2. { He / was governor / by electing. }

1. { She / was named | [to be] Mary. }   2. { She / was Mary / by naming. }

VERBAL ANALYSIS.

1206. Programme for Verbal Analysis.

1. Describe the sentence { as to structure { Simple, Complex, Compound. } as to proposition { Declarative, Imperative, Interrogative. } }
2. Give the complex subject.
3. Give the simple subject.
4. Describe the modifiers of the subject as to { Structure, Relation, and Base. }
5. Give the base of the modifier and describe its modifiers.
6. Give the complex predicate.
7. Give the simple predicate.
8. Describe the modifiers of the predicate as to { Structure, Relation, and Base. }
9. Give the base of the modifier and describe its modifiers.

1207. Verbal Analysis Exemplified.

EXPLANATION.—The numbers of the sentences in the verbal analysis correspond to those of the same sentences in the diagrammed analysis, and the figures in parentheses correspond to the 'steps' in the programme for verbal analysis given above.

1208. Simple Sentences.

1. (1) 'I write' is a simple declarative sentence, of which (3) 'I' is the simple subject unmodified, and (7) 'write,' the simple predicate unmodified.

2. 'The merchant fulfilled his contract,' (1) is a simple declarative sentence, of which (2) 'the merchant' is the complex subject, of which (3) 'merchant' is the simple subject, (4) modified by 'the,' a simple adjective element of the first class; (6) of which sentence also 'fulfilled his contract' is the complex predicate, of which (7) 'fulfilled' is the simple predicate, modified by (8) 'his contract,' a complex objective element of the first class, of which (9) 'contract,' the base, is modified by 'his,' a simple adjective element of the first class.

4. (1) 'A man less diligent in business would have failed in the enterprise,' is a simple declarative sentence of which (2) 'a man less diligent in business' is the complex subject, of which (3) 'man' is the simple subject, (4) modified by 'a,' a simple adjective element of the first class, and 'less diligent' a complex adjective element of the first class, of which (5) 'diligent,' the base, is modified by 'less,' a simple adverbial element of the first class, and by 'in business,' a simple adverbial element of the second class, of which sentence also (6) 'would have failed in the enterprise,' is the complex predicate, of which (7) 'would have failed' is the simple predicate, (8) modified by 'in the enterprise,' a complex adverbial element of the second class, of which (9) 'enterprise,' the noun of the base, is modified by 'the,' a simple adjective element of the first class.

5. (1) 'Experience gives maxims of utility, but rather bitterly sometimes,' is a simple declarative sentence, of which (3) 'experience' is the simple subject unmodified, of which sentence also (6) 'gives maxims of utility, but rather bitterly sometimes,' is the complex predicate, of which (7) 'gives' is the simple predicate, (8) modified by 'maxims of utility,' a complex objective element of the first class, (9) of which 'maxims,' the base, is modified by 'of utility,' a simple adjective element of the second class. 'Gives' is also (8) modified by 'rather bitterly sometimes,' a complex adverbial element of the first class, (9)

of which 'bitterly,' the base, is modified by 'rather,' a simple adverbial element of the first class. The complex base 'rather bitterly' is modified by 'sometimes,' a simple adverbial element of the first class.

6. (1) 'Follow the path to honor' is a simple imperative sentence, of which (2) 'you,' understood, is the simple subject, unmodified, of which sentence also (6) 'follow the path to honor' is the complex predicate, of which (7) 'follow' is the simple predicate, (8) modified by 'the path to honor,' a complex objective element of the first class, of which (9) 'path,' the base, is modified by 'the,' a simple adjective element of the first class, and by 'to honor,' a simple adjective element of the second class unmodified.

7. (1) 'Will he deny the charges?' is a simple interrogative sentence, of which (3) 'he' is the simple subject unmodified, of which sentence also, (6) 'will deny the charges,' is the complex predicate, of which (7) 'will deny' is the simple predicate, (8) modified by 'the charges,' a complex objective element of the first class, of which 'charges,' the base, is (9) modified by 'the,' a simple adjective element of the first class.

8. (1) 'To read well is most certainly a valuable accomplishment,' is a simple declarative sentence, of which (2) 'to read well' is the complex subject of the second class, of which (3) 'to read' is the simple subject, (4) modified by 'well,' a simple adverbial element of the first class, (6) of which sentence also, 'is most certainly a valuable accomplishment,' is the complex predicate, of which (7) 'is accomplishment' is the simple predicate, of which 'is,' the copula, is modified by 'most certainly,' a complex adverbial element of the first class, of which 'certainly,' the base, is modified by 'most,' a simple adverbial element of the first class, (8) and 'accomplishment,' the attribute, is modified by 'valuable,' a simple adjective element of the first class.

1209. Complex Sentences—Third Class Elements.

1. (1) 'A man who is honest will be respected,' is a complex declarative sentence, of which (2) 'a man who is honest,' is the complex subject, of which (3) 'man' is the simple subject, (4) modified by 'a,' a simple adjective element of the first class, and by 'who is honest,' a simple adjective element of the third class. It is also a simple declarative subordinate sentence, of which (3) 'who' is the simple subject, unmodified, also the subordinate connective, and 'is honest' the simple predicate. 'Will be respected' is the simple predicate of the principal sentence, unmodified.

3. (1) 'The hope that better news would come raised their sinking spirits,' is a complex declarative sentence, of which (2) 'the hope that better news would come,' is the complex subject, (3) of which 'hope' is the simple subject, (4) modified by 'the,' a simple adjective element of the first class, and by 'that better news would come,' a simple adjective element of the third class. It is also a simple declarative subordinate sentence, of which (2) 'better news' is the complex subject, and (7) 'would come,' the simple predicate unmodified. 'That' is a connective. The predicate of the principal sentence presents no difficulties.

4. (1) 'That the way is difficult is evident,' is a complex declarative sentence, of (3) 'that the way is difficult' is the simple subject of the third class, also a simple declarative subordinate sentence, of which 'that' is an introductory expletive, and (3) 'way,' the simple subject modified, etc.; (7) 'is difficult' is the simple predicate unmodified, 'is' being the copula, 'difficult' the attribute. 'Is evident' is the simple predicate of the principal sentence.

5. (1) 'His wish is that they should improve,' is a complex declarative sentence, of which (2) 'his wish' is the complex subject, etc., and (6) 'is that they should improve' is the simple predicate, of which 'is' is the copula, and 'that they should improve' the attribute of the third class. It is also a simple declarative subordinate sentence, of which (3) 'they' is the simple subject unmodified, and (7) 'should improve,' the simple predicate unmodified; 'that' is an introductory expletive.

6. (1) 'The joys that cheer us most in life spring from worthy acts and good deeds which we have performed,' is a complex declarative sentence, of which (2) 'the joys that cheer us most in life,' is the complex subject, of which (3) 'joys' is the simple subject, (4) modified by 'the,' a simple adjective element of the first class, and by 'that cheer us most in life,' a simple adjective element of the third class; it is also a simple, declarative, subordinate sentence, of which (3) 'that' is the connective and simple subject unmodified, (6) of which sentence also, 'cheer us most in life' is the complex predicate, of which (7) 'cheer' is the simple predicate, (8) modified by 'us,' a simple objective element of the first class, and by 'most,' a simple adverbial element of the first class; also by 'in life,' a simple adverbial element of the second class, of which sentence also (6) 'spring from worthy acts and good deeds which we have performed' is the complex predicate, of which (7) 'spring' is the simple predicate, (8) modified by 'from worthy acts and good deeds which we have performed,' a com-

pound adverbial element of the second class, of which (9) 'acts,' one noun of the base, is modified by 'worthy,' a simple adjective element of the first class, and 'deeds,' the other noun of the base, is modified by 'good,' a simple adjective element of the first class; 'acts' and 'deeds' are also modified by 'which we have performed,' a simple adjective element of the third class. It is also a simple declarative subordinate sentence, of which (3) 'we' is the simple subject unmodified, of which sentence also (6) 'have performed which' is the complex predicate, of which (7) 'have performed' is the simple predicate, (9) modified by 'which,' a simple objective element of the first class, also the connective of the subordinate sentence.

7. (1) 'The faithful dog came when he was called,' is a complex declarative sentence, of which (2) 'the faithful dog' is the complex subject, etc., of which sentence also (6) 'came when he was called' is the complex predicate, of which (7) 'came' is the simple predicate, (8) modified by 'when he was called,' a simple adverbial element of the third class; (1) 'when he was called' is also a simple declarative subordinate sentence, of which (3) 'he' is the simple subject, and (7) 'was called' the simple predicate (8) modified by 'when,' a simple adverbial element of the first class, also the connective of the subordinate sentence.

1210. Compound Sentences—Compound Elements.

1. (1) 'Frankness is certainly commendable, but impudence is very offensive,' is a compound declarative sentence, of which 'frankness is certainly commendable' is the leading sentence, of which (3) 'frankness' is the simple subject unmodified, of which sentence also (6) 'is certainly commendable' is the complex predicate, of which 'is,' the copula, is modified by 'certainly,' a simple adverbial element of the first class; 'but impudence is very offensive' is the co-ordinate declarative sentence, of which 'but' is the co-ordinate connective, and (3) 'impudence' the simple subject unmodified, of which sentence also (6) 'is very offensive' is the complex predicate, of which (7) 'is offensive' is the simple predicate, (8) of which 'offensive,' the attribute, is modified by 'very,' a simple adverbial element of the first class.

2. (1) 'The children came with laugh and shout, and filled the halls with glee,' is a compound declarative sentence, of which 'the children came with laugh and shout' is the leading declarative sentence, of which (2) 'the children' is the complex subject, etc., of which sentence also (6) 'came with laugh and shout' is the complex pred-

icate, of which (7) 'came' is the simple predicate, (8) modified by 'with laugh and [with] shout,' a compound adverbial element of the second class, connected by 'and,' a co-ordinate connective. (1) 'And [they] filled the halls with glee,' is the co-ordinate declarative sentence, of which 'and' is the co-ordinate connective, and (3) 'they,' understood, the simple subject. The analysis of the predicate presents no difficulties.

1211. Partial Compound Sentences.

1. (1) 'The fire blazed and sparkled in the great chimney,' is a partial compound sentence, of which (2) 'the fire' is the complex subject, of which (3) 'fire' is the simple subject, (4) modified by 'the,' a simple adjective element of the first class, of which sentence also (6) 'blazed and sparkled in the great chimney,' is the complex compound predicate, of which (7) 'blazed and sparkled' is the compound predicate, (8) modified by 'in the great chimney,' a complex adverbial element of the second class, of which (9) 'chimney,' the noun of the base, is modified by 'the,' and 'great,' two simple adjective elements of the first class.

1212. Expletives — Double Relatives — Independent Forms.

1. (1) 'It was not surely very wise to begin in that manner,' is a simple declarative sentence, of which (2) 'it' is an introductory expletive, and 'to begin in that manner' the complex subject of the second class, of which (3) 'to begin' is the simple subject, (4) modified by 'in that manner,' a complex adverbial element of the second class, of which (5) 'manner,' the noun of the base, is modified by 'that,' a simple adjective element of the first class, of which sentence also (6) 'was not surely very wise' is the complex predicate, of which (7) 'was wise' is the simple predicate, of which (8) 'was,' the copula, is modified by 'not surely,' a complex adverbial element of the first class, of which 'not,' the base, is modified by 'surely,' a simple adverbial element of the first class; (8) 'wise,' the attribute, is modified by 'very,' a simple adverbial element of the first class.

2. (1) 'I will grant what you request,' is a complex declarative sentence, of which (3) 'I' is the simple subject unmodified, of which sentence also (6) 'will grant what you request' is the complex predicate, of which (7) 'will grant' is the simple predicate, (8) modified by 'what you request,' a complex objective element of the first class:

it is equivalent to, 'the thing which you request,' of which (8) 'thing,' the antecedent part, modifies 'will grant' as an objective element of the first class, (9) and is modified by 'which you request,' a simple adjective element of the third class. (1) It is also a simple declarative subordinate sentence, of which (3) 'you' is the simple subject unmodified, of which sentence also (6) 'request which' is the complex predicate, of which (7) 'request' is the simple predicate, (8) modified by 'which,' a simple objective element of the first class, also the subordinate connective.

3. (1) 'Heaven and earth! must I remember,' is a simple interrogative sentence, of which 'heaven and earth' are independent forms of exclamation; (3) 'I' is the simple subject unmodified, and (7) 'must remember' the simple predicate unmodified.

1213. Second and Third Class Objective Elements.

1. (1) 'I expected to go to the city,' is a simple declarative sentence, of which (3) 'I' is the simple subject unmodified, of which sentence also (6) 'expected to go to the city' is the complex predicate, of which (7) 'expected' is the simple predicate, (8) modified by 'to go to the city,' a complex objective element of the second class, of which (9) 'to go,' the infinitive base, is modified by 'to the city,' a complex adverbial element of the second class, of which 'city,' the noun of the base, is modified by 'the,' a simple adjective element of the first class.

3. (1) 'They desired him to accept doctrines which he disbelieved,' is a complex declarative sentence, of which (3) 'they' is the simple subject unmodified, of which sentence also (6) 'desired' and all that follows is the complex predicate, of which (7) 'desired' is the simple predicate, modified by 'him to accept doctrines which he disbelieved,' a complex objective element of the second class, of which (8) 'to accept,' the infinitive base, is modified by 'him,' a simple subjective element of the first class, and by 'doctrines which he disbelieved,' a complex objective element of the first class, of which 'doctrines,' the base, (9) is modified by 'which he disbelieved,' a simple adjective element of the third class, also a simple declarative subordinate sentence, of which 'he' is the simple subject unmodified, of which sentence also (6) 'disbelieved which' is the complex predicate, (7) of which 'disbelieved' is the simple predicate, (8) modified by 'which,' a simple objective element of the first class, also the connective of the subordinate sentence.

H. Gram.—20.

5. 'I learned many years ago who was the first President,' is a complex declarative sentence, of which (3) 'I' is the simple subject unmodified, of which sentence also (6) 'learned' and all that follows is the complex predicate, of which (7) 'learned' is the simple predicate, (8) modified by '[at] many years ago,' a complex adverbial element of the second class, of which 'years,' the noun of the base, (9) is modified by 'many' and 'ago,' two simple adjective elements of the first class; 'learned' is also (8) modified by 'who was the first President,' a simple objective element of the third class; it is also a simple interrogative sentence, of which 'who' is the simple subject, an interrogative, of which sentence also (6) 'was the first President' is the complex predicate, (7) of which 'was President' is the simple predicate, of which 'President,' the attribute, is (8) modified by 'the' and 'first,' two simple adjective elements of the first class.

1214. Peculiar Predicate Constructions.

1. He was elected governor.

1′. { He
was elected | [to be] governor.

1″. { He
was governor
⎯⎯⎯⎯⎯
{ by electing = elected.

REMARK.—Sentences of this character *seem* to contain two attributes, but they may be analyzed according to both methods given in the diagrams, considering either the participial form of the verb the attribute, and the predicate noun the attribute of a subordinate adverbial sentence, or the predicate noun the attribute, and the participial form in the passive as modifying the copula, as shown by its equivalent as given in the second method of diagramming.

1. 'He was elected governor,' is a simple declarative sentence, of which (3) 'he' is the simple subject unmodified, of which sentence also 'was elected [to be] governor' is the complex predicate, of which (7) 'was elected' is the simple predicate, (8) modified by '[to be] governor,' a simple adverbial element of the second class; (1) also an abridged simple declarative sentence, which, expanded, becomes 'that he should be governor,' of which 'that' is the subordinate connective, and (3) 'he' the simple subject, of which sentence also (7) 'should be governor' is the simple predicate, of which 'should be' is the copula and 'governor' the attribute. The second method

makes the first sentence equivalent to, 'He was governor by electing.' Thus 'governor' is put in the predicate after 'was,' meaning the same thing as the subject, and 'elected' is resolved into the equivalent adverbial phrase 'by electing.' (1) 'He was governor by electing,' is a simple declarative sentence, of which (3) 'he' is the simple subject unmodified, of which sentence also (6) 'was governor by electing' is the complex predicate, of which (7) 'was governor' is the simple predicate, of which (8) 'was,' the copula, is modified by 'by electing,' a simple adverbial element of the second class; 'governor' is the attribute unmodified.

1215. "**Grammatical and Logical Subjects**"—"**Indirect Objects.**"

1. He gave me an apple.
2. They awarded him a diploma.
3. She taught me grammar.

1216. Explanations.—The *Logical Subject* is the real or true subject of the action of state or being expressed by the verb, and is generally the grammatical subject also.

1217. The *Grammatical Subject* is that subject with which the verb agrees; it is sometimes only the apparent subject, in consequence of an illogical arrangement of the sentence, sanctioned by good usage.

REMARK.—It is an incorrect use of terms to call the simple subject of a sentence the grammatical subject, and the complex subject the logical, since both the simple and complex subjects are generally both equally grammatical and logical.

In the sentence, 'He gave me an apple,' 'he' is both the logical and grammatical subject; but when the construction is changed from the active to the passive, as, *An apple was given me by him*, the grammatical subject is changed, being 'apple,' which is the logical or true subject also. This other passive form is also very common. 'I was given an apple.' Here 'I' is the grammatical subject, but evidently not the logical or true subject, since 'I' does not represent the receiver of the action. This last expression is therefore rejected by most grammarians, but is in my opinion warranted by sufficient usage. Even Dr. Bullions, though rejecting this arrangement as 'loose' and 'illogical,' in his critical discussions uses the same form of expression repeatedly.

1218. The second sentence may be diagrammed in three ways. Thus:

$$2'. \quad \left[\begin{array}{l} \text{They} \\ \text{awarded} \end{array} \left\{ \begin{array}{l} \text{[to] him} \\ \text{diploma | a.} \end{array} \right\} \right. \text{(actively.)}$$

$$2''. \quad \left[\begin{array}{l} \text{diploma | A} \\ \text{was awarded} \end{array} \left\{ \begin{array}{l} \text{[to] him} \\ \text{by them.} \end{array} \right. \right\}$$

$$2'''. \quad \left[\begin{array}{l} \text{He} \\ \text{was awarded} \end{array} \left\{ \begin{array}{l} \text{[with] diploma | a} \\ \text{by them.} \end{array} \right. \right\} \text{(passively.)}$$

In the active sentence, 'they' is both the *logical* and *grammatical* subject. In the second diagram, 'diploma' is the grammatical and logical subject. In the third diagram, 'he' is the grammatical subject, while the true *object* of the active verb 'diploma' (which ought logically to become the subject of the passive—see Sec. 1010) has become an adverbial element. The first and third sentences are diagrammed thus:

$$1'. \quad \left[\begin{array}{l} \text{He} \\ \text{gave} \end{array} \left\{ \begin{array}{l} \text{[to] me} \\ \text{apple. | an} \end{array} \right. \right.$$

$$1''. \quad \left[\begin{array}{l} \text{apple | An} \\ \text{was given} \end{array} \left\{ \begin{array}{l} \text{[to] me} \\ \text{by him.} \end{array} \right. \right.$$

$$1'''. \quad \left[\begin{array}{l} \text{I} \\ \text{was given} \end{array} \left\{ \begin{array}{l} \text{[with] apple | an} \\ \text{by him.} \end{array} \right. \right.$$

$$3'. \quad \left[\begin{array}{l} \text{She} \\ \text{taught} \end{array} \left\{ \begin{array}{l} \text{grammar} \\ \text{[to] me.} \end{array} \right. \right.$$

$$3''. \quad \left[\begin{array}{l} \text{Grammar} \\ \text{was taught} \end{array} \left\{ \begin{array}{l} \text{[to] me} \\ \text{by her.} \end{array} \right. \right.$$

$$3'''. \quad \left[\begin{array}{l} \text{I} \\ \text{was taught} \end{array} \left\{ \begin{array}{l} \text{[in] grammar} \\ \text{by her.} \end{array} \right. \right.$$

REMARK.—Sentences of this character *seem*, at first, to have two objects; but the diagrams plainly show one of them to be an adverbial element. There can be no indirect object, it is a contradiction in terms. The word *object* signifies placed against or opposed, not on *one side* or indirectly, but *directly*. This modifier, then, that some grammarians call the indirect object, is always very plainly an adverbial element. There is no special objection, however, to calling the object of a preposition the 'remote object' of a verb.

ABRIDGMENT.

1219. Abridgment is that part of analysis which treats of contracting sentences by rejecting connectives, suppressing subjects of verbs, and changing the verbs from the finite modes into infinitives and participles.

1220. An **Abridged Sentence** is one whose verb is an infinitive or participle; as,

They came *to see the city;* We had not thought *of his coming so soon.*

1221. Classes.—As to *Function*—As to *Structure.*

1222. As to *Function,* abridged sentences are *substantive, adjective,* and *adverbial.*

1223. A **Substantive** abridged sentence is one that is used as the subject or object of a verb; as,

To play is pleasant; They expected *him to deliver an address.*

1224. An **Adjective** abridged sentence is one that modifies a noun or pronoun; as,

A man *acting dishonestly* will fail in business.

1225. An **Adverbial** abridged sentence is one that fills the office of an adverb; as,

They came *to ask a favor.*

1226. As to *Structure* abridged sentences are divided into *infinitive, participial,* and *absolute.*

1227. An **Infinitive** abridged sentence is one whose leading word of construction is an infinitive.

1228. A **Participial** abridged sentence is one whose leading word of construction is a participle.

1229. An **Absolute** abridged sentence is one whose leading word of construction is the nominative case absolute.

1230. Method of Abridgment.—Remove the connective, change the subordinate finite verb to an infinitive or participle, and suppress its subject, provided it is the same as the subject or object of the finite verb on which the infinitive depends.

1231. Subject of the Subordinate Clause.

1232. When the subject of the subordinate sentence is different from the subject or object of the leading sentence, the subject of the abridged sentence may be in the *nominative, possessive,* or *objective* case. Thus:

1233. In the nominative; as, When night comes, animated nature seeks repose. Equivalent to, *Night coming*, animated nature seeks repose.

1234. In the possessive; as, I was not aware that he had left. Equivalent to, I was not aware of *his* leaving.

1235. In the objective; as, I desired that he might read. Equivalent to, I desired *him* to read.

1236. Attribute of the Subordinate Clause.

1237. The attribute of the predicate in the abridged clause is put in the objective when the subject is in the objective; as, We thought it to be *them*.

1238. The attribute of the abridged clause is in the nominative when its subject is in the nominative or possessive; as, *John*, being a boy, was unable to labor continuously; *His* being a *student* was no reason for *his* being a *savage*.

1239. Analysis of Abridged Sentences.

1240. Order of Analysis.—1. Analyze in the abridged form. 2. Expand the sentence by supplying the connective and subject, and changing the verb to a finite mode. 3. Analyze in the complete form.

In diagramming give both forms. Thus:

1. I wish to read law.
2. They detected his dissembling.

1. { I
   wish | to read | law.

1″. I wish that I could read law.

1″. $\left\{\begin{array}{l}\text{I}\\\text{wish}\end{array}\right.\left\{\begin{array}{l}\text{(that)}\\\text{I}\\\text{could read | law.}\end{array}\right.$

2. $\left\{\begin{array}{l}\text{They}\\\text{detected | dissembling. | his}\end{array}\right.$

2″. They detected that he dissembled.

2″. $\left\{\begin{array}{l}\text{They}\\\text{detected}\end{array}\right.\left\{\begin{array}{l}\text{(that)}\\\text{he}\\\text{dissembled.}\end{array}\right.$

MISCELLANEOUS EXAMPLES FOR PARSING AND ANALYSIS.

1241. 1. Horses run. Girls study.
2. Great men inspire us.
3. Such beauty is transitory.
4. A competence is doubtless desirable.
5. Genius is enthusiasm.
6. Talent is perseverance.
7. Industry is the primal blessing.
8. The love of work is the love of truth.
9. Laziness is a living lie.
10. A man of ideas is a man of study and observation.
11. A successful man controls circumstances, and is not controlled by them.
12. A little mind attends to several things at once.
13. A great mind gives itself solely to one thing at a time.
14. Knowledge may be weakness.
15. Power is knowledge put in practice.
16. A man should reflect on his life.
17. He descended to the luxuriant plain.
18. The natural world contains the most beautiful scenery.
19. Man has always worshiped something.
20. Our real wants are not numerous.
21. Pride goes before a fall.
22. I can not go to the city to-day.
23. The greatest men very frequently have striking peculiarities.
24. He will be with you in prosperity and adversity.
25. A woman less vigorous in intellect would not have succeeded at all in so difficult an enterprise.
26. English literature is no common debtor to the Bible.
27. The Puritans were a brave, wise, and useful body of men.
28. No vicious family regards the Sabbath.
29. Where was there a braver army than that under Julius Cæsar?
30. The style of Bunyan is delightful to every reader.

31. The same God is the author of the visible and invisible world.
32. He who stands up and fights for the right, will always be abused.
33. To debate with your conscience is not wise.
34. That you are able to find gross errors within the church, does not justify you in condemning it.
35. It is no easy task to learn to play well upon an instrument.
36. It is not safe for a young man to spend all he can earn.
37. Christianity does not teach that it is wrong to enjoy the good things of this life.
38. It is evident to all that the mind of the judge was biased.
39. Why will day never come?
40. Can we expect a useful life without earnest preparation?
41. Where shall we look for aid in case of his failure to help us?
42. Bring all thy tithes into the store-house.
43. A stranger who was weary stopped at our gate.
44. An idea which was pressing its way onward he could not withstand.
45. An employer prefers an employe whom he can trust out of sight.
46. Where is the man who will deny it?
47. What possesses the boy that he should act so?
48. That I was wrong is evident.
49. I am confident that you will soon see it as I do.
50. Be careful that you attend to my directions.
51. If you come early you will get the best seat.
52. The truly great man does not scorn little acts of kindness.
53. It is necessary for you to come early.
54. It is thought that he will succeed beyond all precedent.
55. It is enough for him to say so.
56. It is imprudent for us all to be absent from the house to-night.
57. What will it avail that he promises aid?
58. Let it be understood that I am unchangeably opposed to the measure.
59. It is warm enough to melt the snow.
60. It is ten o'clock now.
61. It is Jane. Is it they?
62. Was it you? Is it possible that it was you that knocked?
63. Harley sat down on a large stone, by the way-side, to take a pebble from his shoe, when he saw, at some distance, a beggar approaching him.

64. All that the wisdom of the proud can teach is, to be stubborn or sullen under misfortunes.—GOLDSMITH.

65. The most covetous of mankind would, with small exultation, I presume, accept riches of this kind on these terms.—RUSKIN.

66. Political economy consists simply in the production, preservation, and distribution, at fittest time and place, of useful or pleasurable things.—*Id.*

67. The perfect liberty of any faculty of the mind lies within the range of its office.—HOLLAND.

68. The mind that has become a treasure house of truth and beauty speaks a world into existence with every utterance.—*Id.*

69. It is not difficult to conceive, however, that for many reasons a man writes much better than he lives.—JOHNSON.

70. When we consider the liberty of man, we see that he is free to accept or reject the life that has been given to him.—BARING-GOULD.

71. The traveler stopped to ask what was the matter.

72. The witness pretended to tell what he knew about the matter.

73.   Said he, "They're only pegs,
   But there's as wooden members quite
   As represent my legs."—HOOD.

74. He asked who broke the window.

75. Well did they know who was the first aggressor.

76. Is it not sweet to think, hereafter,
   When the spirit leaves this sphere,
   Love, with deathless wings, shall waft her
   To those she long hath mourned for here?—MOORE.

77.   Not only around our infancy
   Doth heaven with all its splendors lie;
   Daily with souls that cringe and plot
   We Sinais climb and know it not.—LOWELL.

78. I know where the timid fawn abides
   In the depths of the shaded dell,
   Where the leaves are broad and the thicket hides
   With its many stems and its tangled sides,
   From the eye of the hunter well.—BRYANT.

79.   Other creature here,
   Beast, bird, insect, or worm, durst enter none.—MILTON.

80. I wish it to be distinctly understood that I know nothing of his whereabouts.

81. He declared it to be his opinion that the man only claimed what was his own.

82. It should always be borne in mind that, in order to the intelligent study of grammar, whose office it is to teach "to speak and write correctly," pupils must be constantly exercised in this practical use, that the principles which the grammar teaches may be practically exemplified, and power be gained in their application.—BULLIONS' GRAMMAR.

83. As it is the business of the philosopher not to *make* a law of nature, or to *dictate* how her operations should be performed, but by close observation to *ascertain what those laws are*, and to state them for the information of others; so the business of the grammarian is, not to *make* the laws of the language, for *language is before grammar*, but to observe and note those principles, and forms, and modes of speech, by which men are accustomed to express their sentiments, and to arrange the results of his observation into a system of rules for the guidance and assistance of others.—*Id.*

84. For thee, who, mindful of the unhonored dead,
    Dost in these lines their artless tale relate,
If chance, by lonely contemplation led,
    Some kindred spirit shall inquire thy fate,

85. Haply some hoary-headed swain may say,
    "Oft have we seen him at the peep of dawn,
Brushing, with hasty step, the dews away,
    To meet the sun upon the upland lawn."—GRAY.

86.   When thoughts
Of the last bitter hour, come like a blight
Over thy spirit, and sad images
Of the stern agony, and shroud, and pall,
And breathless darkness, and the narrow house,
Make thee to shudder and grow sick at heart;
Go forth into the open sky, and list
To nature's teaching, while from all around
Comes a still voice . . . . .

87.   The hills,
Rock-ribbed, and ancient as the sun; the vales,
Stretching in pensive quietness between

>   The venerable woods; rivers that move
>   In majesty, and the complaining brooks
>   That make the meadows green; and, poured round all,
>   Old ocean's gray and melancholy waste,
>   Are but the solemn decorations all
>   Of the great tomb of man.   .   .   .   .

88. Winding along, at break of day,
        And armed with helm and spears,
     Along the martyr's rocky way,
        A king comes, with his peers;
     Unto the eye a splendid sight,
     Making the air all richly bright,
        Seen flashing through the trees;
     But to the heart a scene of blight,
        Sadder than death were these.—MISS JEWSBURY.

89. It was not what I stated, if he asserted it to be his opinion that I was mistaken, in declaring it to be mine, that John Smith is involved in irretrievable ruin.

90. O woman! lovely woman! Nature made thee
     To temper man; we had been brutes without you.
     Angels are painted fair to look like you;
     There's in you all that we believe of heaven,
     Amazing brightness, purity, and truth,
     Eternal joy, and everlasting love.—OTWAY.

91. Misses, the tale that I relate,
        This lesson seems to carry;
     Choose not alone a proper mate,
        But proper time to marry.—COWPER.

92. There is in souls a sympathy with sounds;
     And as the mind is pitched, the ear is pleased
     With melting airs, or martial, brisk, or grave;
     Some chord in unison with what we hear
     Is touched within us and the heart replies.
     How soft the music of those village bells,
     Falling at intervals upon the ear
     In cadence sweet!—COWPER.

93. Me, let the tender office long engage
     To rock the cradle of reposing age,
     With lenient arts extend a mother's breath,

>   Make languor smile, and smooth the bed of death;
>   Explore the thought, explain the asking eye,
>   And keep a while one parent from the sky.—POPE.

94.
>   Teach me to feel another's woe,
>   To hide the fault I see;
>   That mercy I to others show,
>   That mercy show to me.—*Id.*

95.
>   How loved, how honored once avails thee not,
>   To whom related, or by whom begot;
>   A heap of dust alone remains of thee;
>   'Tis all thou art and all the proud shall be!—*Id.*

96.
>   Vice is a monster of so frightful mien,
>   As, to be hated, needs but to be seen;
>   Yet seen too oft, familiar with her face,
>   We first endure, then pity, then embrace.—*Id.*

97. To be or not to be, that's the question. It is better to be a king and die than to live and be a prince. Whatever thy hand findeth to do, do it with thy might. We have to do it. Lycurgus, the Spartan lawgiver, is said to have been born in the nine hundred and twenty-sixth year before Christ. Romulus is said to have founded Rome.—SELECTED FROM BULLIONS' GRAMMAR.

98. *Simonides being asked* by Dionysius *what* God was, desired a day's time to consider of it before he made his reply. . . . .

99. I shall only add, under this head, *that* when we have raised our notion of this infinite Being *as* high *as it* is possible for the *mind* of man *to go*, it will fall infinitely short of *what* he really is. . .

100. This would imprint in our minds such a constant and uninterrupted awe and veneration *as that which* I am here recommending.—ADDISON.

101. I was quickly distinguished *as a wit* by the ladies, a *species* of beings only *heard of* at the university, *whom* I had no sooner the *happiness of approaching* than I devoted all my faculties to the ambition of pleasing them. . . . .

102. He that hopes to be conceived *as* a wit in female assemblies, should have a form neither so amiable as *to strike* with admiration, nor so coarse as *to raise* disgust; with an understanding too feeble *to be dreaded*, and too forcible to be despised.—JOHNSON.

103. There were betwixt the trees, growing naturally on their own roots, some stakes *fixed* in the earth, which, with the trees, were in-

terwoven with ropes, *made* of heath and birch twigs, up to the top of the Cage, *it* being of a round or rather oval shape.—SCOTT.

104. *It* is difficult for the most cool-headed impostor long to personate an enthusiast, without in some degree believing *what* he is so eager *to have believed.*—*Id.*

105. I was born to a small hereditary estate, which, according to the tradition of the village where it lies, was bounded by the same hedges and ditches in William the Conqueror's time *that* it is at present.—ADDISON.

106. Whether this might proceed from a lawsuit which was then depending in the family, or my father's *being* a *justice* of the peace, I can not determine.—*Id.*

107. Cicero remarks that not to know *what* has been transacted in former times, is to continue always a child.—JOHNSON.

108. From beneath the flap of an enormous pocket of a *soiled* vest of embossed silk, heavily *ornamented* with *tarnished* silver lace, *projected* an instrument [a tuning fork], which, from *being seen* in such martial company, might have been easily mistaken for some mischievous and unknown implement of war.—COOPER.

109. Who can flatter himself that the study of a long life would have enabled *him to discover* the principles of geometry, when he sees *them* yet *unknown* to so many nations, whom he can not suppose less liberally *endowed* with natural reason than the *Egyptians* or Grecians.—JOHNSON.

110. O *for* a glance of heavenly day,
    To take this stubborn heart away;
    And thaw, with beams of love divine,
    This heart, this frozen *heart of mine.*—HART.

111. Let then, O God! thy *servant dare*
    Thy truth in all its power *to tell;*
    Unmask the priestly thieves, and tear
    The Bible from the grasp of hell!—WHITTIER.

112. High *Heaven*, that heard the solemn vow,
    That vow *renewed* shall daily hear,
    Till in life's latest hour I bow,
    And bless in death a bond so dear.—DODDRIDGE.

113.   And the plain *ox,*
    That harmless, honest, guileless *animal,*
    In *what* has he offended?—THOMPSON.

EXAMPLES FOR PARSING AND ANALYSIS. 247

114. *Long* in its dim recesses *pines* the spirit,
 '*Wildered* and dark, despairingly alone;
 Though many a shape of beauty wander near it,
  And many a wild and half-remembered tone
 Tremble from the divine abyss to cheer it,
  Yet still it knows that there is only one
 Before whom it can kneel and *tribute* bring,
 At *once* a happy *vassal* and a *King.*—LOWELL.

115. Let *cares like* a wild *deluge* come,
  Let *storms* of sorrow fall,—
 So I *but* safely reach my home,
  My God, my heaven, my all.—WATTS.

116. Now night her course began, and over Heaven
 Inducing darkness, grateful *truce imposed,*
 And silence on the odious din of war.—MILTON.

117. *Behind* us at our evening meal
  The gray bird ate his fill;
 Swung downward by a single claw,
  He *wiped* his hookéd bill.

118. *What* if God, willing to shew his wrath, and to make his *power known, endured* with much long-suffering the vessels of wrath *fitted* to destruction?—ROM. ix: 22.

119. And let this feeble *body fail,*
  And let it faint or die;
 My soul shall quit this mournful vale,
  And soar to worlds on high.

120. O *what* are all my sufferings here,
  If, *Lord,* thou count *me meet*
 With *that* enraptured host *to appear,*
  And worship at thy feet!—C. WESLEY.

121. And when the barbarians saw the venomous *beast hang* on his hand, they said among themselves, No *doubt* this man is a murderer, *whom,* though he hath escaped the sea, yet vengeance suffereth not to *live.*—ACTS xxviii: 4.

122. Each year to ancient friendship adds a ring,
  As to an oak, and *precious more* and more,
 Without deservingness or help of ours,
 They grow, and silent, wider *spread,* each *year,*
  Their unbought ring of shelter or of shade.—LOWELL.

PROGRAMMES AND MODELS FOR PARSING.

NOUNS AND PRONOUNS.

1242. Programme for Parsing Nouns.
(1) Species? (2) Class? (3) (Sub-class?) (4) Person? (5) Number? (6) Gender? (7) Case? (8) Construction? (9) Rule?

1243. Programme for Parsing Pronouns.
(1) Species? (2) Class? (3) (Sub-class?) (4) Antecedent?
(5) Agreement { (6) Person? (7) Number? (9) Rule? (10) Case? (8) Gender? }

(11) Construction? (12) Rule?

NOMINATIVES.

DEPENDENT CONSTRUCTIONS.

1244. Subject of a Finite Verb.

The *messenger* came while *we* were absent.

Messenger is a (1) noun, (2) common, (4) third, (5) singular, (6) common, (7) nominative, (8) subject of the verb 'came,' (9) Rule XV.[1]

We is a (1) pronoun, (2) personal, (4) its antecedent the company[2] of which the speaker is one, (5) with which it agrees in the (6) first, (7) plural, (8) common, (9) Rule VI, (10) nominative, (11) subject of 'were,' (12) Rule XV.

---

[1] The figures in parentheses in the written parsings give the successive steps as laid down in the programme.

[2] The logical idea abbreviated for parsing into the expression "company of which the speaker is one," is "the names of the persons of the company of which the speaker is one." (See page 86, Art. 436, Remark.)

1245. Nominative in the Predicate.

> James is a *lawyer*.

Lawyer is a (1) noun, (2) common, (4) third, (5) singular, (6) masculine, (7) nominative, (8) in the predicate with the intransitive verb 'is' referring to the same thing as its subject, 'James,' (9) Rule XIV.

NOMINATIVES IN APPOSITION.

1246. Nominative in Apposition with a single word.

> Cortez, *he* who tortured Montezuma, was a Spaniard.

He is a (1) pronoun, (2) personal, (4) its antecedent 'Cortez,' (5) with which it agrees in the (6) third, (7) singular, (8) masculine, (9) Rule V, (10) nominative, (11) in apposition with 'Cortez,' (12) Rule XIII.

1247. Nominative in Apposition with a phrase.

> *His opposing the measure,* an *action* attributed to his personal dislike of its originator, was the salvation of the country.

Action is a (1) noun, (2) common, (4) third, (5) singular, (6) neuter, (7) nominative, (8) in apposition with the phrase, 'his opposing the measure,' (9) Rule XIII, Arts. 211, 212, 968.

1248. Nominative in Apposition with a sentence.

> The governor pardoned the criminal, an *act* of clemency which was generally condemned.

Act is a (1) noun, (2) common, (4) third, (5) singular, (6) neuter, (7) nominative, (8) in apposition with the sentence 'The governor pardoned the criminal,' (9) Rule XIII, Arts. 211, 212, 969.

"IT" AS A NOMINATIVE.

1249. It expletive.

> *It* was necessary that he should go.

It is a (1) pronoun, (2) personal, (4) its antecedent the subordinate sentence 'that he should go,' (5) with which it agrees in the (6) third, (7) singular, (8) neuter, (9) Rule V, Art. 920, (10) nominative by expletion, (11) being the apparent or grammatical subject of 'was,' (12) Rules XV, XXIV.

1250. It introductory.

It was James and Henry who were here.

It is a (1) pronoun, (2) personal, (4) its antecedent, James and Henry, which it introduces, but (5) with which it does not agree according to Art. 302, (6) third, (7) singular, (8) neuter, (10) nominative, (11) subject of 'was,' Rule XV.

1251. It suggestive, antecedent understood.

It rains.

It is a (1) pronoun, (2) personal, (4) antecedent, weather understood, (5) with which it agrees in the (6) third, (7) singular, (8) neuter, (9) Rule V, Art. 303, (10) nominative, (11) subject of 'rains,' (12) Rule XV, Art. 303.

In other examples: *It* is nine o'clock; *It* is very muddy to-day; *It* has been a very hard winter; *It* suggests in each connection very *definitely* its antecedent, and thus should rather be called the 'definite *it*,' than '*it* used indefinitely,' as many grammarians designate it.

1252. Double Relatives as Nominatives.

What merely embellishes is not what we want.

The thing which merely embellishes is not the thing which we want.

REMARK.—The words with dotted lines beneath indicate the equivalency of the double relative. The pupil should always be required to expand the sentence before parsing the equivalents of 'what.'

What is a (1) pronoun, (2) relative, (3) double, equivalent to the thing which. *Thing*, the antecedent part, is a (1) noun, (2) common, (4) third, (5) singular, (6) neuter, (7) nominative, (8) subject of 'is,' (9) Rule XV. *Which*, the relative part, is a (1) pronoun, (2) relative, (4) its antecedent 'thing,' (5) with which it agrees in the (6) third, (7) singular, (8) neuter, (9) Rule V, (10) nominative, (11) subject of 'embellishes,' (12) Rule XV.

Whatever money was in the purse is mine.

That money whichever was in the purse is mine.

Whatever is a (1) pronoun, (2) relative, (3) double, compound, equivalent to, that whichever. *That*, the antecedent part, is an adjective pronominal, limits 'money,' Rule I. *Whichever* is a (1) pronoun, (2) relative, (3) compound; (4) its antecedent, 'money,' (5) with which it agrees in the (6) third, (7) singular, (8) neuter, (9) Rule V, (10) nominative, (11) subject of 'was,' (12) Rule XV.

1253. As as a relative.

Such [ ] *as* choose may go.

As is a (1) pronoun, (2) relative, (4) its antecedent 'persons' understood, (5) with which it agrees in the (6) third, (7) plural, (8) common, (9) Rule V, (10) nominative, (11) subject of 'choose,' (12) Rule XV.

INTERROGATIVES.

1254. Who interrogative in a direct question.

Who goes there?

Who is a (1) pronoun, (2) interrogative, its antecedent, the noun which will answer the question, (5) with which it agrees in person, number, and gender unknown (since the answer is not given), Rule V, (10) nominative, (11) subject of 'goes,' (12) Rule XV.

1255. Who interrogative in an indirect question.

I know *who* he was.

Who is a (1) pronoun, (2) interrogative, (4) its antecedent, answer of question, (5) with which it agrees in person, number, and gender unknown (since the answer is not given), (9) Rule V,

(10) nominative, (11) in the predicate with the intransitive verb 'was,' referring to the same thing as its subject, 'he,' Rule XIV.

1256. **What interrogative in an indirect question.**

> I know *what* made the noise.

What is a (1) pronoun, (2) interrogative, (4) its antecedent answer of question, with which it agrees in person, number, and gender unknown (since the answer is not given), (9) Rule V, (10) nominative, subject of 'made,' (12) Rule XV.

1257. **Predicate nominative with a participle.**

> His being a *judge* is no reason why he should violate the law.

Judge is a (1) noun, (2) common, (4) third, (5) singular, (6) masculine, (7) nominative, (8) in the predicate with the participle 'being,' (9) Rule XIV, Art. 984. In the expanded form the subordinate sentence reads, 'that he is a judge,' in which sentence *judge* is nominative in the predicate with the intransitive verb 'is' referring to the same thing as its subject, 'he.' In the abridged form the verb 'is' is changed to the participle 'being' and its subject 'he' to the possessive 'his'; judge, the nominative in the predicate, remains unchanged in construction, and is therefore nominative in the predicate with the participle 'being,' in violation of Rule XIV.

INDEPENDENT CONSTRUCTIONS IN THE NOMINATIVE.

1258. **Nominative absolute by direct address.**

> John, are you going to the city to-day?

John is a (1) noun, (2) proper, (4) second, (5) singular, (6) masculine, (7) nominative, (8) absolute by direct address, (9) Rule XXII.

1259. **Nominative absolute by exclamation.**

> O *mercy!* what will become of us?

Mercy is a (1) noun, (2) common, (4) third, (5) singular, (6) neuter, (7) nominative, (8) absolute by exclamation, (9) Rule XXII.

1260. **Nominative absolute by inscription.**

Paradise Lost (used as a title).

Paradise Lost is a (1) noun, (2) proper, (4) third, (5) singular, (6) neuter, (7) nominative, (8) absolute by inscrip., (9) Rule XXII.

1261. **Nominative absolute by pleonasm.**

The *boys*, they were supposed to be lost.

Boys is a (1) noun, (2) common, (4) third, (5) plural, (6) masculine, (7) nominative, (8) absolute by pleonasm, (9) Rule XXII.

1262. **Nominative absolute with a participle.**

The *moon* rising, the ghostly trees threw their long shadows across the silent landscape.

Moon is a (1) noun, (2) common, (4) third, (5) singular, (6) neuter, (7) nominative, (8) absolute with the participle 'rising,' (9) Rule XXII.

POSSESSIVES.

1263. **Limiting a noun of different signification.**

John's hat was lost, but mine is here.

John's is a (1) noun, (2) proper, (4) third, (5) singular, (6) masculine, (7) possessive, (8) limiting 'hat,' (9) Rule XIX.

1264. **Limiting a noun as its attribute.**

That book is *yours*.

Yours is a (1) pronoun, (2) personal, (4) its antecedent, the person spoken to, (5) with which it agrees in the (6) second, (7) singular, (8) common, (9) Rule V, (10) possessive, in the predicate limiting the subject 'book' as its attribute, (12) Rule XIX.

1265. **Limiting a participle.**

There is no necessity for *their* leaving so soon.

Their is a (1) pronoun, (2) personal, (4) its antecedent the persons spoken of, (5) with which it agrees in the (6) third, (7) plural, (8) common, (9) Rule V, (10) possessive, (11) limiting the participle 'leaving,' Rule XIX, and Art. 1060.

> O for a glance of heavenly day,
> To take this stubborn heart away;
> And thaw, with beams of love divine,
> This heart, this frozen heart of *mine*.

1266. **Mine** is a (1) pronoun, (2) personal, (4) its antecedent the person speaking, (5) with which it agrees in the (6) first, (7) singular, (8) common, (9) Rule V, (10) possessive, (11) limiting 'being' understood, (12) Rule XIX.

REMARK.—'Mine,' in the above example, may be more properly parsed as a possessive used by enallage for the objective; thus,

1267. **Mine** is a (1) pronoun, (2) personal, (4) its antecedent the person speaking, (5) with which it agrees in the (6) first, (7) singular, (8) common, (9) Rule V, (10) possessive by enallage used for the objective, me, object of the preposition 'of,' Rule XVIII.

1268. Limiting a noun of the same signification.

> He stopped at Mr. Norton, the *tailor's* shop.

Tailor's is a (1) noun, (2) common, (4) third, (5) singular, (6) masculine, (7) possessive, (8) in apposition with Norton, *which* does not take the possessive sign, Art. 232, (9) Rule XIII.

1269. Possessive expletive.

> I never thought of *its* being wrong that I should smoke.

Its is a pronoun; its antecedent is the clause 'that I should smoke,' etc.

OBJECTIVES.

1270. Object of a transitive verb.

> Henry brought a new *book* from the city to-day.

Book is a (1) noun, (2) common, (4) third, (5) singular, (6) neuter, (7) objective, (8) object of 'brought,' (9) Rule XVII.

1271. Object of a preposition.

> Our friend came to *town* yesterday.

Town is a (1) noun, (2) common, (4) third, (5) singular, (6) neuter, (7) objective, (8) object of the preposition 'to,' (9) Rule XVIII.

1272. Objective subject of an infinitive.

I took *him* to be an honest man.

Him is a (1) pronoun, (2) personal, (4) its antecedent the person spoken of, (5) with which it agrees in the (6) third, (7) singular, (8) masculine, (9) Rule V, (10) objective, (11) subject of the infinitive 'to be,' (12) Rule XVI.

1273. Objective in the predicate with an infinitive.

The nation thought him to be a *statesman*.

Statesman is a (1) noun, (2) common, (4) third, (5) singular, (6) masculine, (7) objective, (8) in the predicate with the intransitive verb 'to be' referring to the same thing as its subject, 'him,' (9) Rule XIV.

1274. Objective in apposition.

The officers captured Smith, the *leader* of the gang.

Leader is a (1) noun, (2) common, (4) third, (5) singular, (6) masculine, (7) objective, (8) in apposition with 'Smith,' Rule XIII.

1275. It expletive as an objective.

I thought *it* [ ] absurd that he should advocate such claims.

It is a (1) pronoun, (2) personal, (4) its antecedent the clause 'that he should advocate such claims,' (5) with which it agrees in the (6) third, (7) singular, (8) neuter, (9) Rule V, (10) objective, expletive, (11) apparent or grammatical subject of the infinitive 'to be' understood, (12) Rule XVI, Art. 306, the antecedent clause being the real or logical subject of the verb 'to be.'

OBJECTIVES BY ENALLAGE.

1276. Objective subject of finite verb.

Angel songs, *me*thinks I hear them.

Me is a (1) pronoun, (2) personal, (4) its antecedent is the person speaking, (5) with which it agrees in the (6) first, (7) singular, (8) common, (9) Rule V, (10) objective by enallage, (11) subject of the verb 'thinks,' Art. 325.

1277. **Objective used for nominative absolute.**

> Ah *me!* what a pity!

Me is a (1) pronoun, (2) personal, (4) its antecedent the person speaking, (5) with which it agrees in the (6) first, (7) singular, (8) common, (9) Rule V, (10) objective by enallage, (11) used for the nominative *I* by enallage, Art. 326.

1278. **Objective in the predicate with a finite verb.**

> It is *them*.[1]

Them is a (1) pronoun, (2) personal, (4) its antecedent the persons spoken of, (5) with which it agrees in the (6) third, (7) plural, (8) common, (9) Rule V, (10) objective by enallage, used for the nominative 'they,' (12) Art. 327, in the predicate with the intransitive verb 'is' referring to the same thing as its subject, 'it.'

1279. **Objective "whom" used for "who."**

> Solomon, than whom there never was a wiser, says, "Wisdom is more precious than rubies."

Whom is a (1) pronoun, (2) relative, (4) its antecedent 'Solomon,' (5) with which it agrees in the (6) third, (7) singular, (8) masculine, Rule V, (9) objective, (11) used by enallage for the nominative 'who,' and is equivalent to 'and he,' Art. 328. By expanding, the above sentence reads, Solomon, and there never was a wiser than he [was], says, etc., thus separating 'whom' into its elements, the conjunction *and* and the pronoun *he*. It is thus shown that the objective 'whom' is used by enallage for the nominative *who*, and is not the object of the conjunction 'than,' as some grammarians affirm.

1280. **Objective limiting a participle.**

> We never thought of *them* coming so soon.

Them is a (1) pronoun, (2) personal, (4) its antecedent the persons spoken of, (5) with which its agrees in the (6) third, (7) plural, (8) common, (9) Rule V, (10) objective, (11) limiting the participle 'coming,' used by enallage for the possessive, Arts. 329 and 1060.

---

[1] For the parsing of *it* in this sentence, see *it* introductory, Sec. 1240.

1281. Objective in the predicate with a participle.

I never thought of its being *him*.

Him is a (1) pronoun, (2) personal, (4) its antecedent the person spoken of, (5) with which it agrees in the (6) third, (7) singular, (8) masculine, (9) Rule V, (10) objective, (11) used by enallage for the nominative *he* in the expanded form of the sentence, 'I never thought that it was he.'

ARTICLES.

1282. Programme for parsing articles.

(1) Species? (2) Class? (3) Construction? (4) Rule.

1283. Definite article.

The horse ran away.

The is an (1) article, (2) definite, (3) limits 'horse,' (4) Rule I.

1284. Indefinite article.

The boy was making *a* sled.

A is an (1) article, (2) indefinite, (3) limits 'sled,' (4) Rule I.

ADJECTIVES.

1285. Programme for parsing adjectives.

(1) Species? (2) Class? (3) (Sub-class?) (4) (Degree of Comparison?) (5) (Number?) (6) Construction? (7) Rule?

1286. Descriptive adjective.

A *white* flag was displayed by the garrison.

White is an (1) adjective, (2) descriptive, (6) limits 'flag,' (7) Rule I.

1287. Adjective in the predicate.

William is *taller* than George.

Taller is an (1) adjective, (2) descriptive, (4) comparative, (6) in predicate with the intransitive verb *is*, limiting its subject, William, (7) Rule I.

H. Gram.—22.

1288. Pronominal adjective.

Each may report for himself.

Each is an (1) adjective, (2) pronominal, (6) limits 'person' understood, (7) Rule I.

1289. Reciprocal pronominal adjectives.

Let them assist *one another* in the work.

Let them assist *one* [person] *another* [person] in the work.

One is an (1) adjective, (2) pronominal, (6) limits 'person' understood, (7) Rule I.
Person (understood) is a (1) noun, (2) common, (4) third, (5) singular, (6) common, (7) objective, (8) in apposition with 'them,' (9) Rule XIII.
Another is an (1) adjective, (2) pronominal, (6) limits 'person' understood, (7) Rule I.
Person (understood) is a (1) noun, (2) common, (4) third, (5) singular, (6) common, (7) objective, (8) object of the active transitive verb 'assist,' (9) Rule XVII.

1290. Pronominal adjective with the possessive sign.

I exhort you to be each *other's* joy.

I exhort you to be each [person] [the] other [person]'s joy.

Other's is an (1) adjective, (2) pronominal, (6) limits 'person' (understood), the possessive sign being transferred from 'person' to 'other,' Art. 494.

1291. Numeral adjective.

Five men were injured by the accident.

Five is an (1) adjective, (2) numeral, (3) cardinal, (6) limits 'men,' (7) Rule I.

VERBS.

FINITE MODES.

1292. Programme for Parsing Verbs.

(1) Species? Classes? {(2) Regularity? (3) Transivity?} (4) (Principal Parts?) (5) (Style?) (6) Voice? (7) Mode? (8) Tense? (9) Person? (10) Number? (11) Construction? (12) Rule?

1293. Ordinary style; active voice.

The orator of the occasion *prepared* a speech.

Prepared is a (1) verb, (2) regular, (3) transitive, (6) active, (7) indicative, (8) past tense, (9) third, (10) singular, (11) agreeing with its subject, 'orator,' (12) Rule IX.

We *have* never *seen* a more auspicious beginning.

Have seen is a (1) verb, (2) irregular, (3) transitive, (4) see, saw, seen, (6) active, (7) indicative, (8) present perfect, (9) first, (10) plural, (11) agreeing with its subject, 'we,' (12) Rule IX.

The children *may go* and play.

May go is a (1) verb, (2) irregular, (3) intransitive, (4) go, went, gone, (6) active, (7) potential, (8) present, (9) third, (10) plural, (11) agreeing with its subject, 'children,' (12) Rule IX.

Let them depart in peace.

Let is a (1) verb, (2) irregular, (3) transitive, (4) let, let, let, (6) active, (7) imperative, (8) present, (9) second, (10) plural, (11) agreeing with its subject, 'you,' understood, (12) Rule IX.

1294. Ordinary style; passive voice.

Preparations for the journey *were* already *made* by the party.

Were made is a (1) verb, (2) irregular, (3) transitive, (4) make, made, made, (6) passive, (7) indicative, (8) past, (9) third, (10) plural, (11) agreeing with its subject, 'preparations,' (12) Rule IX.

1295. Compound verbs: passive voice.

James *was* often *laughed at* for his awkwardness.

Was laughed at is a (1) verb, (2) regular, (3) transitive, (6) passive, (7) indicative, (8) past, (9) third, (10) singular, (11) agreeing with its subject, 'James,' (12) Rule IX.

1296. Complex verbs: passive voice.

The farm *has* not yet *been taken possession of* by its owner.

Has been taken possession of is a (1) verb, (2) irregular, (3) transitive, (4) take, took, taken, (6) passive, (7) indicative, (8) present perfect, (9) third, (10) singular, (11) agreeing with its subject, 'farm,' (12) Rule IX.

1297. Solemn style.

Thou, even thou, *art* Lord alone.

Art is a (1) verb, (2) irregular, (3) intransitive, (4) be, was, been, (5) solemn style, (6) active, (7) indicative, (8) present, (9) second, (10) singular, (11) agreeing with its subject, 'thou,' (12) Rule IX.

1298. Emphatic style.

The pupils certainly *did succeed* well in the effort.

Did succeed is a (1) verb, (2) regular, (3) intransitive, (5) emphatic style, (6) active, (7) indicative, (8) past, (9) third, (10) plural, agreeing with its subject, 'pupils,' (12) Rule IX.

1299. Progressive style.

I *was writing* a letter when my friend called.

Was writing is a (1) verb, (2) irregular, (3) transitive, (4) write, wrote, written, (5) progressive style, (6) active, (7) indicative, (8) past, (9) first, (10) singular, (11) agreeing with its subject, 'I,' Rule IX.

INFINITIVES.

1300. Programme for parsing infinitives and participles.

(1) Species? (2) Classes? (3) Principal Parts? (4) Voice? (5) Mode? (6) Tense? (7) Construction? (8) Rule?

1301. *With the construction of nouns.*

1302. Infinitive subject of a finite verb.

To think clearly is a necessary qualification of a business man.

To think is a (1) verb, (2) irregular, transitive, (3) think, thought, thought, (4) active, (5) infinitive, (6) present, (7) construction of a noun, (8) Rule XX, subject of 'is,' Rule XV.

1303. Infinitive, the logical subject of a finite verb.

It is necessary for students *to cultivate* mutual forbearance.

To cultivate is an (1) infinitive, (2) active, (3) present, (4) with the construction of a noun, Rule XX, being the logical subject of 'is,' Rule IX, Art. 644. The grammatical subject 'it' is an expletive, Rule XXIV.

1304. Infinitive attribute of a sentence.

To die is *to sleep*.

To sleep is a (1) verb, (2) irregular, intransitive, (3) sleep, slept, slept, (4) active, (5) infinitive, (6) present, (7) construction of the noun, (8) Rule XX, in the predicate with the intransitive verb 'is' referring to the same thing as its subject, 'to die,' Rule XIV.

1305. Infinitive object of a transitive verb.

Boys love *to swim*.

To swim is a (1) verb, (2) irregular, intransitive, (3) swim, swam, swam, (4) active, (5) infinitive, (6) present, (7) construction of a noun, (8) Rule XX, object of the transitive verb 'love,' Rule XVII.

1306. *With the construction of an adjective.*

Each one, however humble, has a mission *to fulfill*.

To fulfill is a (1) verb, (2) regular, transitive, (4) active, by enallage for the passive 'to be fulfilled,' (5) infinitive, (6) present, (7) construction of an adjective, (8) Rule XX, limits 'mission,' Rule I.

1307. *With the construction of adverbs.*

1308. Limiting a verb.

He immediately returned *to assist* his companions.

To assist is a (1) verb, (2) regular, transitive, (4) active, (5) infinitive, (6) present, (7) construction of an adverb of purpose, (8) Rule XX, limits 'returned,' Rule II.

1309. Limiting an adjective.

The clerk was anxious *to secure* a situation.

To secure is a (1) verb, (2) regular, transitive, (4) active, (5) infinitive, (6) present, (7) construction of an adverb of purpose, (8) Rule XX, limits 'anxious,' Rule II.

1310. Limiting an adverb.

This fruit is ripe enough *to use*.

To use is a (1) verb, (2) regular, transitive, (4) active, by enallage for the passive 'to be used,' (5) infinitive, (6) present, (7) construction of an adverb of purpose, (8) Rule XX, limits 'enough,' Rule II.

PARTICIPLES.

1311. *With the construction of nouns.*

1312. Subject of a finite verb.

Playing croquet is a pleasant pastime.

Playing is a (1) verb, (2) regular, (3) intransitive, (4) active, (5) participial, (6) present, (7) construction of a noun, (8) Rule XX, subject of 'is,' Rule XV.

1313. Attribute of a sentence.

Reading is not *understanding*.

Understanding is a (1) verb, (2) irregular, transitive, (4) active, (5) participial, (6) present, (7) construction of a noun, (8) Rule XX, in the predicate with the intransitive verb 'is,' referring to the same thing as its subject, 'reading,' Rule XIV.

1314. Object of a transitive verb.

Commence *reading* on the tenth page.

Reading is a (1) verb, (2) irregular, transitive, (3) read, read, read, (4) active, (5) participial, (6) present, (7) construction of a noun, (8) Rule XX, object of 'commence,' Rule XVII.

1315. Object of a preposition.

The enemy desisted from firing on the town, after *having been repulsed* in the attack.

Having been repulsed is a (1) verb, (2) regular, transitive, (4) passive, (5) participial, (6) perfect, (7) construction of a noun, (8) Rule XX, object of the preposition 'after,' Rule XVIII.

1316. *With the construction of an adjective.*

1317. Participle directly limiting its noun.

A *cause* based on principles of right ought not to rely on force.

Based is a (1) verb, (2) regular, transitive, (4) passive, (5) participial, (6) past, (7) construction of an adjective, (8) Rule XX, limits 'cause,' Rule I.

1318. Participle in the predicate.

He seemed not well *instructed*.

Instructed is a (1) verb, (2) regular, transitive, (4) passive, (5) participial, (6) past, (7) construction of an adjective, (8) Rule XX, in the predicate limiting 'he,' Rule I.

1319. *With the construction of an adverb.*

The pupils came *hurrying* into the room.

Hurrying is a (1) verb, (2) regular, intransitive, (4) active, (5) participial, (6) present, (7) construction of an adverb, (8) Rule XX, limits 'came,' Rule II.

ADVERBS.

1320. Programme for parsing adverbs.

(1) Species? (2) Class? (3) Degree of comparison? (4) Construction? (5) Rule?

MODIFYING ADVERBS.

1321. Limiting a verb.

The orator dwelt *pathetically* on the wrongs of his nation.

Pathetically is an (1) adverb, (2) of manner, (4) limits 'dwelt,' (5) Rule II.

1322. Limiting an adjective.

The stranger wore a *remarkably* tall hat.

Remarkably is an (1) adverb, (2) of degree, (4) limits 'tall,' (5) Rule II.

1323. Limiting an adverb.

He called much the *loudest*.

Loudest is an (1) adverb, (2) of manner, (3) superlative, (4) limiting 'called,' (5) Rule II.

Much and **the** are adverbs of degree, limiting 'loudest,' Rule II.

CONJUNCTIVE ADVERBS.

The exercise will close *when* the bell rings.

When is an (1) adverb, (2) of time, (4) limits 'rings,' (5) Rule II, Art. 865; 'when' is also the connective of the subordinate sentence.

The camp will be located *where* the ground is most suitable.

Where is an (1) adverb, (2) of place, (4) limits 'is,' (5) Rule II, Art. 865; 'where' is also the connective of the subordinate sentence.

PREPOSITIONS.

1324. Programme for parsing prepositions.

(1) Species? (2) Class? (3) Relation? (4) Rule.

1325. Simple prepositions.

The snowflakes float *through* the air.

Through is a (1) preposition, (3) shows the relation of 'air' to 'float,' (4) Rule IV.

He came *as* an embassador.

As is a (1) preposition, (3) shows the relation of 'embassador' to 'came,' (4) Rule IV, Art. 975, remark.

REMARK.—'As' in this sentence is equivalent to 'in the relation of,' a complex preposition.

1326. Compound prepositions.

He jumped *aboard of* the train at the last moment.

Aboard of is a (1) preposition, (2) compound, (3) shows the relation of 'train' to 'jumped,' (4) Rule IV.

1327. Complex prepositions.

Little need be said *in regard to* his previous career.

In regard to is a (1) preposition, (2) complex, (3) shows the relation of 'career' to 'said,' (4) Rule IV.

CONJUNCTIONS.

1328. Programme for parsing conjunctions.

(1) Species? (2) Class? (3) (Sub-class?) (4) Connection? (5) Rule?

1329. Co-ordinate conjunctions.

The team ran away *and* broke the wagon.

And is a (1) conjunction, (2) co-ordinate, (4) connects the sentences 'The team ran away' and '[the team] broke the wagon,' (5) Rule III.

1330. Subordinate conjunctions.

The attack was unsuccessful *because* the general's orders were misunderstood

Because is a (1) conjunction, (2) subordinate, (4) connects the sentences, 'The attack was unsuccessful' and 'the general's orders were misunderstood,' (5) Rule III.

1331. Correlative conjunctions.

Both the vessel *and* the cargo were a total loss.

Both and **and** are (1) conjunctions, (2) co-ordinate, (3) correlative, (4) together they connect 'vessel' and 'cargo,' (5) Rule III, Art. 780.

INTERJECTIONS.

1332. Programme for parsing interjections.

(1) Species? (2) Construction? (3) Rule?

Hark! did you hear that cry?

Hark is an (1) interjection, (2) used independently, (3) Rule XXIII.

INDEX.

A

A with few and little, 815.
ABRIDGED SENTENCE, absolute, 1229; adjective, 1224; adverbial, 1225; classes, 1221; defined, 1220; expanded, 650; infinitive, 1227; participial, 1228; sub-classes, 1222; substantive, 1223.
ABRIDGMENT, defined, 1219.
ACTIVE VOICE (see Voice).
ACCENT, common, 59; defined, 58; discriminative, 60; emphatic, 61; marks, use of, poetic. 62; primary, 106, rem.; secondary, 106, rem.
ADJECTIVES, apparently become nouns, 445; as nouns, 440; become adverbs, 449; cardinal, 459; comparison, 473; compounded, 438; construction, 827; defective, 480; defined, 436; errors in use of, 841; in comparison after *than*, 833; independent, 832; instead of adverbs, 844; limiting adjectives, 830; modifications, 463; number, 464; numeral, 458; *one* as a noun, 493; ordinal, 460; other parts of speech used as, 439; parsed, descriptive, 1285; pronominal, 1288; pronom. in poss., 1290; reciprocal, 1289; participial, 453; participial distinguished from participles, 454; peculiarities of construction, 489; pronominal, defined, 455; pronominal, list of, 457; proper, redundant, 478; two forms of comparison, 485; with intransitive verbs, 829.
ADVERBS, apparently limit nouns, 859; as other parts of speech, 862; 715; comparison, 737; conjunctive, 727; defined, 711; errors in use of, 871; for adjectives, 872; formation, 729; how parsed in comparisons, 486; independent, 743; limit prepositional phrases, 860; limit sentences, 861; may limit what, 712; modifications, 736; parsed, 1320; peculiarities, 740; position, 853; sub-classes, 716.
ADVERBIAL PHRASES, 714.
ALLEGORY, defined. 1124.
AMEN, how used, 743.
ANADIPLOSIS, defined, 1116.
ANALYSIS, defined, 1159; diagrammed notation of, 1199; of abridged sentences, 1229; of double relatives, diagrammed, 1203; written, 1212; of predicate constructions, diagrammed, 1205; written, 1214; of second and third class obj. elements, diagrammed, 1204; written, 1213; of simple sentences, diagrammed, 1198; written, 1208; of complex sentences, diagrammed, 1200; written, 1209; of compound sentences, diagrammed, 1201; written, 1210; of partial compound sentences, diagrammed, 1202; written, 1211; verbal programme for, 1206.
ANAPHORA, defined, 1117.
ANTECEDENT, of a pronoun, defined, 254; may be what, 255; position, 256.
ANTITHESIS, defined, 1134.
ANTI-CLIMAX, defined, 1136.
ANTONOMASIA, defined, 1141; examples, 1141.
APOSTROPHE, defined, 1130; example, 1130; mark, use of in possessives, 225.
APHTHONG, defined, 73.
APHERESIS, defined. 1102.
APOCOPE, defined, 1104.
ARCHAISM, defined, 1100.
ARTICLES, before a vowel or consonant, 505; classes, 498; defined, 496; definite, derivation, 501; indefinite, derivation, 504; in comparison. 813; parsed. 1282; *the*. denoting a class. 816; use of, with appositives, 812; with plurals 815.

ARTICULATION, defined, 57.
As, as an adv., 745; as a preposition, 746, 1325; as a relative, 274; used with so-called appositives, 975.
AS AND LIKE, 876.
ASPIRATE, obstructed, 46; pure, 45.
ASYNDETON, defined, 1112.
ATTRIBUTE, can not be an adverb, 552; defined, 1181; may be what, 551; of an abridged clause in the objective, 1227.
AUXILIARIES, 678; as principal verbs, 681; *had, should,* and *would,* 685; having participles, 683; not used as principal verbs, 670; origin, 682.

B

BASE, of a syllable, 87; of compound word, 96; of derivative, 98.
BID, *dare, feel,* etc., without infinitive sign, 1070.
BREVE, use of, 1152.

C

CAPITALS, rules for use of, 118.
CARET, 1150.
CASE, absolute, 214; absolute of pronouns, 1076; nominative, use of, 207.
CATACHRESIS, defined, 1140.
CLIMAX, defined, 1135; examples, 1135.
COALESCENT, defined, 42.
COLON, use of, 1147.
COMPARISON, degrees of, 467; of two objects by comp. or superl., 470; terms of include what, 836.
COMMA, use of, 1147.
CONJUGATION, defined, 695; of verb *be,* 708; of verb *love,* 709.
CONJUNCTIONS, classes, 768; co-ordinate, 770; copulative, 773; correlative, 780; defined, 767; disjunctive, 774; introductory, 778; list of, 776; parsed, 1318; peculiarities of, 778; subordinate, 771; use of, 880.
CONNECTIVE, co-ordinate, 1196; defined, 1194; subordinate, 1197.
CONSEQUENT or SUBSEQUENT, 898.
CONSONANT, defined, 72.
CONTINUANT, 52.
COPULA, defined, 1182.

D

DASHES, use of, 1147.
DECLENSION, of nouns, 252; of pronouns, 310.
DENTAL, defined, 48.
DERIVATIVE WORD, base of, 98; defined, 95; formation with prefix and suffix, 100.
DIERÆSIS, defined, 1151.
DIAGRAMMED ANALYSIS, 1198.
DIGRAPH, combined, 79; conjoined, 76; consonant, defined, 78; disjoined, 77; vowel, 75.
DIPHTHONGS, 74.
DISSYLLABLES, 103.
DICTATION EXERCISE, 117.
DOUBLE RELATIVE, 277; parsed, 1252.
DOUBLE COMPARATIVES and SUPERLATIVES, 845.

E

EACH OTHER, 493; parsed, 1290.
EITHER, referring to more than two objects, 840.
ELEMENTS, sentential, adjective, adverbial, 1176; complex, 1186; compound, 1187; objective, 1190; of the first class, 1191; second class, 1192; third class, 1193; principal, 1177; simple, 1185; subordinate, 1184.
ELLIPSIS, defined, 1111.
ENALLAGE, defined, 1119; obj. by for nom., 324; for possessive, 329.
EPIZEUXIS, defined, 1115.
ETYMOLOGY, defined, 25.
EUPHEMISM, defined, 1139.
EVER and NEVER, use of, 870.
EXCLAMATIONS, defined, 1132.
EXPLETIVES, 1093.

F

FIGURES, classes, 1097; of etymology, 1101; of orthography, 1098; of rhetoric, 121; of syntax, 1110.
FIRST TWO, etc., 826.
FOR as an introductory expletive, 763.

G

GENDER, as applied to animals and young children, 199; common, 195; defined, 188; feminine, 193; masculine, 190; neuter, 196; neuter becomes masculine or feminine, 198; of personal pronouns, 295.
GRAMMAR, divisions of, 20; English, 22; general, 20; particular, 21.
GUTTURAL, defined, 50.

H

HYPERBATON, defined, 1118.
HYPERBOLE, defined, 1127.
HYPHEN, omitted in compounds, 235; use of, 1155.

INDEX. 269

I

IMPERATIVE MODE (see Mode).
INDEPENDENT CONSTRUCTIONS, nominative, parsed, 1258; obj., 1277.
INDEX, use of, 1157.
INFINITIVE, as a noun, adjective, or adverb, 1044; as an element of the second class, 1192; as a verb, 1052; attribute, 635; constructions, 1042; construction of adj., 636; denoting purpose, 1050; has no case, 638; in comparisons, 1051; introduced by *for*, 644; limiting an adjective, 637; limiting an adverb, 637; limiting a verb, 637; modes, 629; not absolute, 641; object of a verb, 635; sign, omission of, 576, 634; after *have*, 1074; after *need*, 1070; after passive of *bid*, *dare*, etc., 1071; subject, 646; subject of finite verb, 644; time of, 643; used as logical sub., 645; with the verb *be*, 1045.
INFLECTION, defined, 696; of *be*, 708.
INTERJECTIONS, defined, 782; followed by pronoun, 1092; list of, 786; parsed, 1332; rule, 1089; use of, 783, 1091.
INTERROGATION, defined, 1133; point, 1147.
INTERROGATIVE PRONOUNS, defined, 287; parsed, 1254; parsed in indirect questions, 1255.
INTRANSITIVE VERBS, have no passive, 571.
IRREGULAR AND REDUNDANT VERBS, 710.
IRONY, defined, 1128.
IT as a nominative expletive, 1249; expletive obj., 1275; for obvious ant. understood, 303; introductory, 1250; introductory expletive, 305; introduces ant. of diff. per., num., gen., 915; suggestive, 1251; used for animals and children, 301; uses of, 300.

L

LABIAL, defined, 47.
LANGUAGE, alphabetic, 16; artificial, 8; diversity, 3; equivocal, 17; gesticulate, 19; hieroglyphic, 14; highest development of, 4; history, 1; natural, 7; origin, 1; phonic, 12; pictorial, 13; spoken, 1; syllabic, 15; symbolic, 11; unequivocal, 18; local, 9; written, 10.
LETTERS, defined, 67; grammatical forms, 69; power, 70; sounds, drill on, 63; typical forms, 68.
LEXICOGRAPHY, defined, 26.

LIKE and AS, 876.
LIQUID, defined, 53.
LITOTES, defined, 1138.

M

MACRON, use of, 1152.
MANY A, parsed, 495.
METAPHOR, defined, 1123.
METONYMY, defined, 1125.
MIMESIS, defined, 1099.
MINE, THINE, YOURS, etc., 315.
MODES, classes, 577; finite, defined, 578. infinitive, 629; names, 630.
MODE, imperative, 589; referring to the future, 619; sign of, 590; subject in third person, 591; indicative, 579; use, 579; infinitive constructions, 635; tenses, 633; tense signs, 633; participial, 651; tenses, 651; tense signs, 651; potential, 580; signs, 612; use. 603; subjunctive, 583; implies what, 586; obsolescent, 588; signs of, 584.
MONOSYLLABLE, defined, 102.

N

NASAL, defined, 54.
NEED, peculiarities in agreement, 940.
NEGATIVES, use of, 866.
NEVER and EVER, use of, 870.
NO, how used, 864.
NOMINATIVE, absolute, 1076; parsed, by direct address, 1258; by exclamation, 1259; by inscription, 1260; by pleonasm, 1261; with a participle, 1252; in apposition, 210, 963; parsed, 1246; with a phrase, 1247; with a sentence, 1248; with a single word, 1246; in the predicate, 209, 977; in the predicate with a participle, parsed, 1257; number of constructions, dependent, 207; independent, 213; parsed, 1234; subject of a finite verb, 208, 986.
NOUNS, abstract, 148; collective, 149; classes, 142; common, become proper, 152; begin with capital, 145; sub-classes, 147; declension, 252; having two plurals of diff. significations, 181; in apposition, 963; in the first person, const. of, 159; in the second person, const. of, 161; in the third person, const. of, 165; in the predicate, 166; plurals, how formed, 174; of compounds, 182; of foreign nouns, 185; of letters, 186; of names with titles, 183; singular and plural alike, 184; two names forming

parsed, 144; verbal, 150; wanting plural, 170; wanting singular, 173; what may be used as, 141.

NUMBER, as applied to auxiliaries, 628; as applied to verbs, 621; formation, 174; plural, singular, 169.

NUMERAL ADJECTIVES, 458.

O

OBELISK or DAGGER, double, 1157.

OBJECTIVE CASE, by enallage, parsed, for nominative absolute, 326; in the predicate with finite verb, 327; in the predicate with participle, limiting a participle, 329; subject of finite verb, 325; *whom* for *who*, 328; constructions, 238; denoting time, weight, etc., so-called independent, 247; introductory, 323; of kindred signification, 1014; of pronouns, peculiarities, 321; parsed, in apposition, 244; predicate with infinitive, 243; subject of infinitive, 241; subject of infinitive can not be object of preposition, 1001; with causative verbs, 1015.

OBJECT, of a preposition, 1017, of a transitive verb, 1003.

OBJECTS, two with verbs of asking, teaching, etc., 1011.

ONE ANOTHER, 838.

ONE, as a pronominal, 494.

ONE, EACH, OTHER, parsed, 493.

ONE, TWO, etc., with first and last, 492.

ONLY, how used, 858.

ORGANS OF SPEECH, articulatory, 33; classes, 33; defined, 32; respiratory, 35; vocal, 34.

ORTHOEPY conspectus of, 15.

ORTHOGRAPHY, defined, 66; teaching by chart, 111; teaching by derivatives, 112.

OUGHT, peculiarities in agreement, 539, 945.

P

PALATAL, defined, 49.

PARAGOGE, defined, 1106.

PARAGRAPH, use of, 1157.

PARALEPSIS, defined, 1137.

PARALLEL, use of, 1157.

PARENTHESIS, use of, 1147.

PARENTHETICAL MARKS, 1147.

PARONOMASIA, defined, 1142.

PARSING, exercises for, 333; of adj., 1285; of adv 1320; of art., 1282; of conj., 1328; of interjection, 1332; of nouns and pronouns, 1242; of prep., 1324; of verbs, 1292.

PARTICIPLES, as attributes, 1062; as nouns, adj., and adv., 1057; become nouns, 151; become other parts of speech, 1061; classes, 651; constructions, 661, 1042; errors in use of, 1064; have no cases, 665; how distinguished, 652; 659; parsed, attribute, 1313; construction of, 1318; of adverb, 1319; object of preposition, 1315; object of verb, 1314; subject of finite verb, 1312; passive, belong only to transitive verbs, 656; preceded by art. or adj., 659; present active in a passive sense, 1063; signs, 651; subject of in poss. or the obj., 1060; tenses, 651; time of, 666; used in conjugation, 652.

PASSIVE VOICE (see Voice).

PEL, 114.

PERIOD, 1146.

PERSONS, first, 157; in all constructions, 165; of auxiliaries, 628; of nouns, 155; of verbs, 620; second, 160; third, 163; third for first and second, 164.

PERSONAL PRONOUNS, discussion, 258; (see Pronoun).

PERSONIFICATION, defined, 1129.

PHENICIA, letters brought from by Cadmus, 2.

PLEONASM, defined, 1113.

POINTS USED IN PUNCTUATION, 1146.

POSSESSIVE CASE, constructions, 220; defined, 219; expletive, 320; formation, 225; introductory, 318; of irregular plurals, 226; of nouns in singular, 225; of plurals like singular, 229; of pronouns, peculiarities, 311; parsed, limiting noun of diff. signif., 1263; limiting noun understood, 1264; limiting noun of same signif., 1268; limiting participle, 224, 1255; position of, 1032; rule, 1031; sign when several nouns in the poss., 1035; sign of, with appositives, 232; with compounds, 231; is what, 230; with letters, 228; with plurals, 230; omitted when, 207, 1035; slang, 234; suggestive, 319; with limited nouns understood, 233.

POSSESSIVES, in the predicate, 312; mine, thine, etc., 312.

POTENTIAL MODE (see Mode).

PREDICATE NOUN or PRONOUN, 978; rule, 977; use of, 982; with infinitives and participles, 984.

PREFIX, defined, 100.

INDEX. 271

PRESS, as a root, 115.
PREPOSITIONS, alphabetical list of, 758; classes, 748; *for*, introductory, 763; formation, 757; how used, 903; miscellaneous relations of, 756; parsed, complex, 1317; compound, 1316; simple, 1315; peculiarities of, 762; sub-classes, 750; two with one object, 1029.
PREPOSITIONAL PHRASES, 1027.
PRINCIPAL PARTS, are what, 672; how used, 675; signs, 677.
PROGRAMMES for PARSING, adjectives, 1285; adverbs, 1320; articles, 1282; conjunctions, 1328; interjections, 1332; nouns, 1232; prepositions, 1324; pronouns, 1233; verbs, 1292.
PRONOMINAL ADJECTIVES, defined, 455; list of, 457.
PRONOMINALS, *each, either, neither*, 839.
PRONOUNS, agreement with antecedent, 294, 910; agreement with nouns used by personification, metaphor, etc., 916; antecedent of, 254; antecedents of connected by *and*, 926; antecedents preceded by *each, every*, etc., 928; antecedents connected by *as well as*, 928; antecedents connected by *or* and *nor*, 932; classes, 257; in apposition, 929; in the predicate, 327; interrogative agreement with antecedent unknown, 297; mistaken for double relative, 290; parsed, 1254; limiting a participle, 329, 1060; masculine including both genders, 922; modifications, 293; order of in a sentence, 308; personal, relative, compound, 275; double, 251; parsed, 1252; simple, 264; referring to collective nouns, 924; refer to antecedents limited by *many a*, 921; simple and compound, 259; *thou* for *you*, 299; use of same style, 913; use of *we* for *I*, 298.
PRONUNCIATION, defined, 56; methods of teaching, 63.
PROSODY, defined, 1095.
PROSTHESIS, defined, 1105.
PUNCTUATION, classes of, 1144; defined, 1143; etymological, 1148; for reference, 1157; for the printer, 1158; points used, 1146; rhetorical, 1145; rules for, 1147.

Q

QUOTATION MARKS, 1147.

R

RECIPROCALS, *Each Other, One Another*, 838.

RELATIVE PRONOUNS, double (see Pronoun).
RELATIVE WHAT, 278.
RULES FOR SPELLING, general, 110; special, 116.
RULES FOR PUNCTUATION, 1147.
RULES FOR USE OF CAPITALS, 118.
RULES OF SYNTAX, act. verbs, *bid, dare*, etc., 1070; appositives, 963; articles and adjectives, 797; adverbs, 852; classified, p. 201; conjunctions, 878; expletives, 1003; infinitives and participles, 1042; interjections, 1080; nom. abs., 1076; obj. of prep., 1017; obj. of trans. verb, 1003; possessive case, 1031; predicate, 977; preposition, 897; pronouns agree with ant., 910; with collective noun, 924.

S

SECTION MARK, use of, 1157.
SENTENCES, abridged, 1164; complex, 1165; complete, 1163; compound, 1168; co-ordinate, 1171; declarative, 1172; imperative, 1173; interrogative, 1174; leading, 1170; partial comp., 1169; principal, 1166; simple, 1162; subordinate, 1167.
SEMICOLON, use of, 1146.
SEX, grammatical distinctions of, 200.
SIMILE, defined, 1122.
SOUND, articulate, 37; aspirate, 44; defined, 31; limit of vibration, 31; rate of progress, 31; subvocal, 43; vocal, 39; voiced, 38.
SOUNDS, cognate, 55; drill on, 63; where obstructed, 48.
SPEECH, organs of, 32.
SPELLING, defined, 107; general rules for, 110; orthographies, 108; phonic, 109; special rules for, 116.
SPLITTING PARTICLES, 1029.
STYLES OF VERBS, emphatic, 561; int. and neg., 565; ordinary, 559; progressive, 563; solemn, 560.
SUBJECT, defined, 1178; grammatical, 1217; logical, 1216; of finite verb, 986; parsed, 1244; of inf., 909; of part., 667; of subordinate clause in nom., 1233; in obj., 1225; in poss., 1224.
SUBSEQUENT OR CONSEQUENT, 899.
SUBVOCAL, defined, 43.
SUBJUNCTIVE MODE (see Mode).
SUCH A, parsed, 495.
SYLLABLE, accented, 106; antecedent, 89; antepenult, 85; base of, 87; classes,

82; consequent, 96; penultimate, 84; preantepenultimate, 86; ultimate, 83.
SYLLEPSIS, defined, 1120.
SYNECDOCHE, defined. 1126.
SYNERESIS, defined. 1108.
SYNCOPE. defined, 1103.
SYNOPSIS, how given, 697.
SYNTAX, defined, 27; rules of, 797.

T

TEACHING ORTHOGRAPHY, advanced methods, 111.
TENSE, future 601; future-perfect, 605; historical present, 598; past, 600; past-perfect, 604; present, 596; present expresses general truths, 597; present-perfect, 602.
TENSES, of the imp., 618; of the ind., how used. 597; signs of, 606; of the part., signs of, 651; of the potential, how used, 608; signs of, 612; of the subjunctive, how used. 614; signs of, 617.
TERMS OF COMPARISON, include what, 835; two referring jointly to another term, 890.
THAN IN COMPARISONS, 833.
THAT, as a conjunction. 272; as an expletive, 1063; as an objective, 273; as a pronom. adj., 271; as a relative, 273.
THE, as an adverb, 744.
THERE, as an expletive, 1093.
TILDE, 1148.
THESE KIND. THOSE SORT, 848.
THIS and THAT, THESE and THOSE, reference of, 837.
THIS HERE, THAT THERE, 847.
TMESIS, defined, 1109.
TO, sign of the infinitive, 640.
TRIGRAPH, disjoined, 81; vowel. 80.
TRISYLLABLE, 104.
TWO FIRST, TWO LAST, 826.

V

VERBS, attribute, 1181; complex, 1296; compound, 1295; copulative, 1182; classes. 532; defective, 381; finite, agreement 934; having collective noun for sub., 948; having phrases for sub's., 956; having sub's. of different persons, 960; forms with different persons, 623; impersonal, 540; intr. all act., 568; intransitive, with an object, 548; irregular, how formed, 535; list of, 710; modifications, 557; of making, choosing, etc., 1012; of giving, teaching, etc., 1011; person and number of, 622; prin. pts., 672; redundant, defined, 541; list of, 710; regular, how formed, 534; resolved into copula and attribute, 553; standing between sub's., 955; styles of, 558; subject may be what, 942; transitive, 543; defined, 543; express action, 546; voice, 566.
VISION, defined, 1131.
VOCAL, compound, 41; simple, 40.
VOICE, active, belongs to passive verbs, when, 571; changed to the passive, 1010; in a passive sense, 573; distinction in meaning of the active and passive, 572; passive, 569; belongs to transitive verbs, 570; formation, 1010; for the act. by enallage, 575; used to conceal actor, 574.
VOICE OR VOCAL SOUND, defined, 36.
VOWEL, defined, 71.

W

WE, used for I, 298.
WHAT, as a double relative, 278; as an interrogative, 290; parsed, 1252.
WHETHER, as an interrogative, 291.
WHICH, as an interrogative pronom. adj., 269; uses of, 267.
WHO, antecedent of, understood, 266; interrogative, 288; parsed, 1254, 1255.
WORDS, analyzed, as to number of syllables. 102; compound, 93; base of, 96; modifier, 97; defined, 91; derivative, 95; base of, 98; modifier, 97; primitive, 94; simple, 92.

Y

YES, how used, 864.

ECLECTIC EDUCATIONAL SERIES.

VAN ANTWERP, BRAGG & CO., Publishers, Cincinnati and New York.

Murdoch's Analytic Elocution. A complete and practical exposition of the only truly scientific method of developing the speaking voice. Fully illustrated by numerous extracts from the best sources, to which are added seventy pages of carefully selected readings. By JAMES E. MURDOCH, *Actor, Reader, and Instructor of Elocution.* 12mo, half roan, 504 pp. Price $1.00; postage and mailing, 17 cts.

Murdoch's Plea for Spoken Language. By the same Author. A Plea for the study of Spoken Language; History of the development of the best system of Elocution, including brief treatment of systems formerly used, and an Appendix containing *Barber's Essay on Rhythmus* and *Hill's Essay on Elocution*. 12mo, cloth, 320 pp. Price $1.00; postage and mailing, 17 cts.

Venable's School Stage.
Venable's Amateur Actor.
Venable's Dramatic Scenes.
These Dialogues and Plays submitted to the young people and their advisors, are designed to amuse quite as much as to instruct. They are derived from widely different sources, dramatized from standard works of fiction, and their production is practicable in any ordinary school-house or parlor.

The selections are varied in style and subjects. Plain and full directions relative to costumes, properties and stage business are given in connection with particular Dialogues and Dramas.

Either vol., 12mo, cloth, price 60 cts.; postage and mailing, 10 cts.

Venable's Standard Exhibition Dialogues and Acting Plays. Many teachers having expressed their desire that Venable's *School Stage, Amateur Actor,* and *Dramatic Scenes* might be obtained in separate parts and cheaper form, so that schools could obtain the separate Plays or Dialogues at a very small cost, the Publishers take pleasure in offering them in convenient shape. *Standard Exhibition Dialogues*, 30 Nos., each 10 cts., by mail post-paid.

Kidd's New Elocution. Revised edition of *Kidd's Elocution*, for many years the popular standard. The New Elocution contains much new and important matter; fuller information on essential points; a greater number of valuable exercises, and of new and appropriate examples for illustration. 504 pp., half roan. Price $1.00; postage and mailing, 17 cts.

McGuffey's New Juvenile Speaker. Two hundred easy and animated exercises for reading or speaking; humorous, instructive, grave and gay. A novel and valuable feature is the introduction of *choruses*, to be spoken, read or sung in concert. Music adapted to them may be found at the close of the book. 12mo, 228 pp. Price 40 cts.; postage and mailing, 7 cts.

McGuffey's New Eclectic Speaker. A collection embracing choice gems of prose and poetry, both humorous and grave. Selected with reference to purity of sentiment, beauty of style, real eloquence, interest, and instructiveness of matter; and especially for their adaptation for drill in declamation and reading. 12mo, cloth, 504 pp. Price 80 cts. Postage and mailing, 14 cts.

ECLECTIC EDUCATIONAL SERIES.

Published by VAN ANTWERP, BRAGG & CO., Cincinnati and New York.

NEW ECLECTIC PENMANSHIP.

ECLECTIC ELEMENTARY COURSE.

The three *Elementary Copy-Books* form a complete series, designed to cover the same ground as the first four or five ordinary copy-books. Nos. 1 and 2 are tracing books. Price by mail, post paid, 7 cents.

ECLECTIC PRIMARY COPY-BOOK.

A complete primary book for second school year. Contains all the small and capital letters and figures. Price by mail, post paid, 7 cents.

NEW ECLECTIC COPY-BOOKS. Revised and Re-engraved.

Nos. 1, 2, 3, 4, 5 Boys, 5 Girls, 6 Boys, 6 Girls, 6½, 7 and 8 Boys, 8 Girls, and No. 9. *Girls'* Copy-Books identical, word for word, with the *Boys'*, but in smaller hand-writing. Best paper, engraving, and ruling.

The simplest, most legible and business-like style of Capitals and Small Letters is adopted. Each letter is given separately at first, and then in combination; the spacing is open; analysis simple, and indicated in every letter when first presented. Price by mail, post paid, 10 cents.

ECLECTIC PRACTICE-BOOK.

With either single or double lines, 24 pp., same size and same paper as Eclectic Copy-Books, and designed to be used with them. Price by mail, post paid, 5 cts.

NEW HAND-BOOK OF ECLECTIC PENMANSHIP.

A Key to the Eclectic System of Penmanship. A complete description and analysis of movement and of the letters, and a brief summary of what is required in teaching penmanship. 12mo, cloth. Price 50 cents; postage and mailing, 8 cents.

ECLECTIC WRITING CARDS.

72 Nos. on 36 Cards. One Letter or Principle on each Card. Capital Letter on one side, Small Letter on the reverse. Each illustration accompanied with appropriate explanations and instructions. Size of Cards, 9 x 13 inches; loop attached for suspending on the walls. In wooden box, $3.50.

ECLECTIC ANGULAR HAND.

A complete course of instruction for ladies in the present fashionable Angular Penmanship. Six Copy-Books by Prof. J. P. Gordon. Price by mail, post paid, 10 cts.
Practice Cards, Four Nos. Price by mail, post paid, 18 cts.

ECLECTIC GERMAN COPY-BOOKS.

A new and complete system of German Penmanship, carefully arranged with reference to use in American schools, engraved on copper in the best style, printed with care on good paper. These books are 7½ x 8½ inches, which is larger than any competing series. 5 Nos. Price by mail, post paid, 9 cents.

ECLECTIC PENS.

These pens are made by the foremost manufacturer in the world, expressly for the scholars using the Eclectic System of Penmanship. No. 100 School Pen. Flexible and moderately fine. No. 200 Commercial Pen. Coarser, for business writing. No. 300 Extra Fine. Ladies and advanced scholars will find this pen admirable for careful writing. Per gross, either number, by mail, post paid, $1.00. Sample card by mail on receipt of 10 cents.

ECLECTIC EDUCATIONAL SERIES.

VAN ANTWERP, BRAGG & CO., Publishers, Cincinnati and New York.

SCIENCE.

ECLECTIC PHYSICAL GEOGRAPHY.
By RUSSELL HINMAN. 382 pp., 12mo, with 30 Charts and Maps, and 151 Diagrams and other illustrations. A text-book on this important subject in a new and convenient form. All irrelevant matter is omitted and the pages devoted exclusively to Physical Geography. Price, $1.00; postage and mailing, 17 c.

ELEMENTS OF PSYCHOLOGY.
Designed especially for Young Teachers, by EDWIN C. HEWITT, author of the Elements of Pedagogy. The book is addressed to young teachers who desire the facts of Psychology to aid them in the work of the school-room. It is written in a popular style. Special attention has been paid to the definitions, making them clear and distinct. 192 pp., full cloth. Price, 85 c.; postage and mailing, 14 c.

NORTON'S PHYSICS.
Elements of Physics for Academies and Common Schools. By S. A. NORTON, A. M., Prof. in Ohio Agricultural and Mechanical College. 12mo, cloth, 286 pp. Price, 80 c.; postage and mailing, 13 c.

NORTON'S NATURAL PHILOSOPHY.
The Elements of Natural Philosophy. By S. A. NORTON, A. M. A new treatise, embracing latest discoveries to date of publication. 12mo, cloth, 458 pp. Price, $1.10; postage and mailing, 18 c.

NORTON'S CHEMISTRY.
The Elements of Chemistry. By S. A. NORTON, A. M. 12mo, cloth, 504 pp. Illustrated. *New Edition, including Organic Chemistry.* Price, $1.10; postage and mailing, 18 c.

ANDREWS'S ELEMENTARY GEOLOGY.
An Elementary Geology, designed especially for the Interior States. By E. B. ANDREWS, LL. D., late of the Ohio Geological Corps, and Professor in Marietta College. 12mo, cloth, 269 pp. and Index. 432 Illustrations. Price, $1.00; postage and mailing, 17 c.

GREGORY'S POLITICAL ECONOMY.
A new Political Economy, by JOHN M. GREGORY, LL. D., Ex-Pres. Illinois Industrial University. Contains many features of striking originality. 12mo, clo., 394 pp. Price, $1.20; postage and mailing, 20 c.

SCHUYLER'S LOGIC.
The Principles of Logic. By A. SCHUYLER, LL. D., Pres't of Baldwin University; author of Algebra, Trigonometry, Surveying, etc. 12mo, cloth, 168 pp. Price, 60 c.; postage and mailing, 10 c.

ANDREWS'S CONSTITUTION.
A Manual of the Constitution of the United States, for the instruction of American Students and General Readers in the Duties, Obligations and Rights of Citizenship. By the late I. W. ANDREWS, LL. D. *Revised to 1888 by the Author.* Reset entire and printed from new type. 12mo, 408 pp. Price, $1.00; postage and mailing, 17 c.

"In each aspect of its usefulness, the work can not fail to meet with approval, and, *as a text-book, it is by all odds the best of its kind.*"—THE NATION.

ECLECTIC EDUCATIONAL SERIES.
Published by VAN ANTWERP, BRAGG & CO., Cincinnati and New York.

THALHEIMER'S HISTORICAL SERIES.

By M. E. THALHEIMER, Teacher of History and Composition in Packer Collegiate Institute. For Graded Schools, High Schools, Academies, and Colleges. These books furnish to teachers, students and general readers the best brief course in History.

NEW ECLECTIC HISTORY OF THE UNITED STATES.

This standard history has been thoroughly revised and brought down to the latest date. New and beautiful illustrations have been introduced, and the style in many places simplified. Brief biographies of important persons and fuller details of some events are furnished in explanatory notes at the ends of chapters. It is copiously illustrated with maps, portraits, etc. The Declaration of Independence and Constitution with questions on the same appear in the appendix. Price, $1.00; postage and mailing, 17c.

THALHEIMER'S HISTORY OF ENGLAND.

12mo, 288 pp. New edition in which the narrative is brought down to 1889. A compact volume, comprehensive in scope, but sufficiently brief to be completed in one school term. Its statements of historical facts are based upon the studies of the most recent authorities. Reliable Maps and pictorial illustrations. Price $1.00; postage and mailing, 17c.

THALHEIMER'S GENERAL HISTORY. (*Revised.*)

12mo, 448 pp. Maps and pictorial illustrations. The wants of common schools, and those of higher grade unable to give much time to the study of history, are here exactly met. The teacher is aided by *Review Questions* at the end of each principal division of the book, and by references to other works in which each subject will be found more fully treated. Price, $1.20; postage and mailing, 20 c.

THALHEIMER'S ANCIENT HISTORY.

A Manual of Ancient History from the Earliest Times to the fall of the Western Empire, A. D. 476. 8vo., full cloth, 365 pp., with Pronouncing Vocabulary and Index. Illustrated with Engravings, Maps and Charts. Price, $1.60; postage and mailing, 27 c.

In compliance with a demand for separate Histories of the Early Eastern Monarchies, of Greece and of Rome, an edition of THALHEIMER'S MANUAL OF ANCIENT HISTORY *in three parts has been published.*

Price, 80c. each part; postage and mailing, 14c.

THALHEIMER'S MEDIÆVAL AND MODERN HISTORY.

A Manual of Mediæval and Modern History. 8vo., cloth uniform with Thalheimer's Ancient History. 455 pp., and very full Index. Numerous double-page Maps. A sketch of fourteen centuries, from the fall of one empire at Ravenna to the establishment of another at Berlin. Price, $1.60; postage and mailing, 27 c.

ECLECTIC PRIMARY HISTORY

Of the United States. By EDW. S. ELLIS, Supt. of Schools, Trenton, N. J. Profusely illustrated with superior engravings and portraits. Square 12mo, full cloth, 224 pp. A most attractive and entertaining volume for pupils of Fourth and Fifth Reader Grades. Price, 50 c.; postage and mailing, 8 c.

www.ingramcontent.com/pod-product-compliance
Lightning Source LLC
Chambersburg PA
CBHW031939230426
43672CB00010B/1972